IMAGES
of America

AROUND CLARKSVILLE

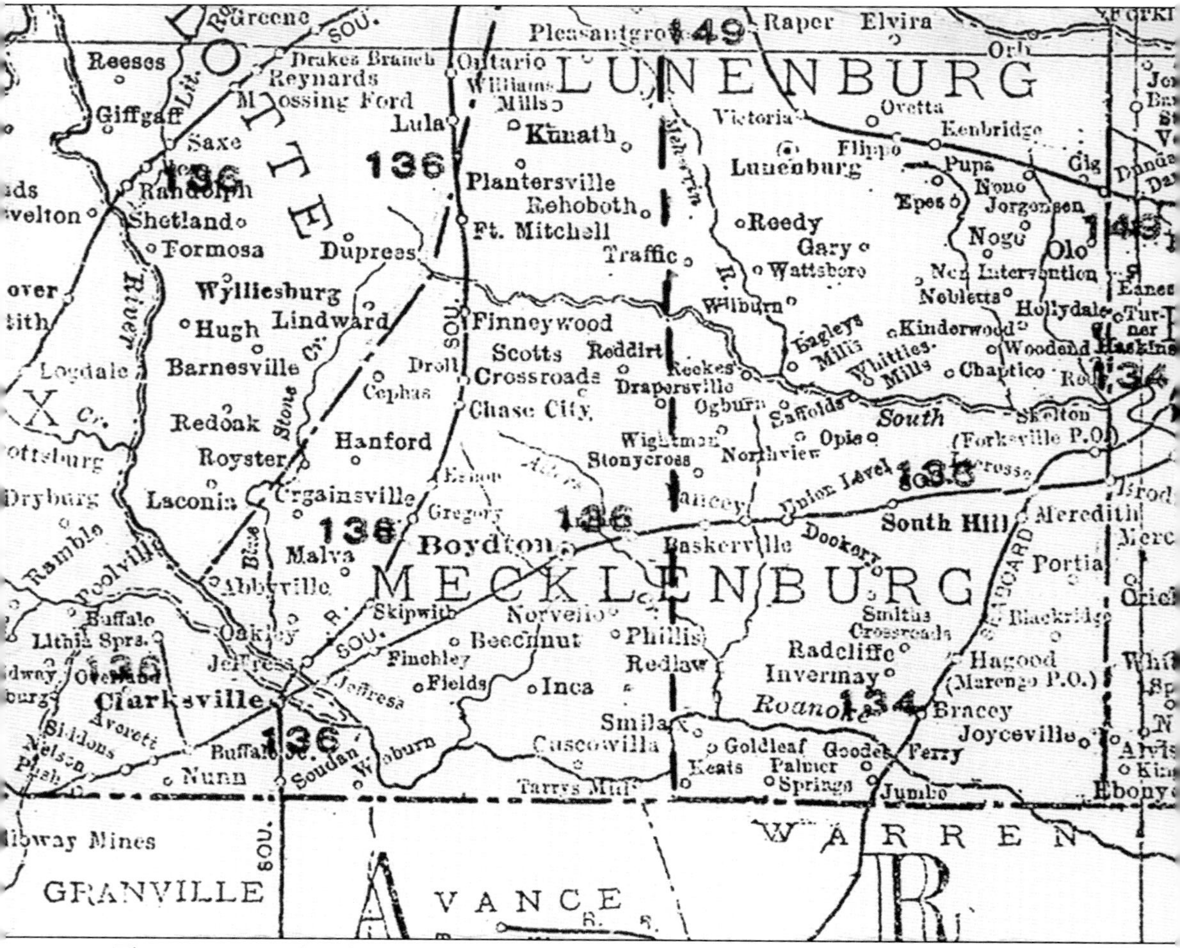

This is a 1916 railroad map cut out section of Mecklenburg County, Virginia. The broken line down the center illustrates the territory (to the left of the line) that is covered in this text. (William C. Gregory.)

ON THE COVER: After World War II, a significant literacy program was begun across the United States. Part of this program was to ensure access in rural communities to the regional library books and resources. The bookmobile, loaded with numerous volumes, would make its rounds to small towns and country store communities on a scheduled two-week basis. (Southside Regional Library.)

IMAGES
of America

AROUND CLARKSVILLE

John Caknipe Jr.

ARCADIA
PUBLISHING

ISBN 978-0-7385-6792-1

Published by Arcadia Publishing
Charleston, South Carolina

Printed in the United States of America

Library of Congress Control Number: 2009922701

For all general information contact Arcadia Publishing at:
Telephone 843-853-2070
Fax 843-853-0044
E-mail sales@arcadiapublishing.com
For customer service and orders:
Toll-Free 1-888-313-2665

Visit us on the Internet at www.arcadiapublishing.com

Contents

ACKNOWLEDGMENTS

There are many special thanks deserved by individuals who helped to bring this text to print: William Gregory sent his collection as soon as I told him I was going to do the book; Bob Howerton provided hours of stories, advice, clarity, and numerous photographs; Rebecca Cary gave me her folders of years of research and publications and told me to return them when done; the volunteers of Clarksville Regional Museum opened their archives, providing photographs with lots of stories. Thank you and likewise to Historic Boydton Renaissance, Inc.; the town hall staff of Clarksville; and the town hall staff of Boydton.

For the many dedicated collections of Mary Ann Boyd Ottinger, Michael Dobbs and the U.S. Army Corps of Engineers, Wanda Brooks and Southside Regional Library, D. Stuart Buchanan Sr., Henry H. Gregory Jr., Thomas and Pat Gryder, Mecklenburg Electric Cooperative, Hugh Lankford, Mark Colgate, Lucille T. Hudson and W. P. Hudgins Sr., Ronnie A. Bugg, Jack Hite, Lucille Tisdale Campbell, and the nearly 100 names captioned with the photographs—thank you. The media and archives of the *News Progress* and *Clarksville Times*; *Mecklenburg Sun*; Greg Thrift at WKSK and local historians James Sheppard, Walter Beales III, and Louis Hite; the deeds and records office of Mecklenburg County; along with hundreds of interviews and notes from current and former residents of the area with their support, history, and encouragement made this small portion of the history possible.

I apologize in advance for omission. The range from 1676 to 2009 encompasses a lot of history.

To Dallas Weston, who meticulously brought my wife's computer back to life after an attack of a mega virus, a big thank you. But, in light of all else, it has been a privilege because of family support and encouragement. "Time for a break, let's go hunting," I heard and responded to. Beverly Wootton Jones said, "Here's my lap-top. Bring it back when you git 'er done," then scanned numerous photographs when my wife's scanner took up the vice of smoking and died. To my wife—my photographer, scanner, printer, support, critic, and inspiration—my life, Betty Caknipe, thank you all (y'all) and I love you.

INTRODUCTION

Western Mecklenburg County, especially the town of Clarksville, Virginia, should be referred to as "the rebound town." Since its beginning in 1818, Clarksville was plagued with floods or fires about every four to five years. Is Clarksville rebounding again? After all, it is the only town on the lake.

In 1676, Nathaniel Bacon led a rebellion against the British royal governor of Virginia, Sir William Berkeley. Enlisting the aide of the Occoneechee Indians, whom he befriended and who were supportive of the colony, Bacon moved west into frontier territory. Moving along the rivers, he was led to the Roanoke. Along the way, his troops killed all the Native Americans they came in contact with. Finally, arriving at Fort Occoneechee in May 1676, Bacon turned on his guides and the families at the fort, killing over 300. This was Bacon's last battle of his rebellion—in the fall, he died.

After Bacon's troops returned to the coast, the first plantation to become settled in the western frontier was China Grove, southeast of the present-day Boydton. The plantation was settled and developed by Samuel Bugg. It was not until 1750 that more rapid expansion took place, and most of this was due to the governor awarding land to those settlers who came and established farms and a ferry system along the Roanoke River.

One of these farmers was William Royster, who settled on the old Fort Occoneechee and Occoneechee Island as an overseer for Col. William Byrd's Bluestone Castle land grant. William Royster died around 1792. His son, Clark Royster, inherited 376 acres of Fort Occoneechee that William had a clear title to and in short order built a tavern, a spring house for his mineral spring, and a tobacco warehouse on First Street.

Before the survey of Col. William Byrd in 1726, the lands south of the rivers were considered part of North Carolina. After the survey, the boundary was changed, and they became part of Virginia.

Tobacco became the principal crop, but getting it to the nearest market in Petersburg, Virginia, was difficult, especially for those farming south of the rivers.

In 1817, Clark Royster laid out a plat of 25 acres with an additional 75 acres set aside for himself and petitioned the Commonwealth of Virginia for a town charter. The General Assembly granted his request in 1818, and the community of Clark's Ferry and Clark's Town became Clarksville, making it the second chartered town in Mecklenburg County. In 1821, it was incorporated and became the first incorporated town in Mecklenburg County.

In 1854, the Roanoke Valley Railroad came through Clarksville on its way to Manson, North Carolina, with connections to Raleigh, North Carolina, or to Norfolk, Virginia. But with the beginning of the Civil War, work on the expansion of the railroad came to a halt, and the track was removed to another location to support the war supply effort. By the 1850s, Clarksville (with nearly 1,000 people, the county's first bank, and three churches) was experiencing very wealthy times. But with the western Mecklenburg surplus of Thoroughbred horses, the changes in slavery issues, the fire of 1857, and the commerce repercussions of the Civil War, the local economy was devastated.

Boydton became Clarksville's "big brother" as early as 1818, with Col. William Townes purchasing the Occoneechee Plantation just across the river to the northeast. Thoroughbred horses became a new market in western Mecklenburg County. When the Boydton Plank Toll Road was built from Petersburg, a local merchant and builder paid for the extension on to Clarksville.

With the newly formed Mecklenburg County, in 1764, a local farmer and magistrate, Richard Swepson, a resident since 1746, was instrumental in securing the location of the courthouse in present-day Boydton on its current site. His rationale was that the courthouse should be in the center of the county but to the south to accommodate those citizens who lived across the river. The first official court session was held on Monday, March 11, 1765, in his home; a courtroom was later added with a jail underneath until the courthouse was completed in 1770. During this first session, local lawyer and tobacco planter Robert Mumford was appointed the first county justice of the peace. The newly formed community was called Mecklenburg Court.

In 1765, Alexander Boyd arrived in Mecklenburg Court from Scotland. He married Swepson's daughter, Ann, began a mercantile business, and purchased a plantation on the Roanoke River. Alexander and Ann had 11 children and are reported to have lived in the original center of the present-day Boyd Tavern. They resided there until Alexander's death in 1801. In 1811, Alexander Boyd Jr. deeded 2 acres of land for the new courthouse and support buildings. Many local residents complained, as Boyd still owned the surrounding property and no other merchants could build or operate businesses in the area. Boydton became the first town developed in Mecklenburg County.

Although located less than 3 miles from the Roanoke River, Boydton's economy relied on "Court Days" and Thoroughbred horses. Several horse racetracks were developed in the region before the War of 1812: Petersburg, Lawrenceville, Hicksford, Raines Tavern, and Halifax. The track at Raines Tavern was developed by Samuel Puryear, a plantation owner, horse breeder, owner of the tavern/ordinary, and the postmaster. The track in Boyd Town was developed by Col. William Townes, owner of the Occoneechee Plantation, a tobacco grower, and a Thoroughbred race horse breeder and racing fan.

The following photographs are the result of extensive research through numerous resources, which resulted in many varied versions of history. Over 1,000 hours of interviews with local and former citizens of western Mecklenburg County were completed. This volume presents a journal overview of an era that is rapidly fading from the memories and graphic collections of our ancestors. With flame, flood, and simple misfortune, our history is slowly fading away.

The following are abbreviated in the courtesy lines:

BH Bob Howerton
BMC Betty McKinney Caknipe
COE U.S. Army Corps of Engineers
CRM Clarksville Regional Museum
HBR Historic Boydton Renaissance, Inc.
RB CW3 Ronnie Bugg, U.S. Air Force (retired)
REC Ruth and Edwin Crowder
WCG William C. Gregory

One

BEFORE THE CIVIL WAR

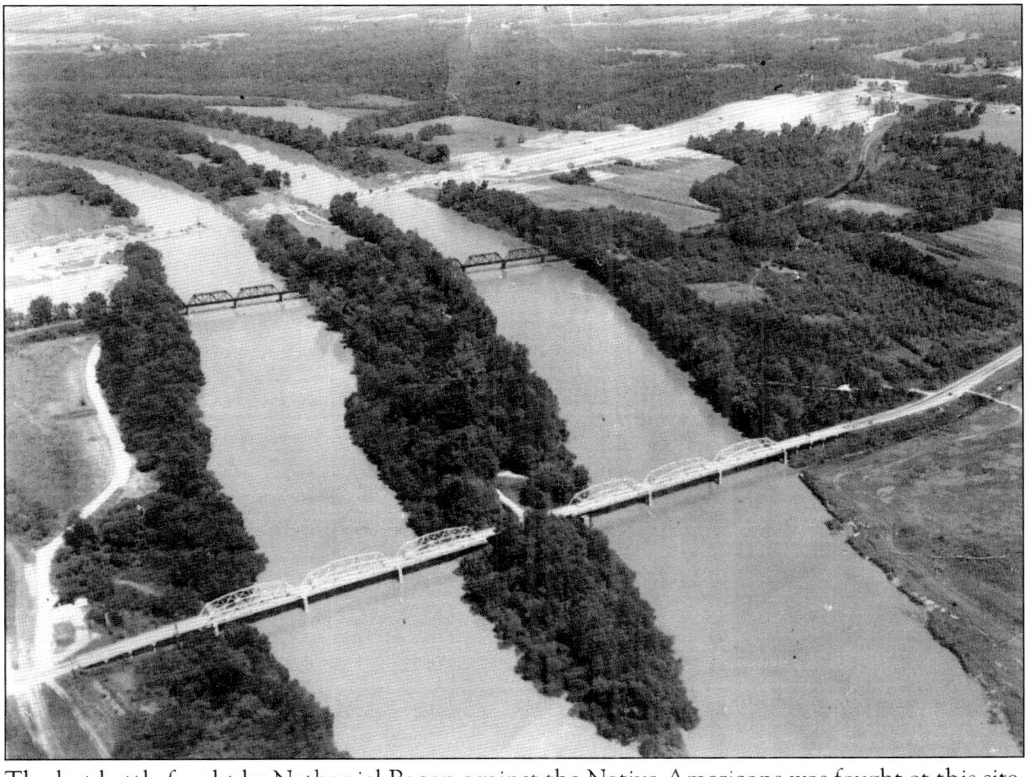

The last battle fought by Nathaniel Bacon against the Native Americans was fought at this site. The two rivers pictured are the Dan River and the Roanoke River. In the center is Occoneechee Island, and at the southern tip of the island is where the rivers converge to become the Roanoke. (Susan W. Guill.)

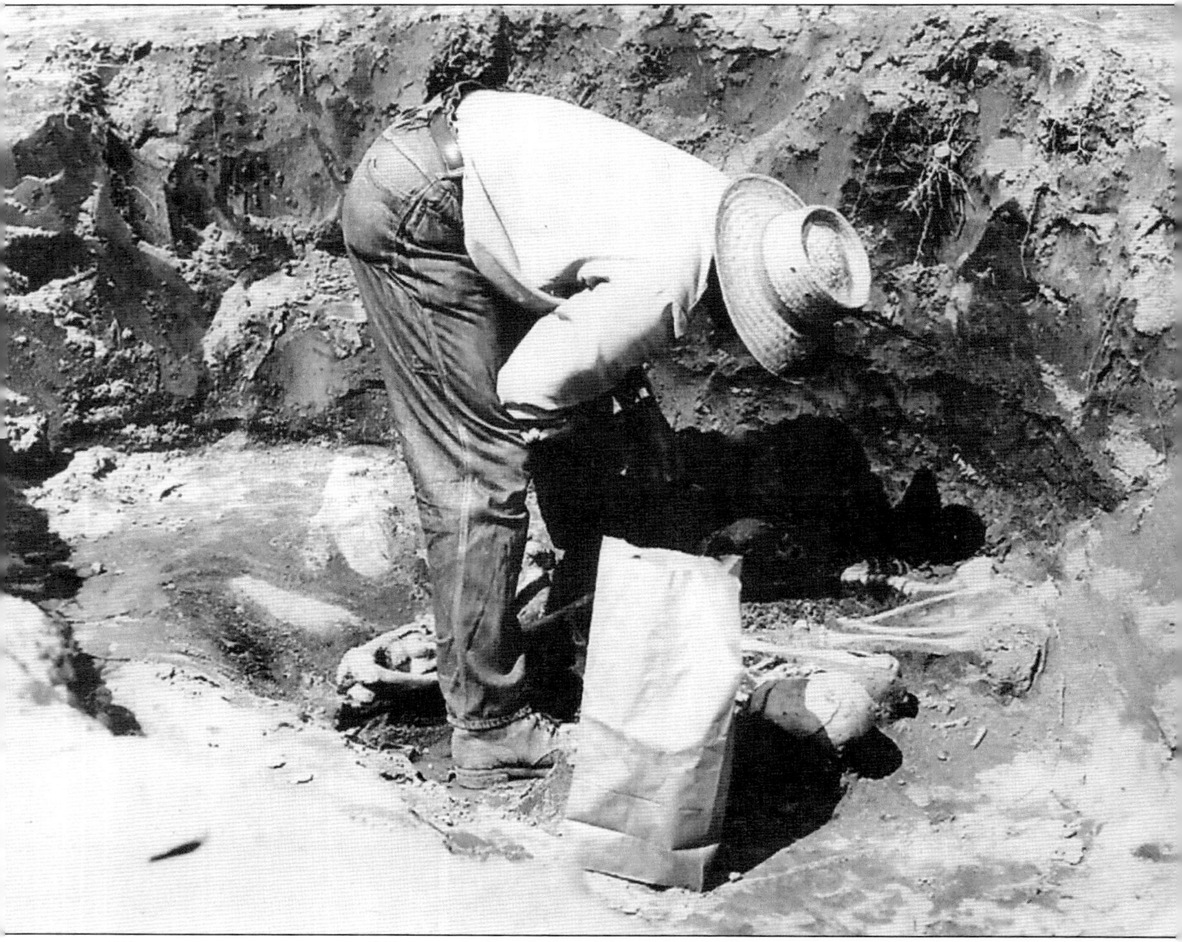

This is an excavation of Occoneechee Island by the Smithsonian in 1948, before the lake was created. They found 80 sites of villages, encampments, and workshops, with 46 human skeletons and 24 dogs. Numerous large collections exist, such as MacCallum More Museum, of over 30,000 prehistoric and American Indian tools, artifacts, and weapons catalogued by the Virginia Department of Historic Resources. (COE.)

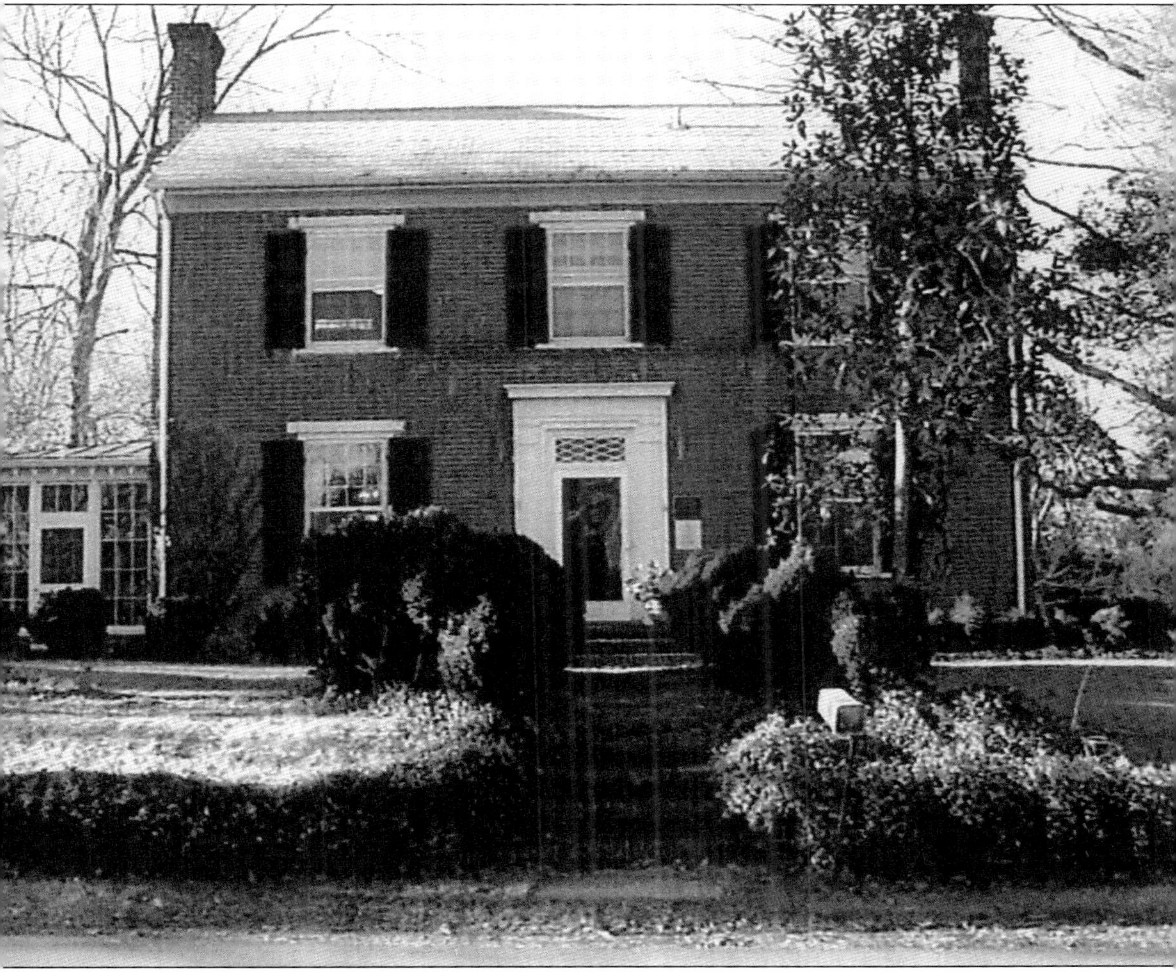

Clark Royster inherited 376 acres of land from his father, William, in 1797—the year of his death. William was encouraged by the governor of Virginia to join several other farmer/merchants to begin a westward expansion of the commonwealth and to develop a ferry system to cross the rivers. The highest point atop the bluff overlooking the rivers is where William chose to build his new home—today this area is called Rose Hill. (BH.)

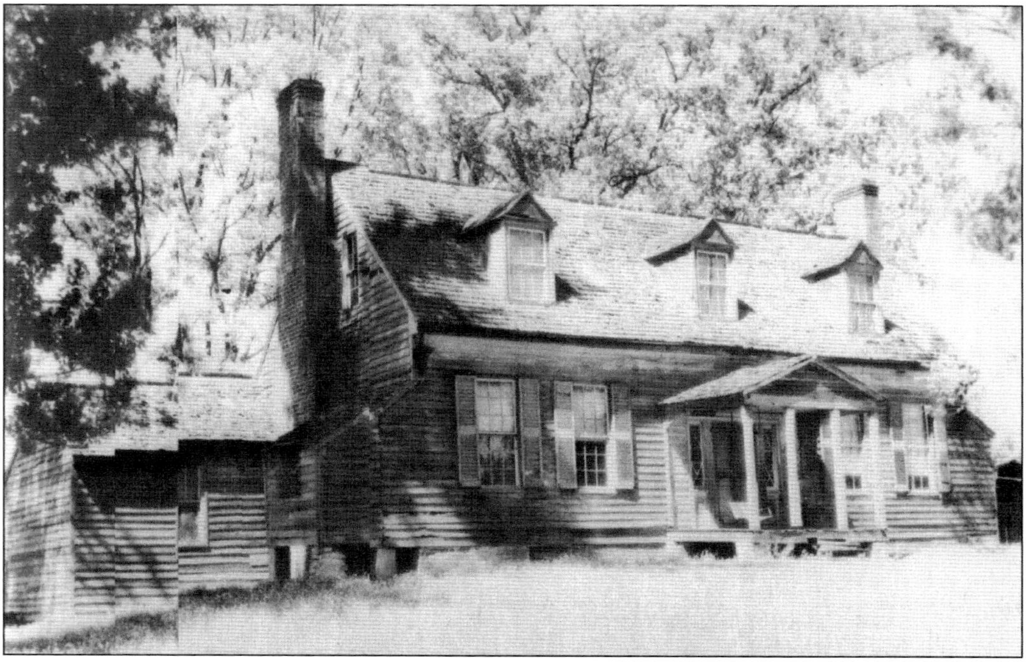

John Speed purchased much of his land in 1811 from Ambrose Gregory and developed Buffalo Springs. He continued the tavern/ordinary but built a "house of entertainment." The area was cited in the book of Col. William Byrd. In 1728, Byrd, with his surveying party, managed to kill a local buffalo drinking from the nearby creek; he named it Buffalo Creek. Around 1916, the highway changed. The front of the house was copied to the back. Front and back are identical. The home is called Rebel Hill. (CRM.)

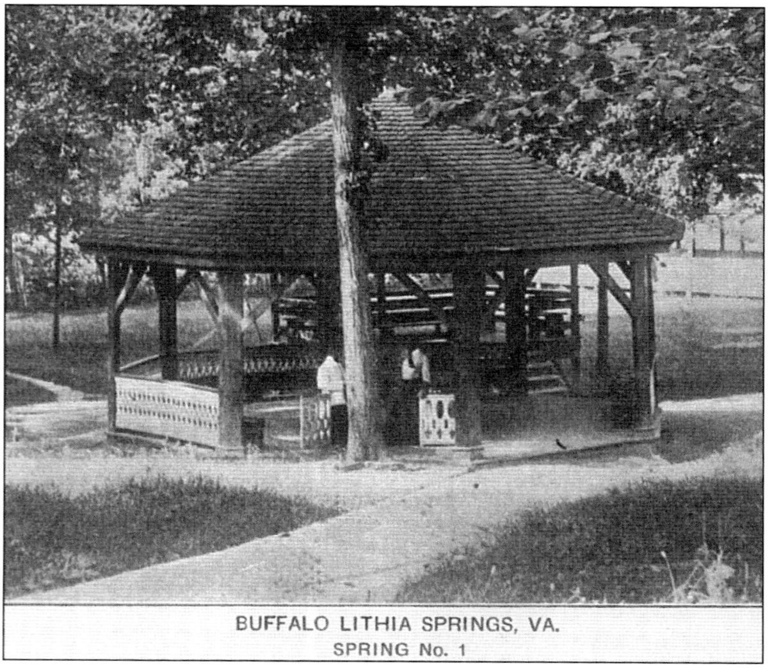

Speed quickly developed the area, first building a new, large home and a tavern/ordinary with gaming room but retaining the two former log structures. He advertised far and wide, but with poor transportation and being south of the rivers, the clientele were few but affluent and loyal. Many notables, including Pres. Thomas Jefferson, have visited the springs for the restful attractions and curative waters. (WCG.)

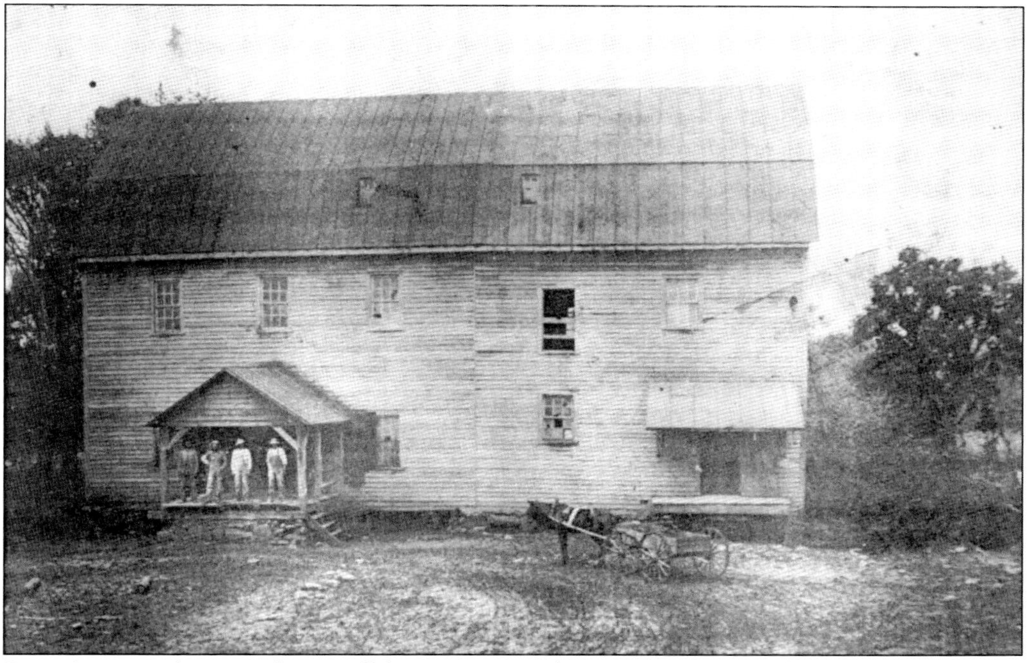

Directly across the rivers from Buffalo Springs was the 1798 community of Nelson, named for its new owner, John Nelson. It was changed to Little York in 1799 and to Abbeyville in 1818. This photograph, taken in 1912, shows, from left to right, C. O. Poole, Walter Poole, Frazier Jones, and unidentified. The mercantile sold fertilizer, seeds, farming implements, and dry goods. (Harry Click, *News Progress*.)

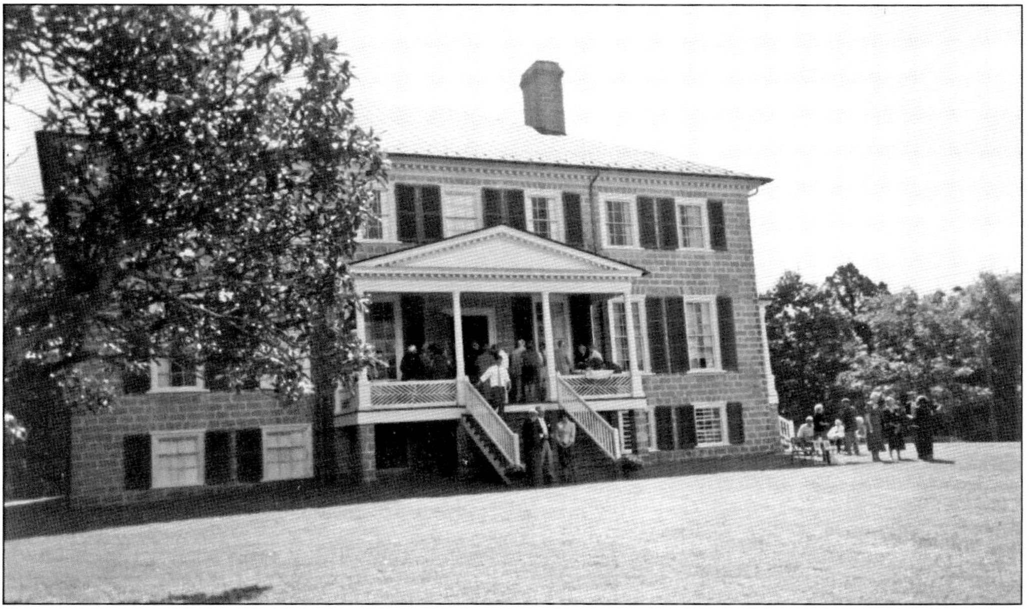

Bluestone Castle, owned by William Byrd, was removed to make way for Prestwood on lands inherited by Sir Peyton Skipwith and his brother. The manor home was built by Jacob Shealor and John Inge, being completed in 1797. (John Caknipe.)

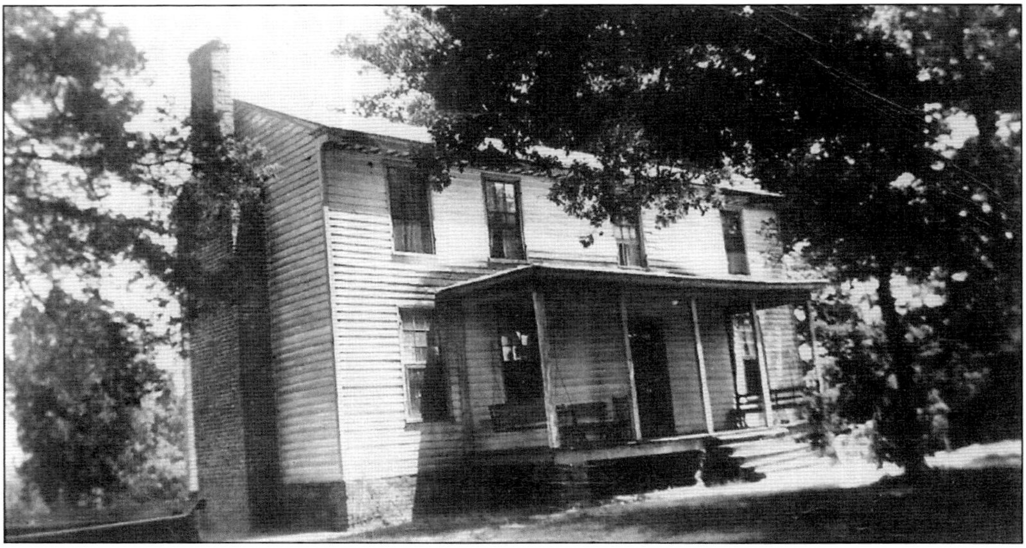

The Crowder family, a very large and prominent family throughout Mecklenburg County, built Kensington in Abbeyville in 1820. With the coming of the lake, Edwin Crowder purchased the home in 1949 and moved it to Boydton. He combined it with the 1820 Boyd cabinet shop to build his home. (REC.)

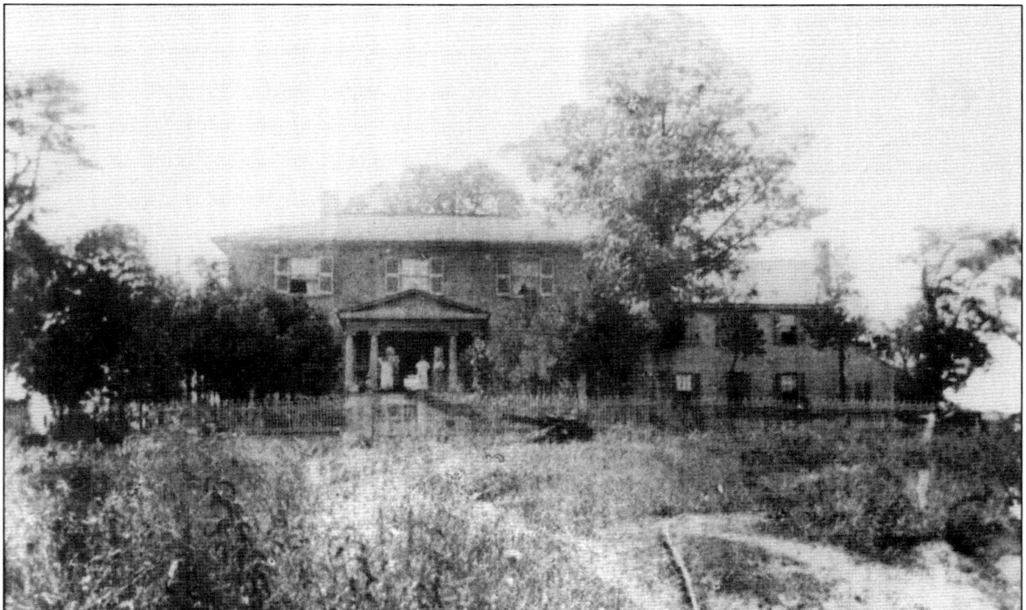

Built in 1839 by William Townes Sr., the Occoneechee Plantation, next to Prestwood, contained over 3,105 acres and was directly across the rivers from Clarksville. A lover of Thoroughbred horses, Townes was president of the Roanoke River Colt Sales Association, and Occoneechee was a breeding stables for many, many colts. After his death, the plantation was sold to Dempsey P. Crudup. When the manor burned on Christmas Eve 1898, Dempsey is said to have died and was buried in an unmarked grave on the property. (Virginia Department of Conservation and Recreation.)

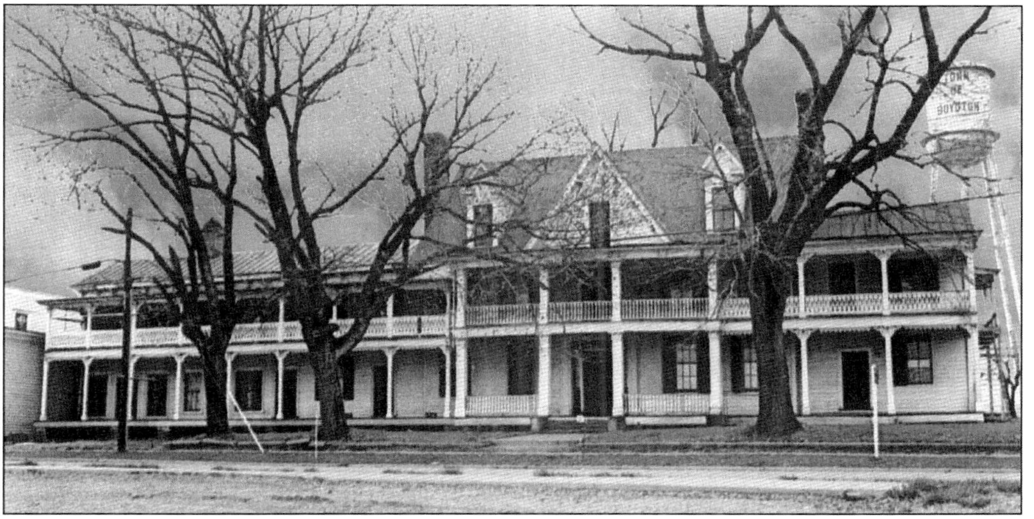

One of the oldest structures remaining in Mecklenburg County is the tavern. Established after the Revolutionary War by Richard Swepson Jr., the tavern included the first county courthouse, where later a jail was added underneath. Across the lawn was the mercantile of Alexander Boyd, recently arrived in town. His mercantile was licensed on March 15, 1787. He later married Swepson's daughter, Ann, and on April 15, 1794, he and Ann purchased the tavern with 480 acres from her father for £1,000. The third floor of the tavern contains 10 apartments. (Posie Hugh Lankford.)

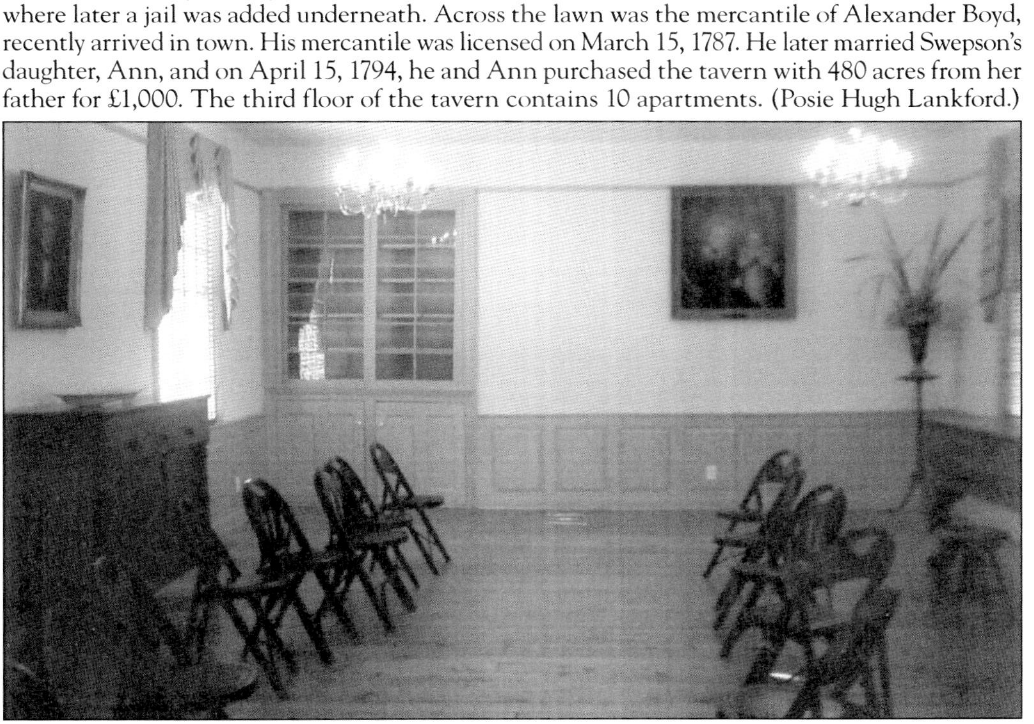

Boyd was appointed commissioner of the peace in 1792, and in 1797, his elder son, Richard, took over managing the hotel/tavern. Boyd died during a trial in this courtroom on August 11, 1801. He and Richard are buried in a private cemetery in the front of the tavern. On August 11, 1801, Alexander Boyd Jr. deeded 2 acres to be used for a new courthouse and supporting services. On February 3, 1812, he platted a parcel of 50 acres and petitioned the Virginia General Assembly for recognition as a town. The petition was granted, and Boyd's Town became the first town in Mecklenburg County. (Boyd Tavern Foundation.)

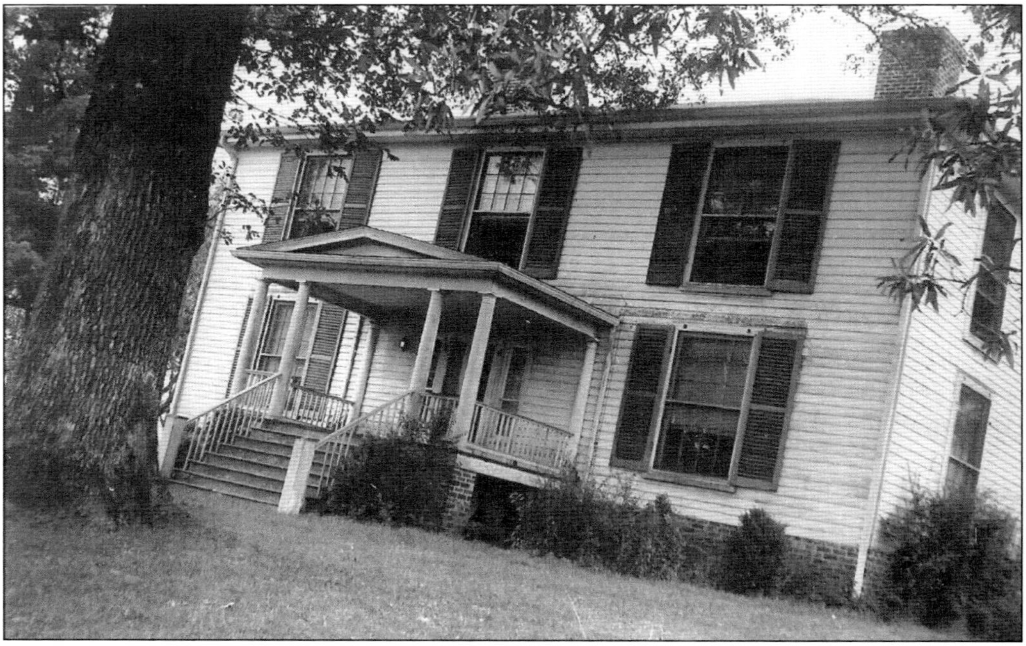

Alexander Boyd Jr. with his wife, Matilda, built their home, Rose Hill, across the courtyard in front of the tavern. Between his home and the tavern is the family cemetery, next to which was his mercantile. Boyd built the store around 1820 and operated it until his death. In 1850, Boyd and James Whitice funded extending the Boydton Plank Toll Road to Clarksville, and Boyd began a stagecoach line from Petersburg with a man named Scoggins. (Mary Ann Boyd Ottinger.)

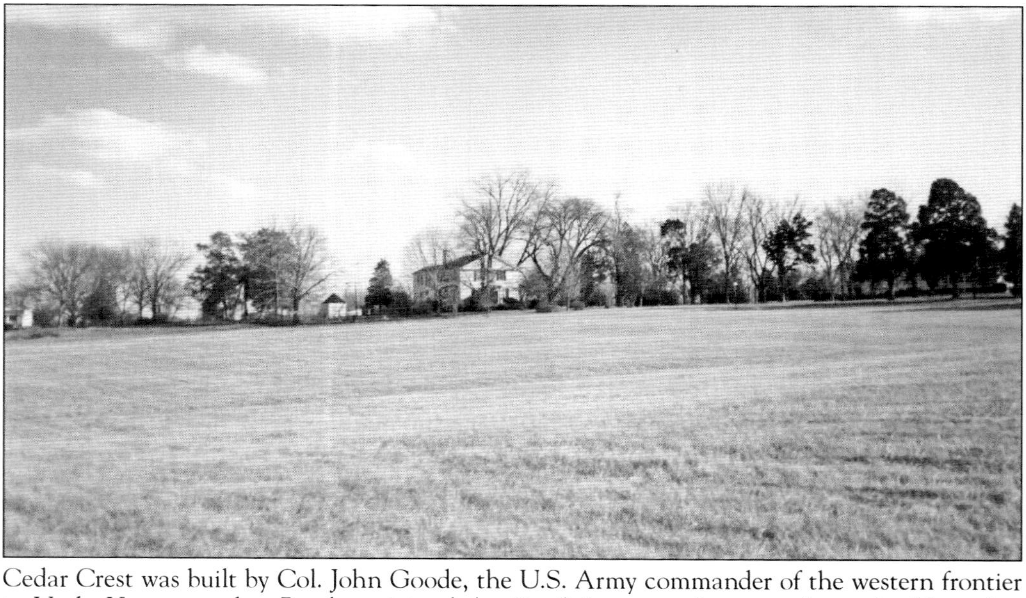

Cedar Crest was built by Col. John Goode, the U.S. Army commander of the western frontier in Utah. He returned to Boydton, joined the Confederacy, and rose to the rank of brigadier general. When Gen. Philip Sheridan came through town between April 20 and 25, 1865, this home was used as his headquarters, and troops camped on the field seen in this photograph. (Landon Crowder.)

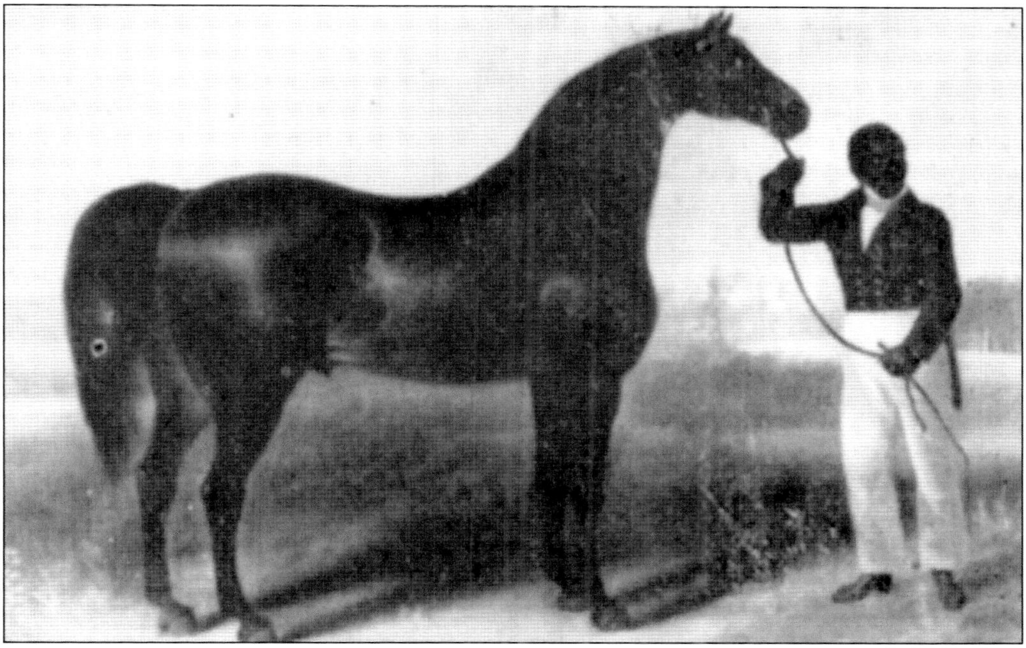

Sir Hal, owned by the William Baskerville family of Boydton, and Bedford were two notable horses of the era. John C. Goode was probably the most prominent breeder in the area. He owned a horse named Bet Bounce, whose bloodline included Gen. Robert E. Lee's horse, Traveler. Goode's fame began in 1765 with Racehorse John, which gave a bloodline of perfection to the American Quarter running horse. (Southside Regional Library.)

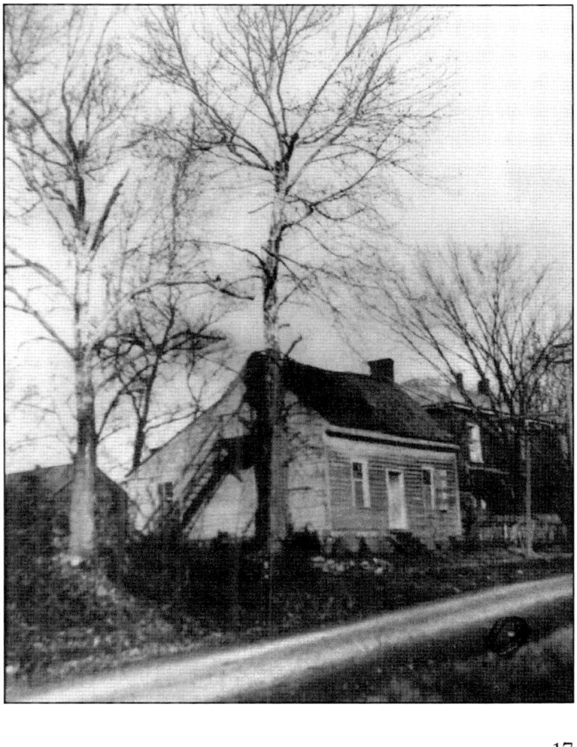

The Washington Tavern and a mercantile store were built in 1820 by James Bruce of Halifax County fame. His local partner was Capt. Beverly Sydnor, who ran the businesses, along with several other enterprises, for nearly 37 years before it became part of the Exchange Hotel complex in 1857. In this c. 1903 photograph is the tavern with the mercantile in the background, facing the courthouse. (REC.)

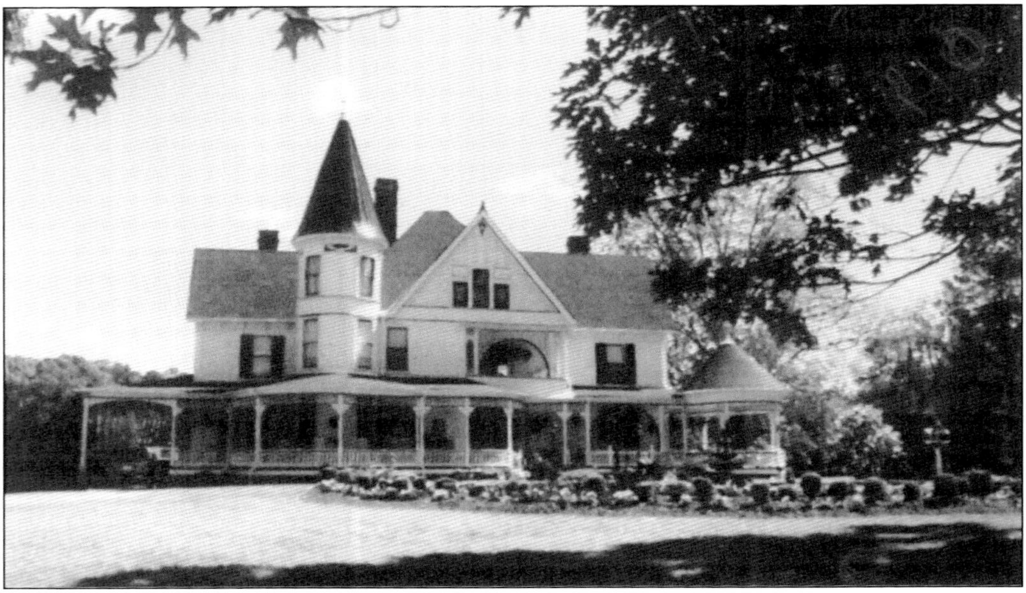

On the Hill or 12 Oaks was an 1830 farmhouse situated on 23 acres inherited by George B. Finch. In 1886, he gave his new bride, Alice Marrow Finch, $5,000 as a wedding gift to remodel the home. She hired William K. Holt and told him the Victorian design she wanted. George Finch was a graduate of Randolph-Macon College, commonwealth's attorney, and also one of the few survivors of Picket's Charge at Gettysburg during the Civil War. (Bob and Jenny Salzmann.)

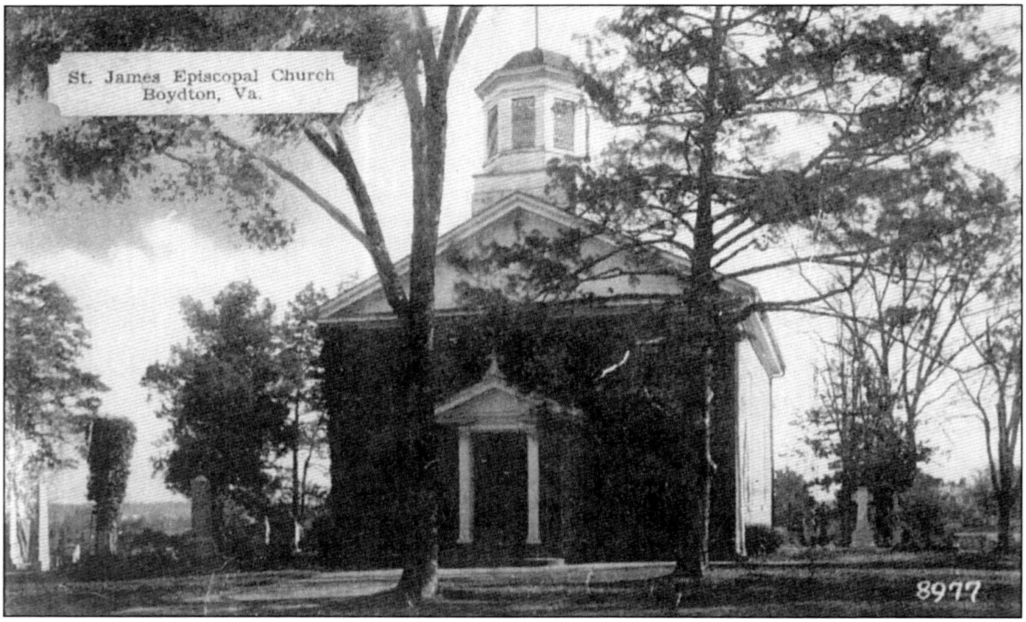

In 1818, Rev. John S. Ravenscroft dedicated a new church at Cabin Point on Old Cox Road; it was named St. James Episcopal Church, as western Mecklenburg County was in the St. James Parish. In 1835, it was moved 4 miles east on Old Cox Road to Butcher's Creek near Wheatland, and then in 1842, it was moved farther along Old Cox Road to Boydton. Remodeled, it is still at its 1842 location. (WCG.)

William O. Goode owned a plantation near present-day Skipwith named Wheatland, having purchased the land from Maj. Thomas Nelson. Goode was the U.S. congressman from the southside district for several years and after purchasing the plantation began to develop the lands with a new home, gristmill, school, and outbuildings. This image, taken around 1910, shows the Wheatland mill and, from left to right, William "Archie" Bland, unidentified, and Carrie Goode Bugg. (Henry H. Gregory Jr.)

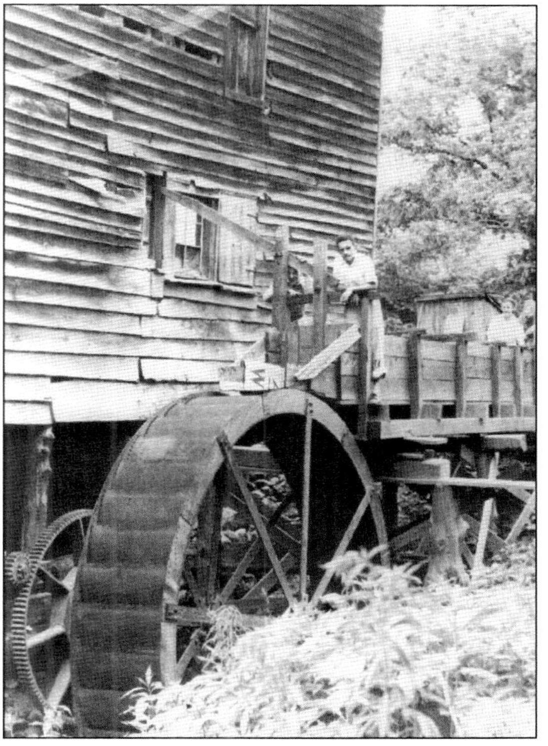

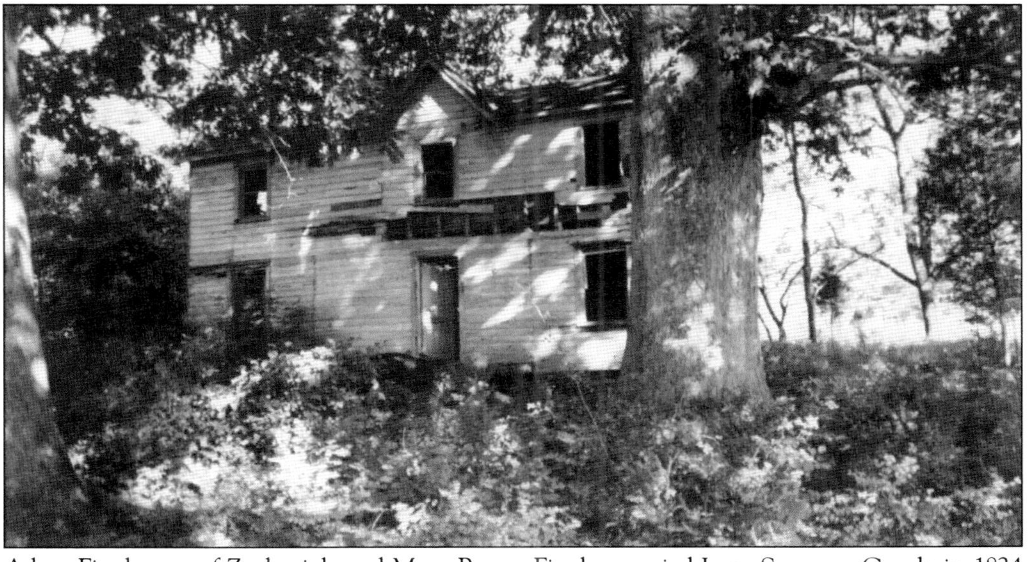

Adam Finch, son of Zachariah and Mary Bacon Finch, married Lucy Swepson Goode in 1824 and built their home on the Finch plantation adjoining Puryear, near where the Christiansville racetrack was located. The home, nearly gone, is still on the original site; in the front yard are reminders of 1902, when it was the training area for Capt. Adam Tyree Finch and the Mecklenburg Guard. Adam Finch was the preacher/teacher at Centenary meetinghouse at the forks of the Boydton Road. His son Adam Tyree Finch, M.D., was born in this home, as was Rev. Dr. William C. Finch. (Thomas and Pat Gryder.)

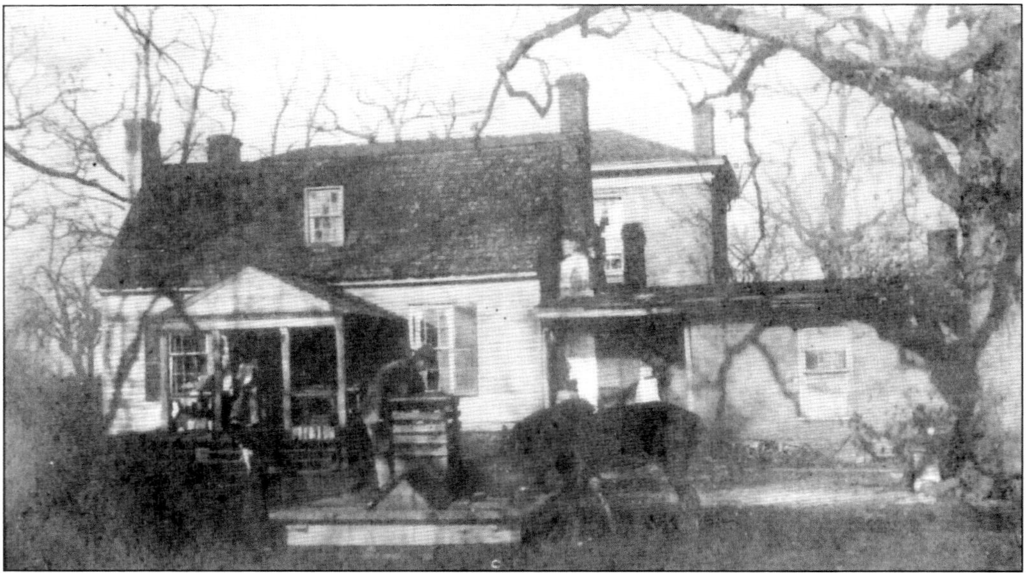

The northwesternmost plantation in Mecklenburg County was the James Carrington land grant of 1767. Carrington sold his lands and acquired new holdings in Charlotte County. The plantation bordered the lands of Dr. John Burwell and Col. Lewis Burwell of Finneywood. A 290-acre parcel was purchased by Robert and Mary Portwood, with their four children, where they built their home around 1820 and continued to operate the mill. The individuals in this photograph are not identified. (John and Roy Wootton.)

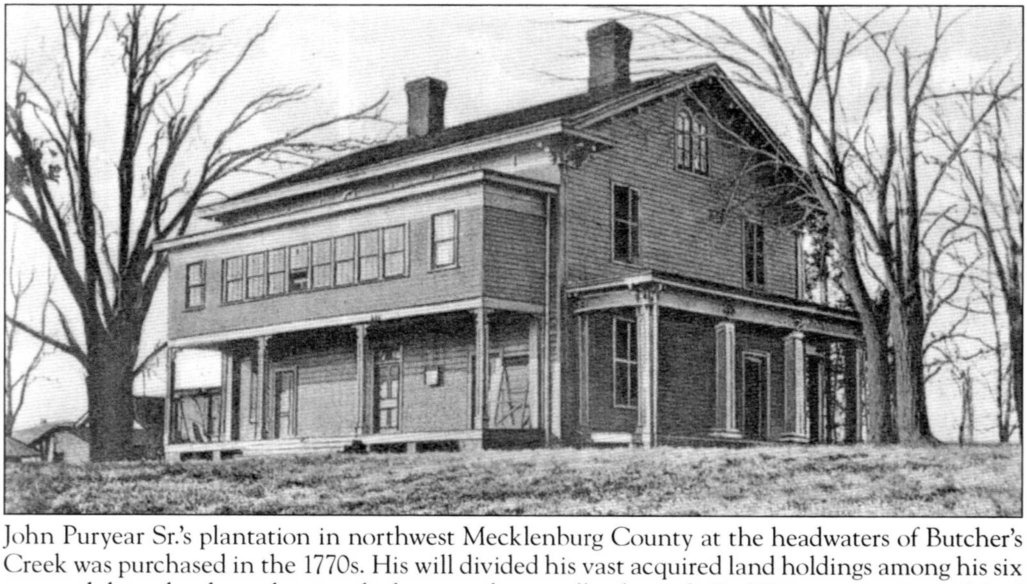

John Puryear Sr.'s plantation in northwest Mecklenburg County at the headwaters of Butcher's Creek was purchased in the 1770s. His will divided his vast acquired land holdings among his six sons and three daughters, leaving the home and gristmill to his wife. By 1790, one son, Samuel, had built a home/ordinary and was operating the gristmill. On the plantation, a racetrack was begun that operated until 1826. Richard Puryear came back to the area, began purchasing property, and later moved the house to the new Abbeyville Road, next to the new Christiansville Academy and Presbyterian church on the south side of his farm, where the town began to develop. In 1809, it was called the "Puryear Gentlemen's house;" today it is Shadow Lawn. (Richard Burnett.)

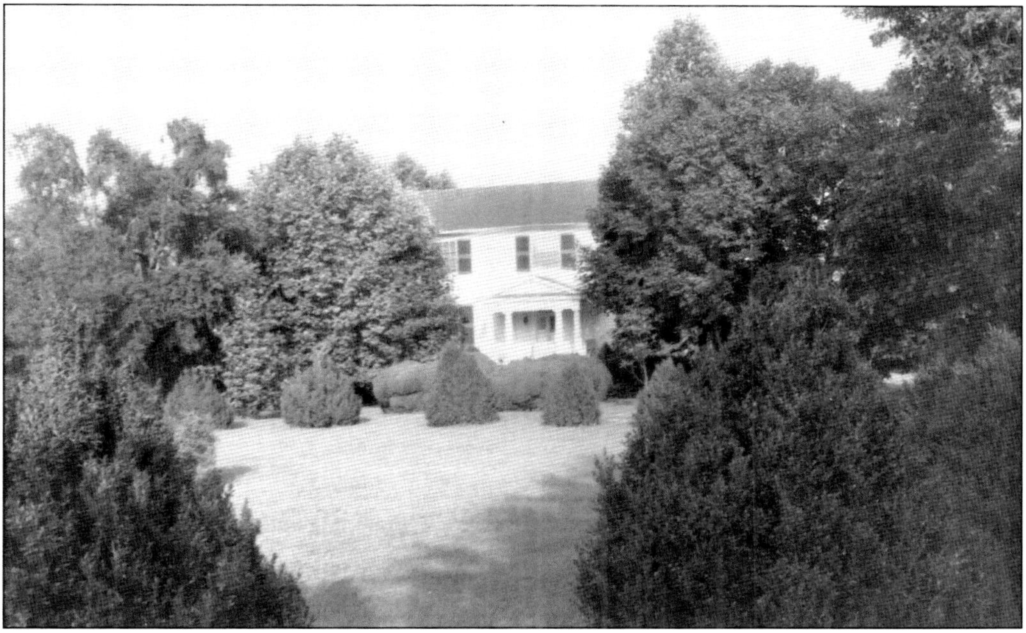

Adjoining the Puryear plantation to the south was a 1,000-acre land grant to Archer Smith, which he named Plainview. After his death in 1840, his son Alexander tore down the home and built a new one on the same site. Alexander's son drowned in the spring in back of the house in 1839 at the age of 3. (Neil Blackwell.)

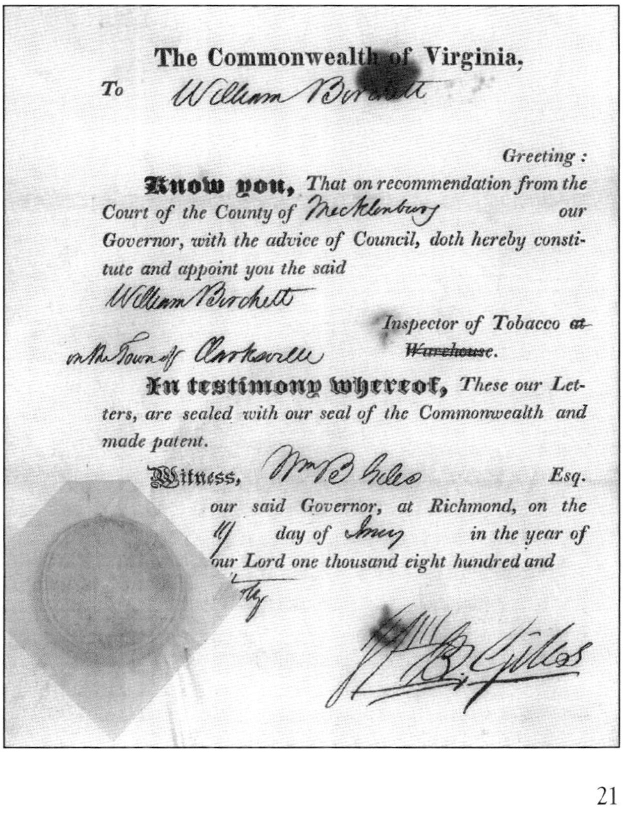

The Commonwealth of Virginia,

To William Brockett

Greeting:

Know you, *That on recommendation from the Court of the County of* Mecklenburg *our Governor, with the advice of Council, doth hereby constitute and appoint you the said* William Brockett *Inspector of Tobacco* ~~*at*~~ in the Town of Clarksville ~~*Warehouse*~~.

In testimony whereof, *These our Letters, are sealed with our seal of the Commonwealth and made patent.*

Witness, Wm B Giles *Esq. our said Governor, at Richmond, on the* 11 *day of* [illegible] *in the year of our Lord one thousand eight hundred and* [illegible]

Wm B Giles

With the great boom in tobacco in 1838, tobacco factories were being developed in Christiansville, Abbeyville, and Clarksville. In 1830, the Roanoke Navigation Company was in full operation, and Clarksville had its first tobacco inspector, appointed by Gov. William Giles. (WCG.)

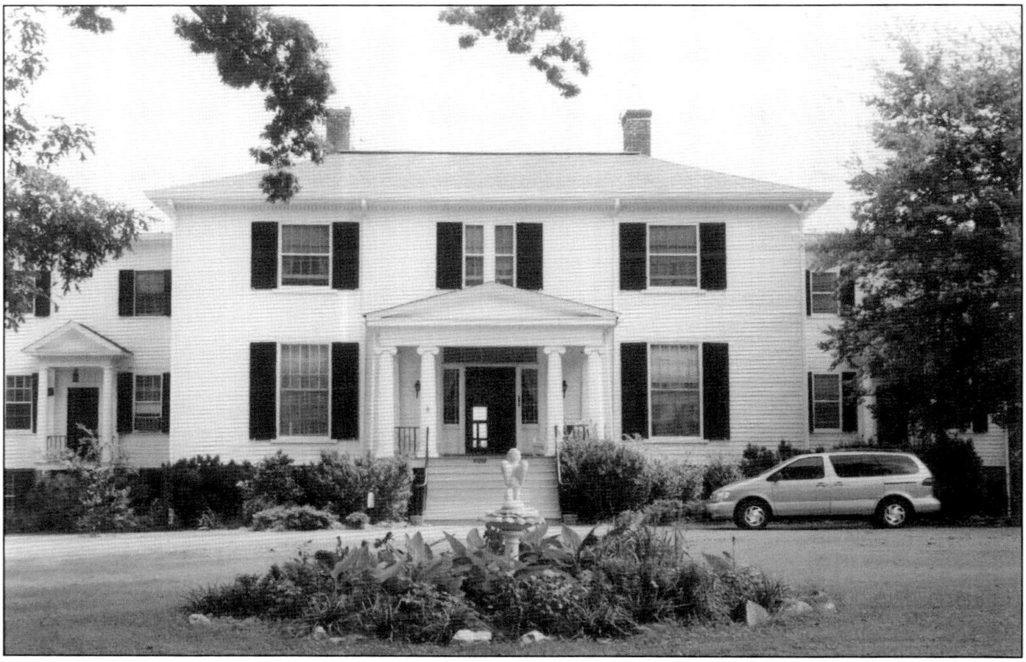

Kinderton Manor house was one of several houses built in the area over a 25-year period of similar ornate and intricate details in style. Abraham W. Venable served in the U.S. Congress and had purchased part ownership of numerous lots, businesses, and parcels in the Clarksville area, but by 1843, all his holdings were seized by the Exchange Bank, put to auction by the bank's manager, Nathaniel Venable, and sold to Robert Y. Overby in 1846. Venable moved to his wife's parents' plantation in Granville County, North Carolina, that same year. (Peter T. Eaton.)

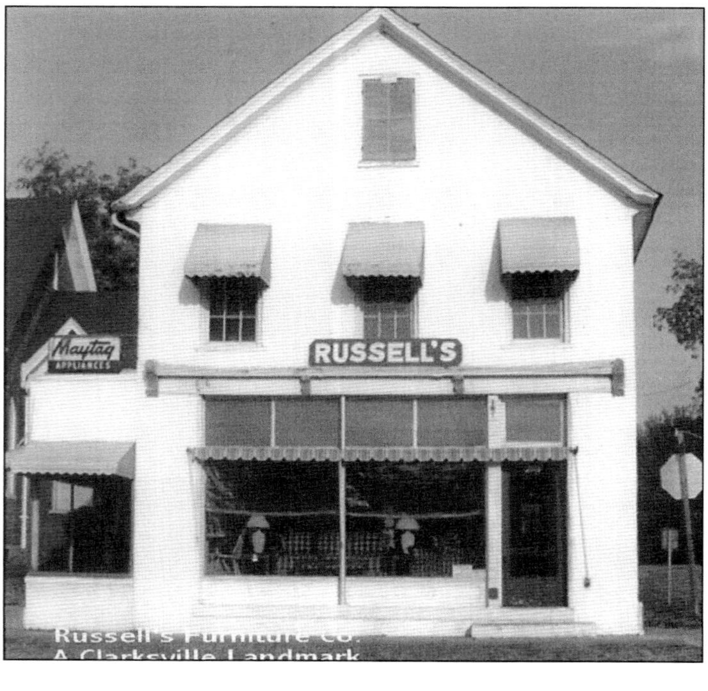

The front section of Russell's Furniture dates to about 1841 as the Robert B. Harris Coach Factory. The factory met with much success, and in 1843, Harris took on two partners—Henry Taliaferro and James Whitice. The company failed and in 1876 was seized by Mechanics Building and Loan Association, whose director, Charles H. Russell, leased the building for a short time to Boyd and Brother leather goods. When it failed, Russell used the building as a showroom and parts manufacturing for his wagons. (BH.)

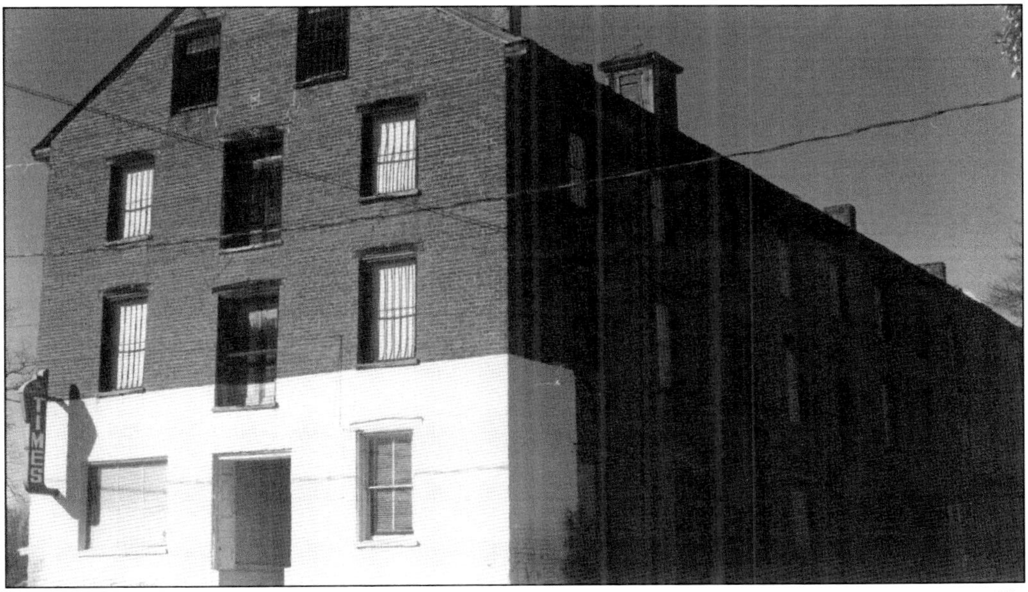

In the 1840s, Robert Moss and partners rented the Royster Warehouse on First Street. By 1853, business had grown to a staff of 73 processing 300,000 pounds of tobacco per year—most of this was sold to seamen and fishermen. In 1854, a new factory was erected, one of the largest warehouses in Virginia at that time. The Moss Tobacco Factory was lost to foreclosure in 1862. The rented warehouse, later purchased from Royster, burned in the great fire of 1857, which destroyed most of First Street and the lower part of town. (Southside Regional Library.)

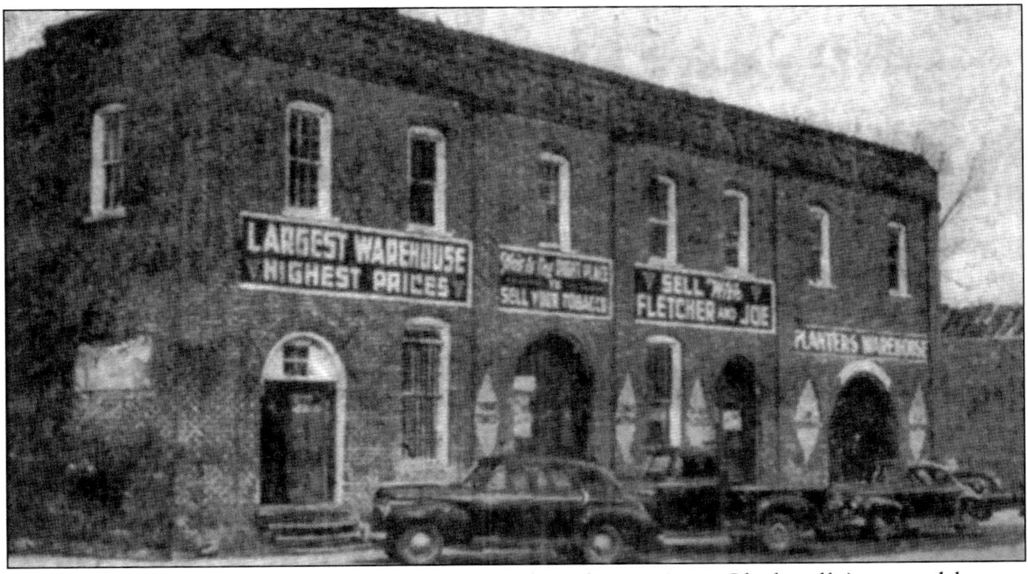

Planter's brick tobacco sales/warehouse opened in the 1840s as Clarksville's second largest warehouse. When it was built, tobacco had to be inspected and put into wooden barrels, which had a post through the center to which wheels could be attached to pull them by mule to market or the wheels removed and loaded onto bateaux for shipping. After 1871, tobacco was sold by the leaf rather than by bulk, and a new process of flue-cured tobacco changed the market forever. Around 1946, this warehouse was owned by Joe Burnett and Fletcher Burton. (BH.)

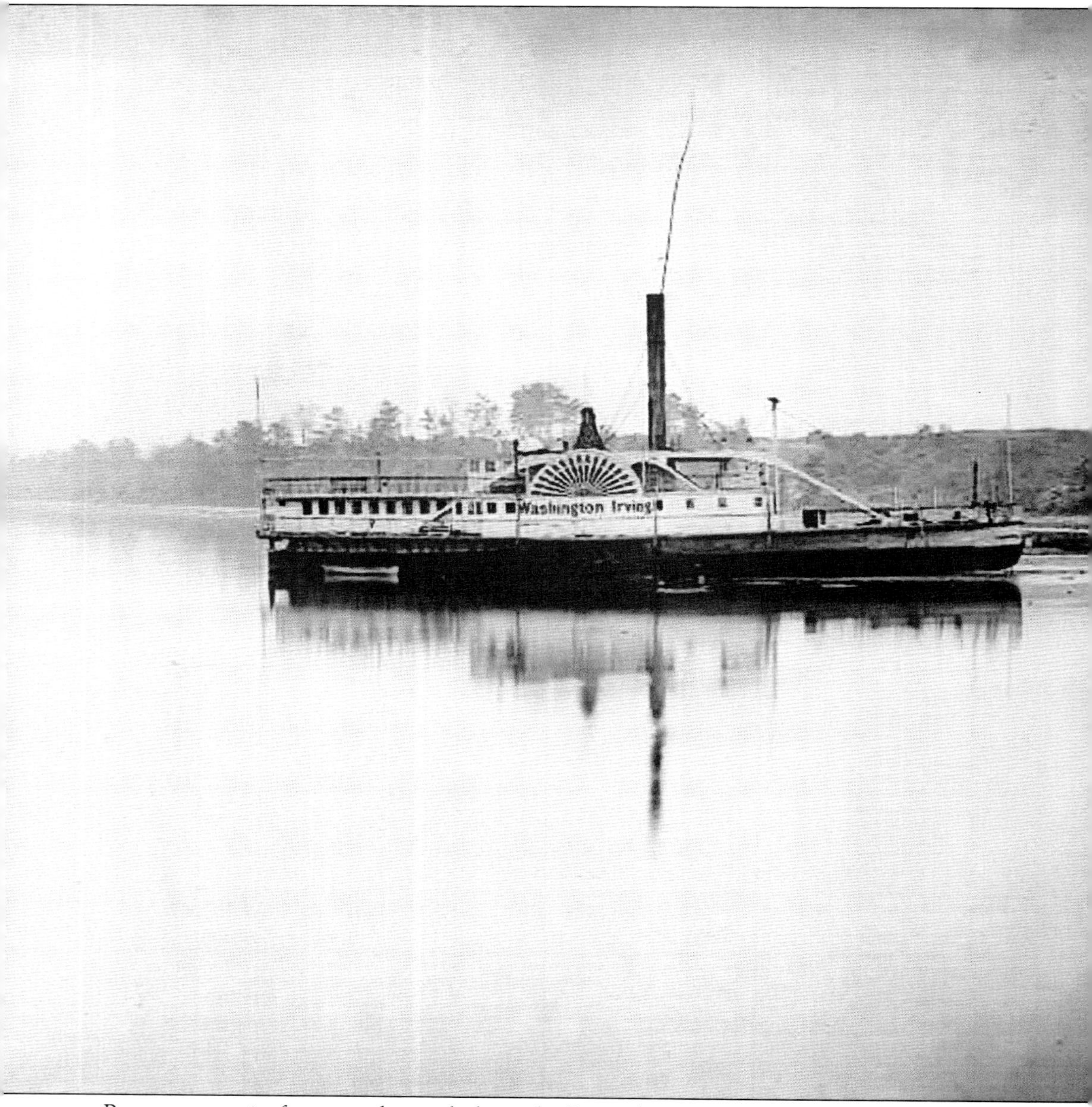

Bateaux were in frequent demand along the Roanoke River. Bateaux operated on the river until the 1890s, but with the war, small steamships were found that could occasionally navigate the canals. Steamboats such as the *Washington Irving* surveyed the rivers for the Confederacy throughout the war and were decommissioned after the war. In May 1872, Thomas F. Goode began the Mecklenburg Boat Line, which operated on the Roanoke River until 1895. (Library of Congress, Civil War Collection.)

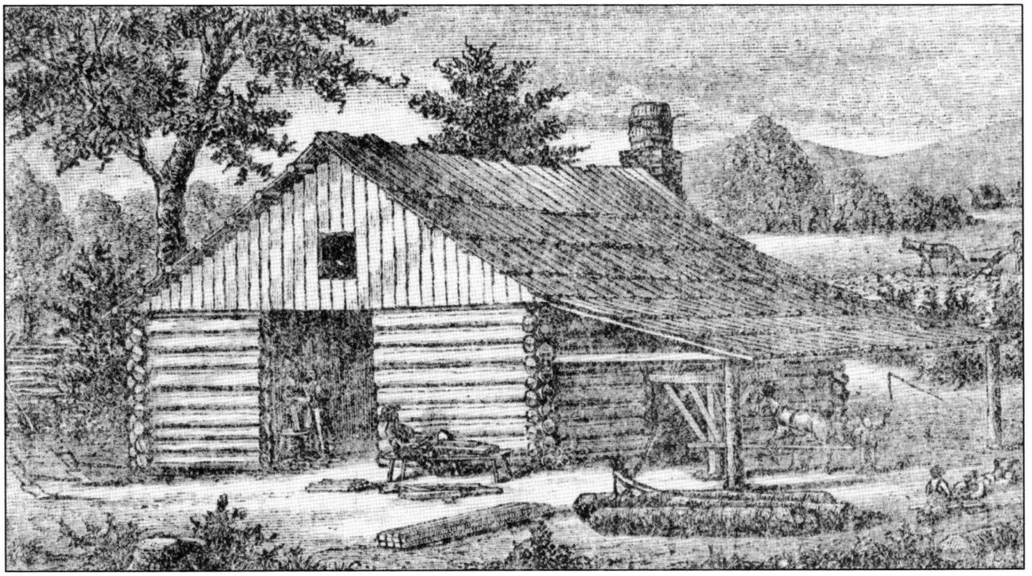

Avery Plow Company began operation in Clarksville in 1825. It was located in a 18-by-20-foot log building atop the hill east of Virginia Avenue on Fourth Street on a lot owned by Clark Royster. In 1848, the factory was moved to Louisville, Kentucky, and in the early 1900s was sold to Minneapolis-Moline Company. In 1956, it was closed. (CRM.)

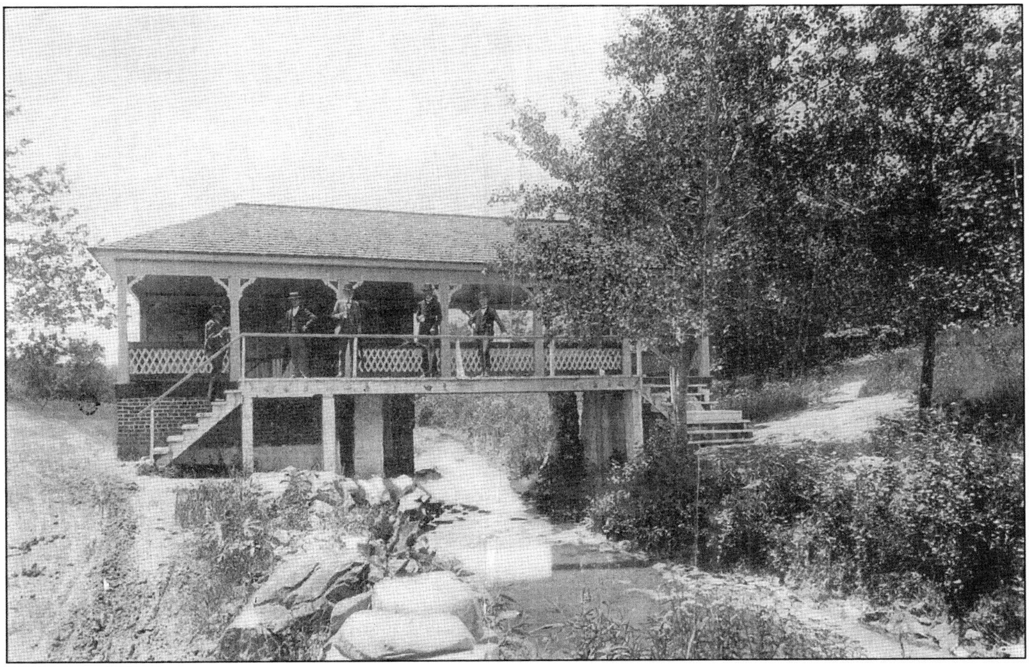

Dr. David Shelton from Clarksville leased the springs from 1824 to 1828. Dr. Shelton began to develop additional springs No. 2 and No. 3. John S. Field and Alexander S. Jones purchased the springs in 1830 and built a ballroom, hotel, and dining hall that could accommodate 300 guests. The grand balls and feasts were well attended by local tobacconists/farmers during market time, even though the resort was seasonal. (CRM.)

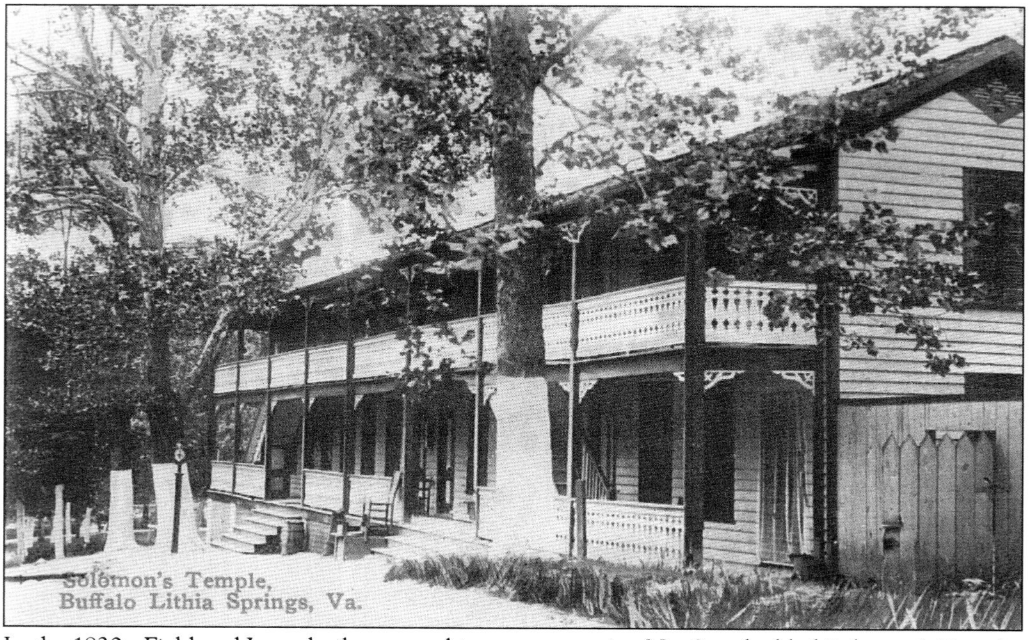

In the 1830s, Field and Jones built more cabins next to spring No. 2 and added Solomon's Temple. Advertisements were for "excellent cuisine, liquor, and entertainment." They boasted "the finest bands have been employed," and they now could accommodate 150 overnight guests. (WCG.)

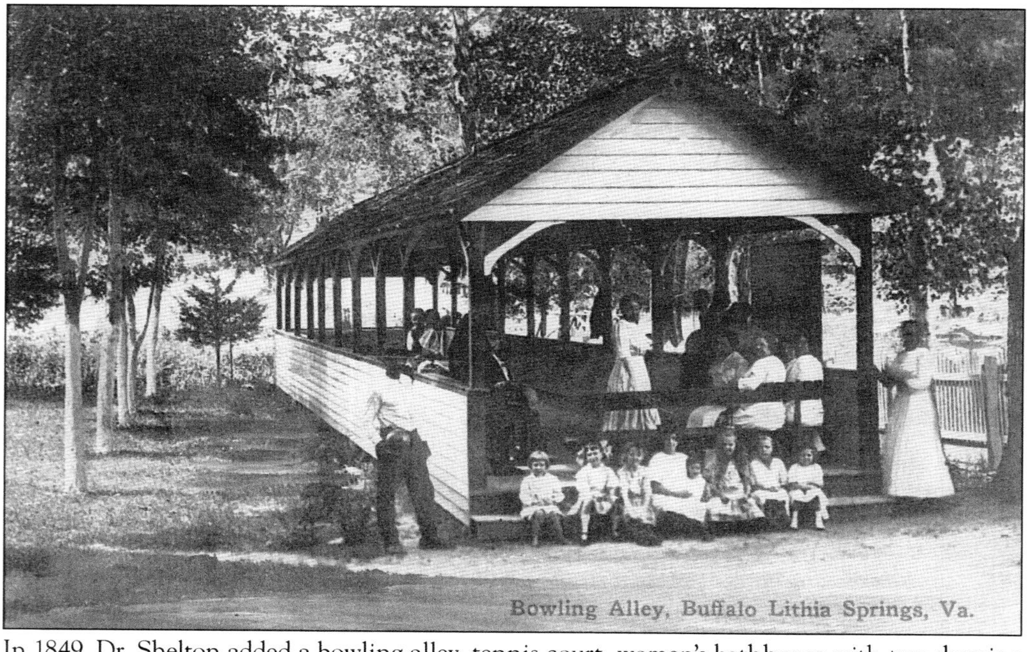

In 1849, Dr. Shelton added a bowling alley, tennis court, women's bathhouse with two dressing parlors, and riding trails. It was during this time that Gen. Winfield Scott and General Santa Anna came to the springs. With the outbreak of the Civil War, the stage line had ceased, the railroad tracks were moved to support a supply train to the troops, and Dr. Shelton was in poor health. He sold the springs in 1863 and died nine months later. (WCG.)

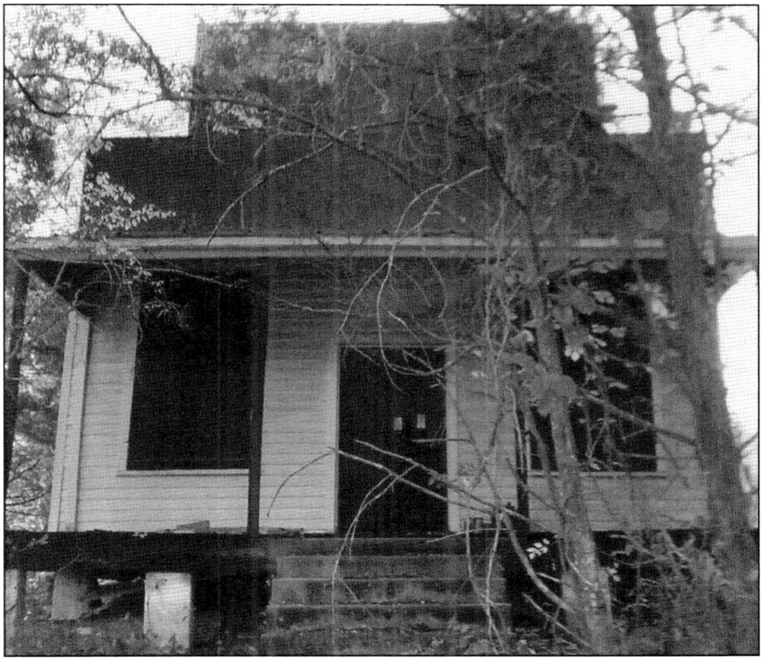

The 1830s demonstrated great prosperity to western Mecklenburg County, which contained 50 plantations. At the intersection of three or four adjoining plantations would generally develop a small community consisting of a post office with general store, a church, or a tavern with distillery. Thus many small communities began to evolve, such as Abbeyville. This is the last surviving store of Abbeyville. (BMC.)

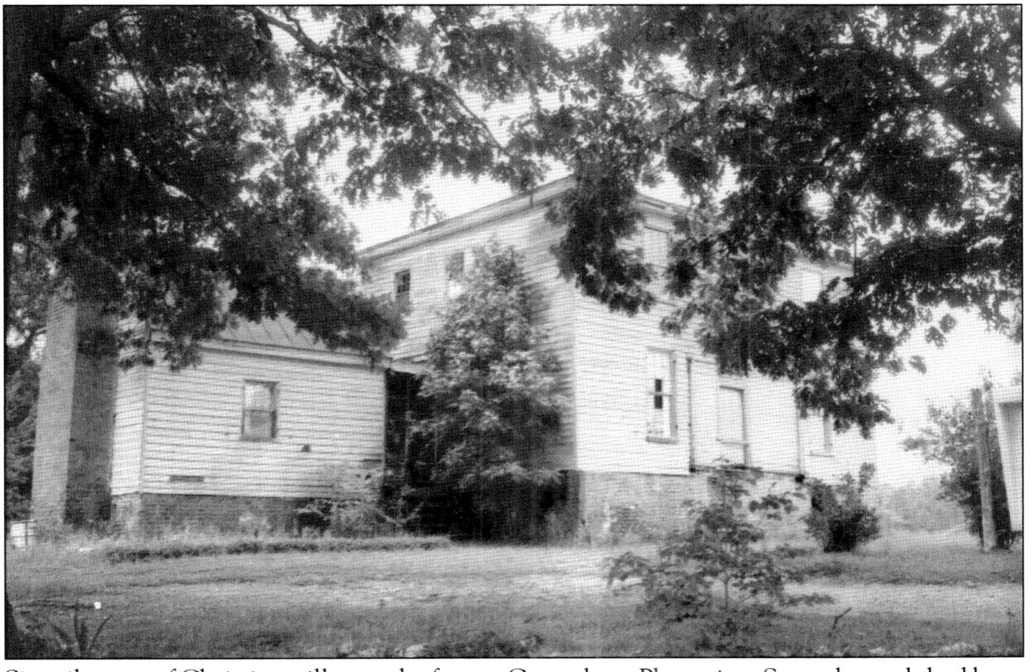

Six miles east of Christiansville was the former Greensboro Plantation. Several parcels had been sold to Quakers who came from England and became involved with the Concord Wesleyan meetinghouse. They included the widowed Sarah Draper, her unmarried daughters Sarah, Elizabeth, and Dorothy, and her son, Dr. John William Draper, with his new bride, Antonia Coetannas de Parva Pereira Gardner of Portugal. As the family were all teachers, in 1833, they opened the Draper Boarding School for girls in their home, pictured here. (Neil Blackwell.)

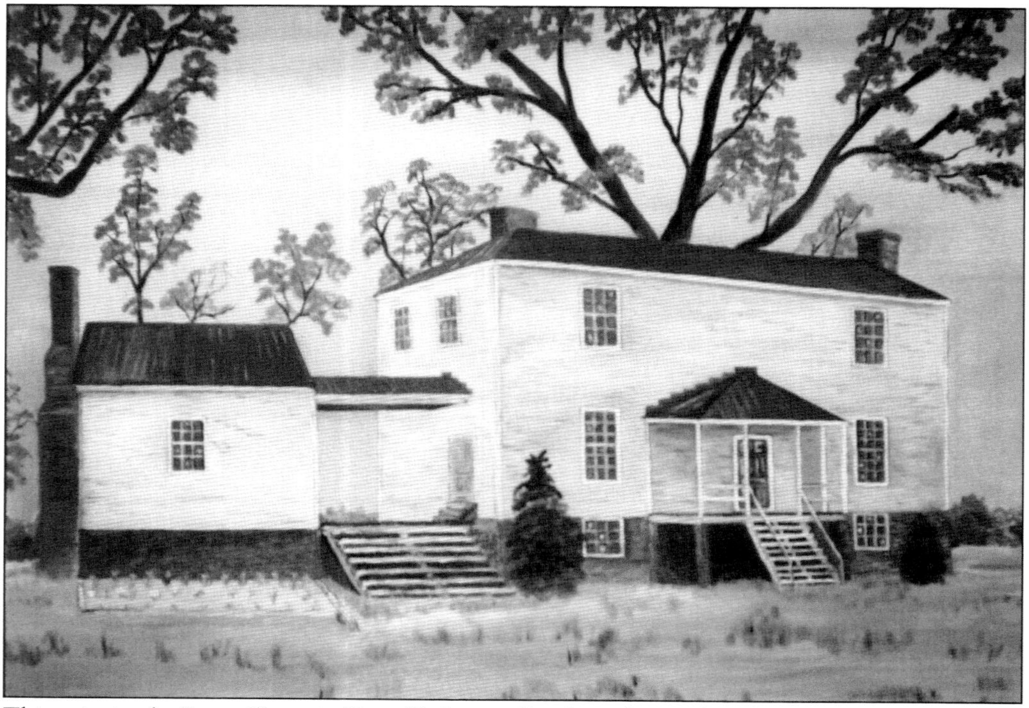

This painting by Farmville artist Doris Dickerson Rowlette shows what the home looked like—the main home where classes were conducted in two rooms downstairs and they ate and lived, the upstairs for sleeping, and the basement for Dr. Draper, who was particularly interested in the science of glass making. It is said this is where Dr. Draper built his first camera. The 1839 addition had a classroom with sleeping quarters upstairs. (Ray Gryder.)

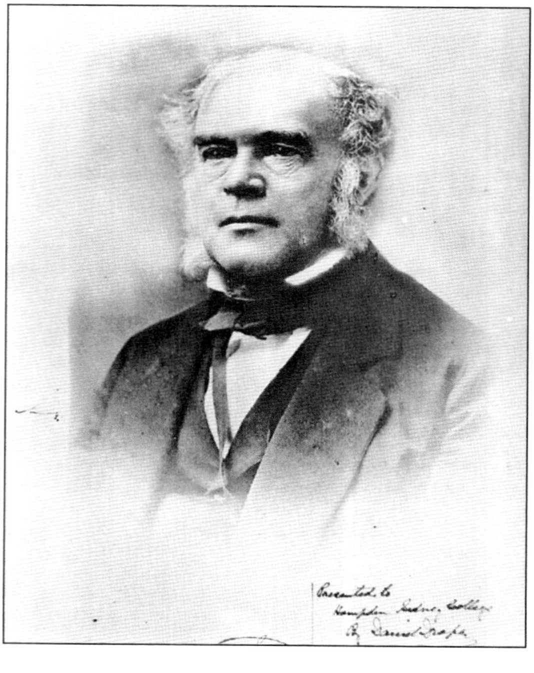

While at the Draper house, from 1834 and 1836, Dr. Draper prepared eight important scientific papers and glass lenses for telescopes, mirror imaging, and reflections, along with his first camera. Not a medical doctor but a scientist, he was called upon to help treat a local smallpox epidemic. Depressed and with fever, Dr. Draper left to attend University of Pennsylvania Medical School in 1835, graduating in 1836. (Atkinson Museum of Hampden-Sydney College.)

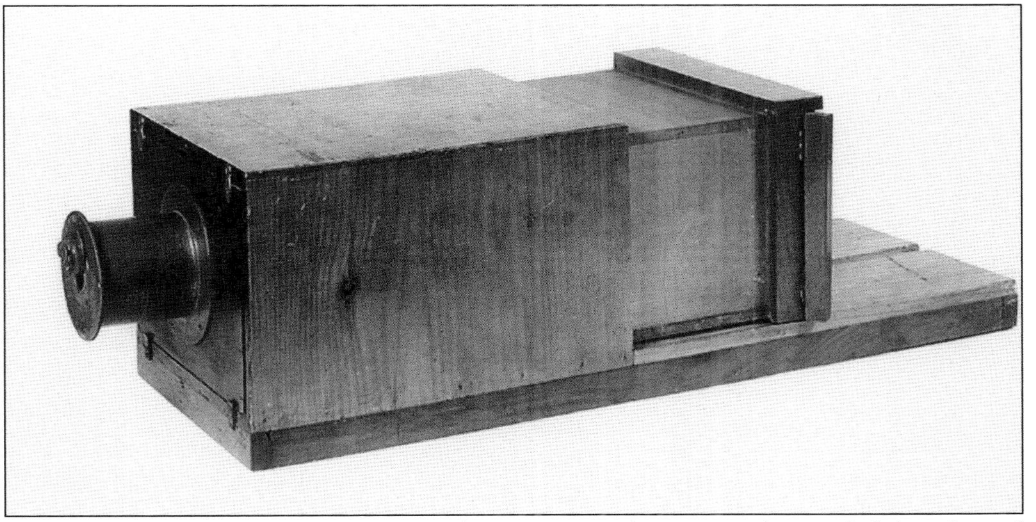

In the fall of 1836, Dr. Draper began a faculty position in chemistry and natural philosophy and became head of the newly formed Mineralogical Society with Hampton-Sydney College near Farmville. He continued to work on his camera, shortening the box, modifying the lenses and mirror, and so on, until the prototype above was developed in 1839. That same year, Dr. Draper left Hampton-Sydney to accept a position with City University of New York. In 1851, his first textbook on chemistry was published. (Atkinson Museum of Hampden-Sydney College.)

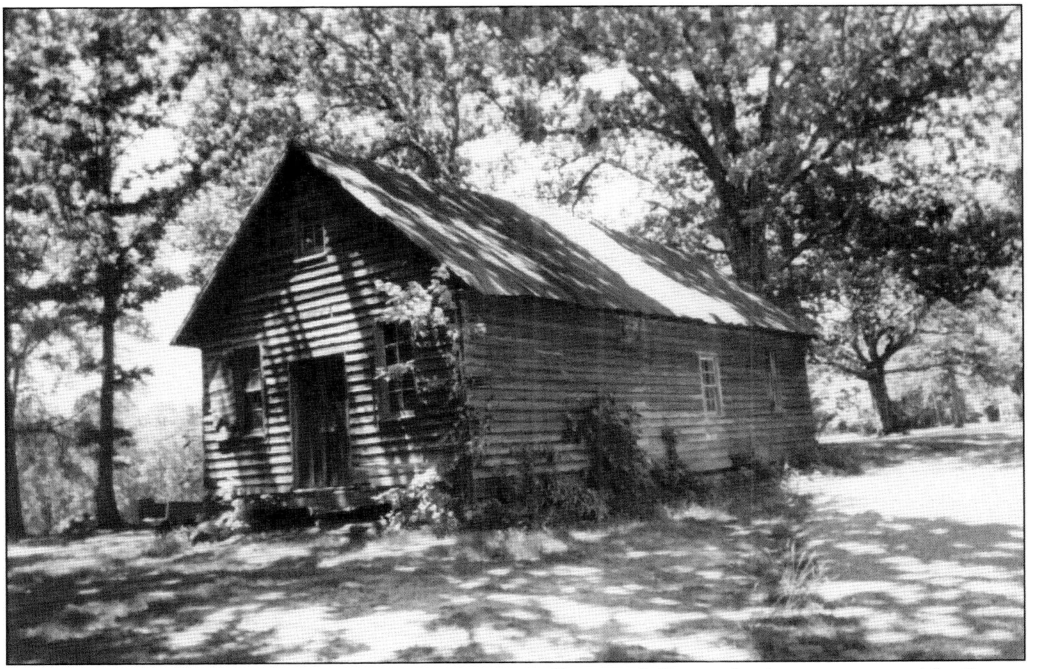

In front of the Draper home was the new Draperville Post Office, which was operated by Lewis Williams from 1837 until June 1866, when he died. The new postmaster was James J. Gregory, who died in 1880. In 1880, the new postmaster, Albert W. Garner, built a new post office and store 1.5 miles east on his farm. This photograph is of the 1880 post office, which still stands. (Ray Gryder.)

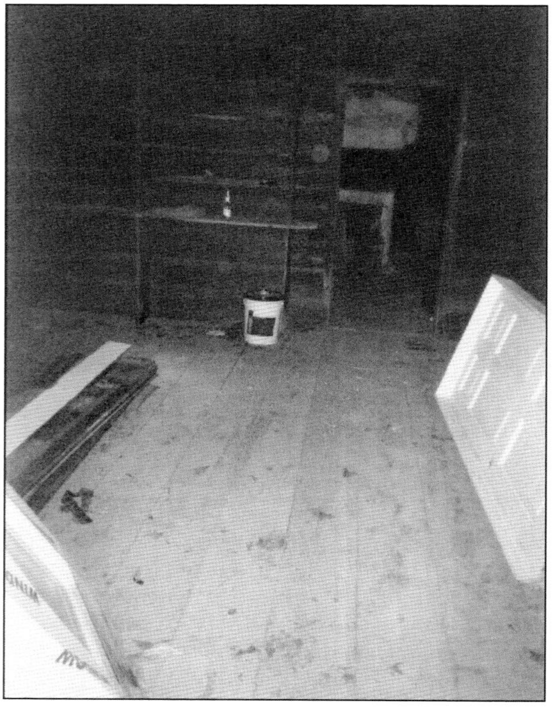

Community post offices were multipurpose buildings in those times. The mail was a very small part, as they also served as a community store, occasionally hosting a weekly Bible study, family social room, and even a tavern. A back room with fireplace and door could host a friendly card game. Some sold prepared foods and local produce. To protect the mail, postmasters lived in the post office. The U.S. government would send a new postmaster funds to build a building, but a smart postmaster would get the neighbors to build it and the money would be invested, usually in land. This is the inside of the Draperville Post Office, showing the back room. The mail boxes were in the left corner. Living quarters were upstairs. (Ray Gryder.)

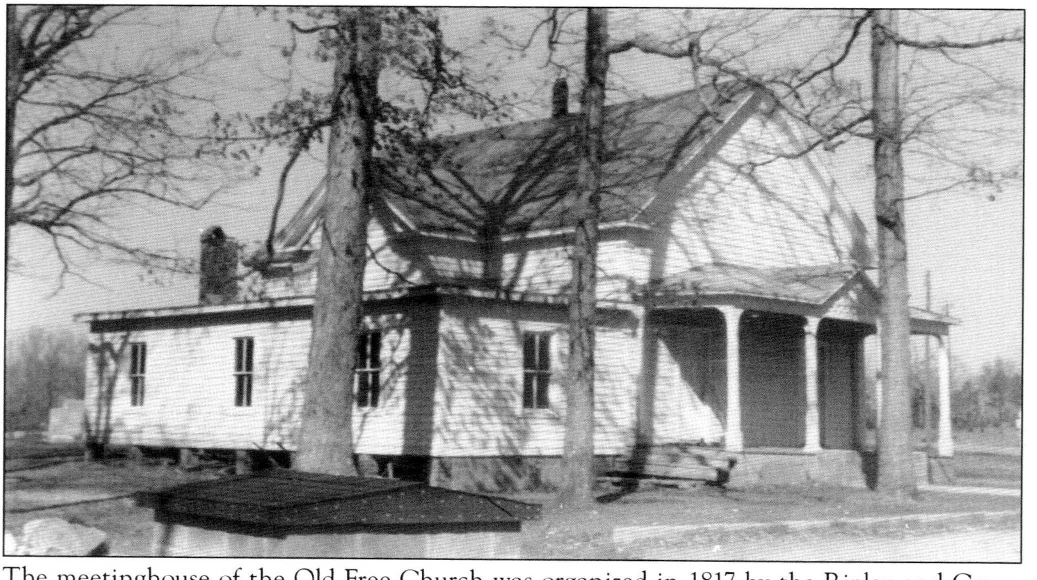

The meetinghouse of the Old Free Church was organized in 1817 by the Ripley and Green families as a Wesleyan church. The meetinghouse was built on land donated by Allen Walker, a farmer and preacher. The fourth Saturday and Sunday of each month was for worship services and business meetings. The building quickly became too small, and a wing was added to the church in 1846 and again in 1868, when attendance was 69 whites and 77 "colored." A new law required that churches be segregated, so the meetinghouse was given to the African Americans and a new church for the whites was constructed 300 yards east. A new meetinghouse was built in 1874. (Pozie Hugh Lankford.)

The first Methodist residential college the United States, Randolph-Macon College opened for the fall semester of 1832. Created in part by a $10,000 donation raised by citizens of Mecklenburg County and a delegation headed by Congressman William O. Goode, the Virginia General Assembly approved the Henry-Mason College (the name was changed to Randolph-Macon before it opened). The primary building was four stories, nearly 80,000 square feet, with 70 rooms and 10 more buildings on the 94-acre campus by 1845. Tuition for the year (10 months) was $30, but with room, board, laundry, wood, and lights, it was $115. (HBR.)

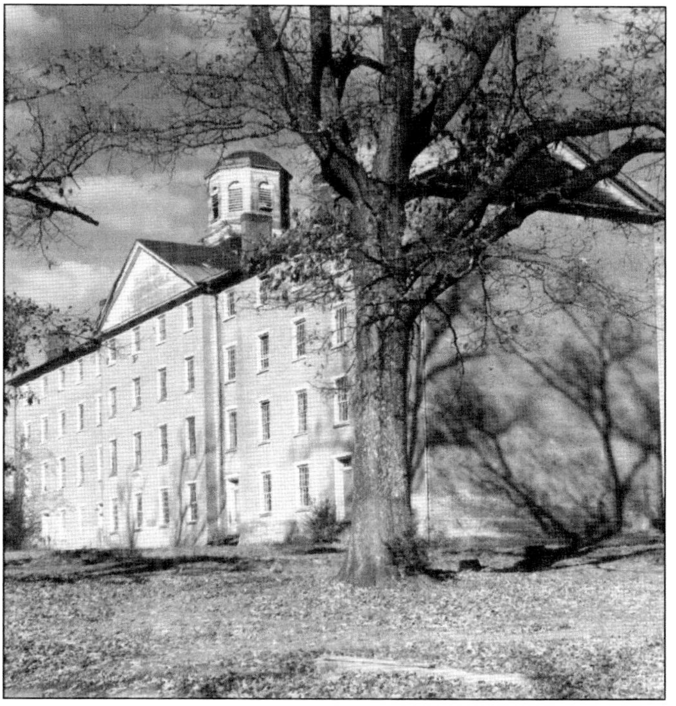

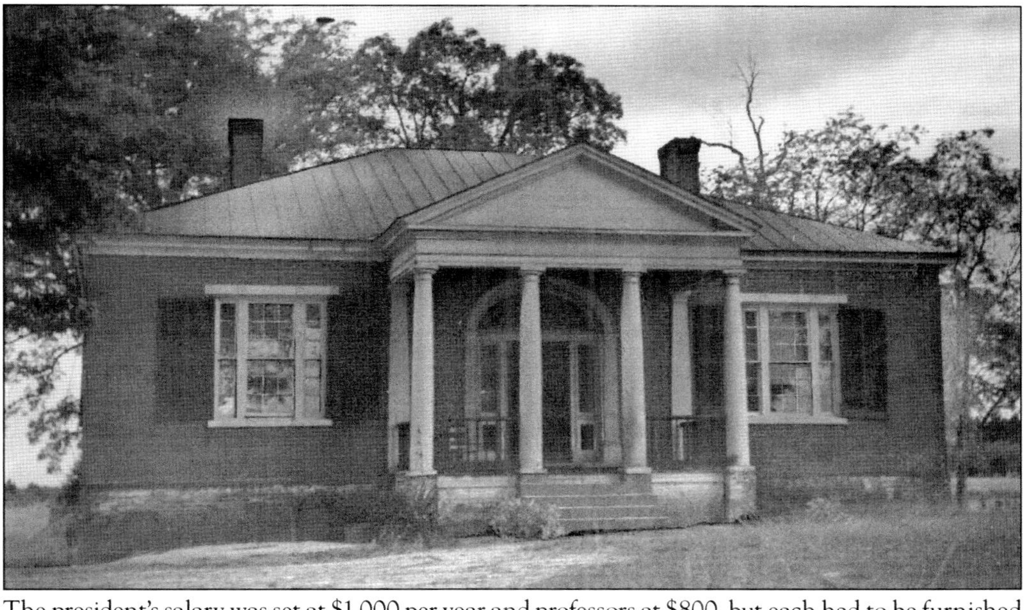

The president's salary was set at $1,000 per year and professors at $800, but each had to be furnished a house with attached yard and garden space. U.S. president John Tyler came to the college in 1841 to present the issues of the time and a gradual end to slavery. Built by Howard and Cosby, later joined by John Whitice with his new apprentice, Jacob Holt, the campus consisted of five tracts of land totaling 232 acres. The first temporary president of the college was Prof. M. P. Parks, and Dr. William A. Smith was the last in 1862. It is said most of the students and faculty enlisted in the Confederate army. (Mary Ann Boyd Ottinger.)

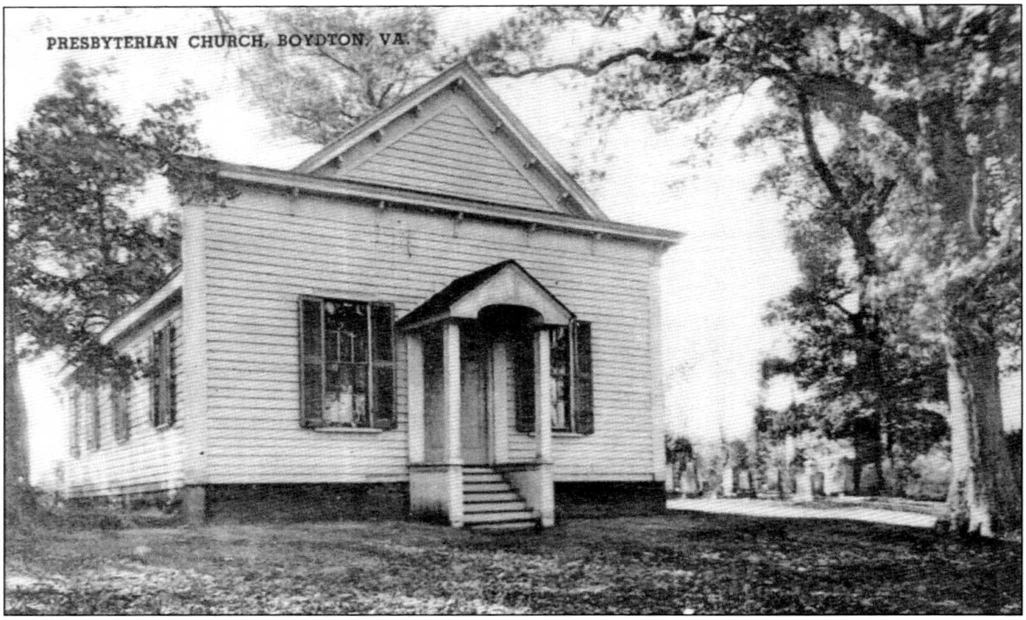

The Presbyterian Church of Boydton was built by Alexander Boyd Jr. on his property in 1819 and was opened to be used by all faiths. The Episcopalians continued to meet in the church until their building was moved and remodeled in 1842. This was the first church established in Boydton, and the surrounding cemetery contains many graves of the earliest settlers of the town. Many of those namesakes are still in town. (REC.)

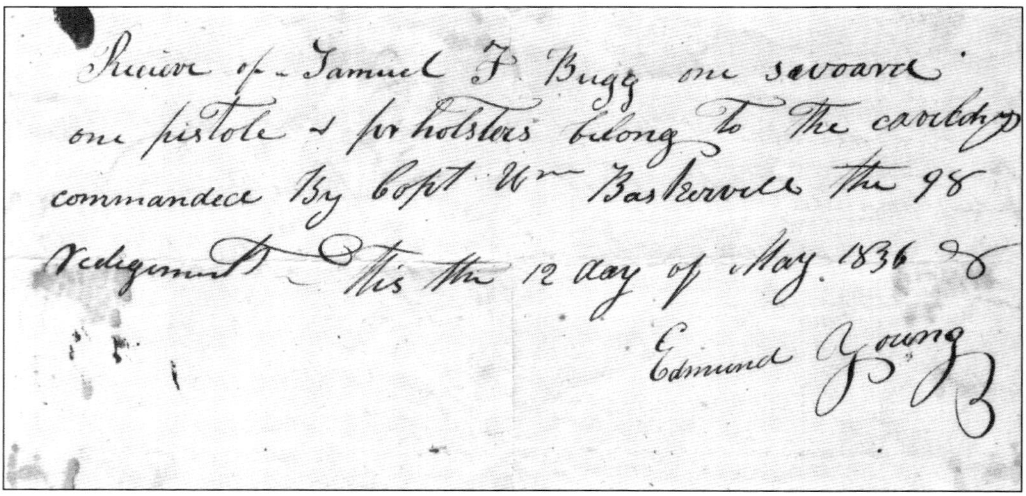

Receive of Samuel F. Bugg one swoard one pistole & for holsters belong to the cavelry commanded By Capt Wm Baskerville the 98 Redigiment This the 12 day of May 1836

Edmund Young

The Boydton Cavalry was organized for the Revolutionary War, continued through the War of 1812, and was still in force during the Mexican Border Campaign. On May 12, 1836, one of its members, resigning, received this receipt for turning in "one swoard one pistole & for holsters belong to the cavalry commanded by Capt Wm Baskerville the 98 Redigiment," signed by Edmund Young. (RB.)

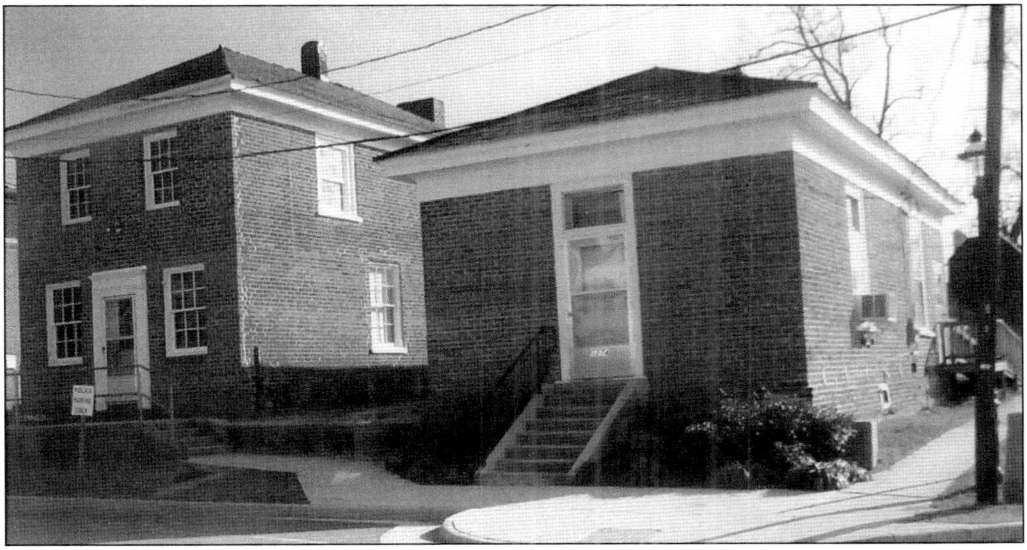

With the opening of the college, Boydton began to grow, adding an additional dry goods store and millinery. In 1842, Brack Duggar's Tailor Shop (left) opened. After the Civil War, it was the Boydton Post Office with the law offices of Thomas F. Goode upstairs. In 1893, the postmaster advertised he had added "a handsome new money order window." In the 1870s, Thomas Goode purchased the Randolph-Macon Lodge and used the brick to build the small law office building (right) next door to Duggar's. (BMC.)

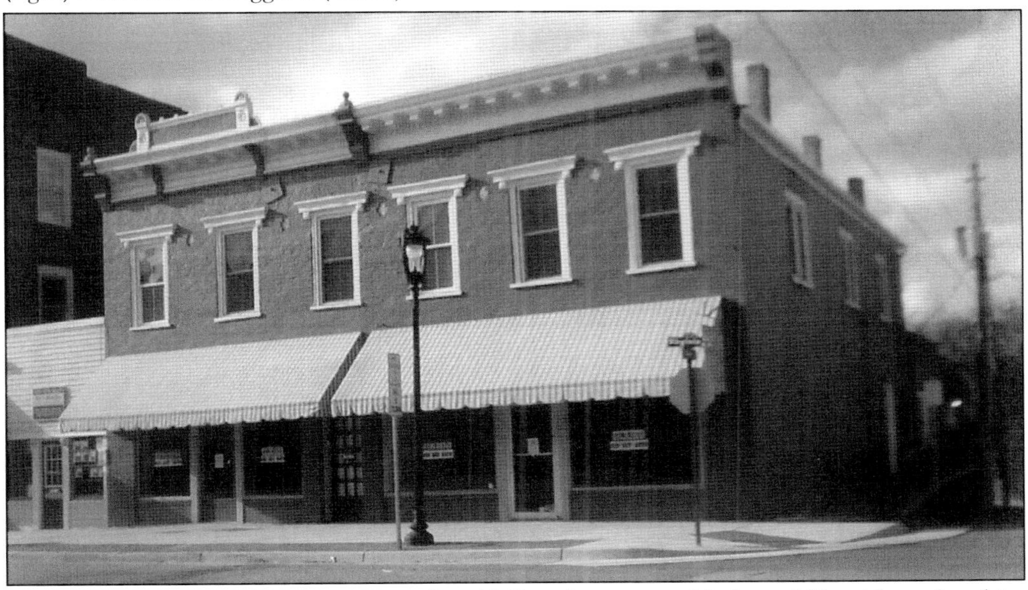

The Exchange Bank of Virginia opened in 1845 with manager Nathaniel Venable and cashier William Gee and operated until 1866. In 1871, it reopened as Bank of Clarksville but was closed by 1879 when purchased by the Mechanics Building and Loan Association. In the 1890s, it became the T. D. Moore Hardware store with Richard B. Humphrey's, jeweler, watchmaker, and optics, upstairs. An addition to the back was for the Farming Implement and Supply Company. In the 1920s, Moore Hardware was purchased by Tom Humphrey, and it became Humphrey's Hardware, stoves, sporting goods, and farm implements. The building is now vacant. (John Caknipe.)

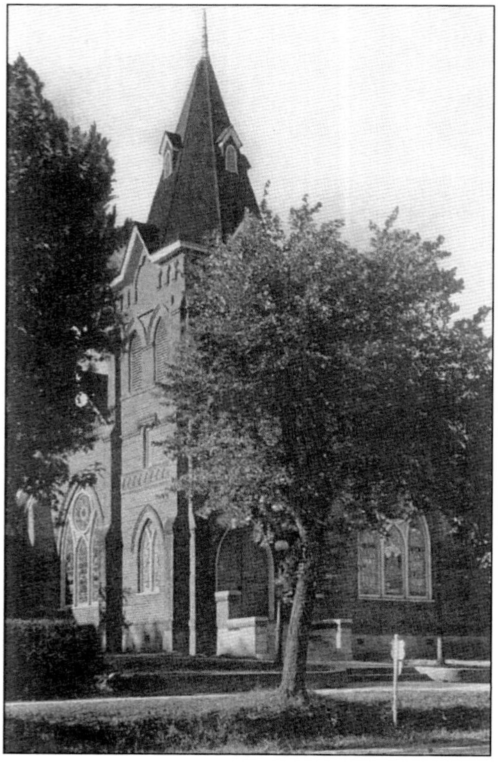

The Presbyterian Church of Clarksville was organized and built in 1832 and dedicated on July 12 on Fourth Street with its first pastor being Rev. Samuel Graham. In 1907, it was sold to the Board of Deacons for the Baptists, and a new church was erected on Fifth Street and Virginia Avenue. By 1893, Dr. Thomas Drew of Chase City was the pastor until his retirement from both churches in 1917. (Kathryne B. Routt.)

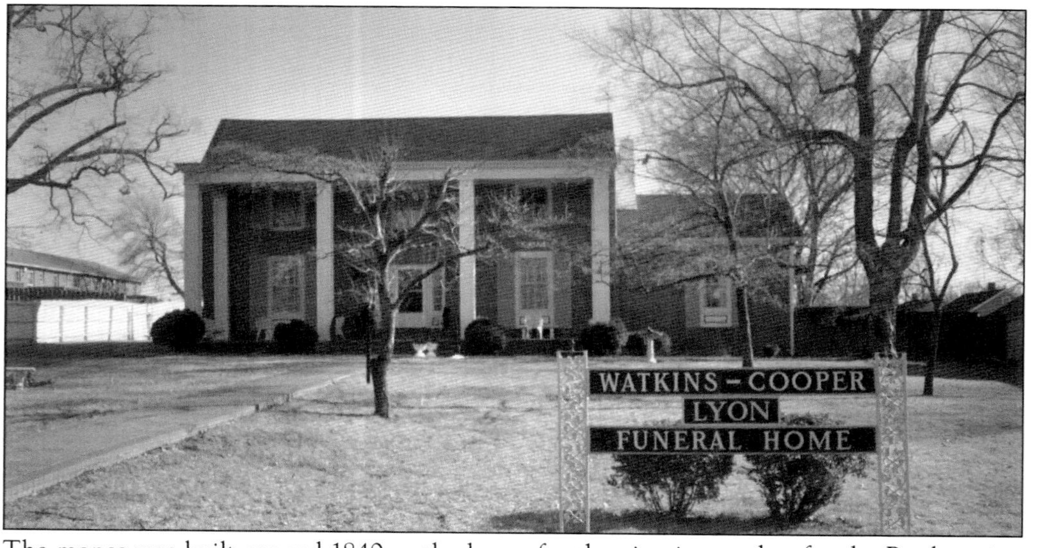

The manse was built around 1840 as the home for the circuit preacher for the Presbyterian churches of the parish. Since Dr. Drew had a residence in Chase City, the manse was sold in 1893. In 1943, Jack Watkins and Jim Cooper purchased the business from D. Webster Yancey's widow and began Watkins-Cooper Funeral Home. This funeral home is a development of what began as "Liipfort—the coffin maker," followed by Yancey and Luther J. Morgan, with several to follow. In the 1930s, this home was the first meeting place for the Catholic community of the area. (Watkins-Cooper Lyon Funeral Home.)

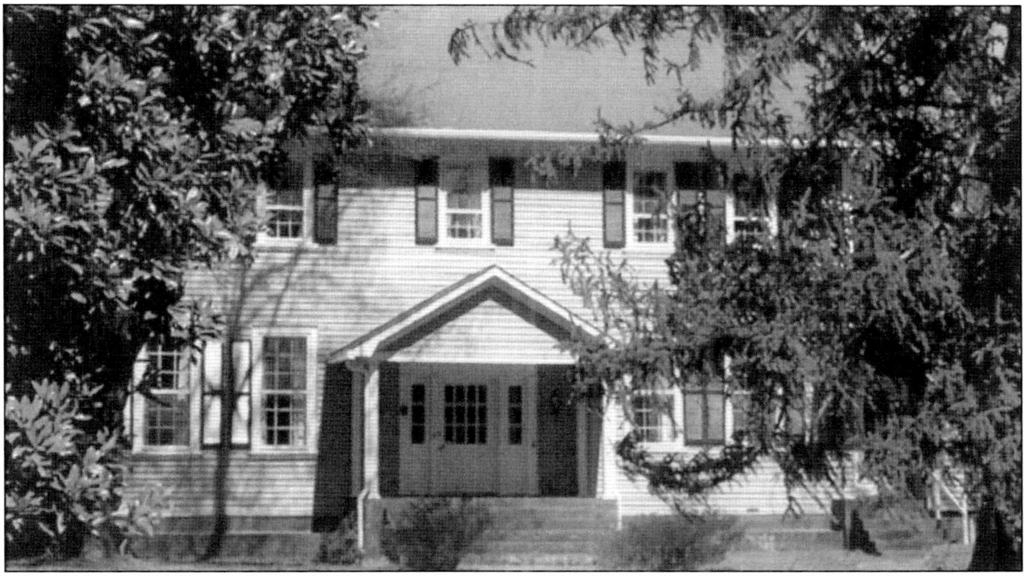

In the 1770s, another settler, later planter and farmer, to the area was Thomas Greenwood. The "Tithing Book" for 1778 shows Thomas in a business transaction with Philip Mealer. His 1,000-acre tract of land was outside Clarksville next to the Oxford Road but provided Clarksville with much of its produce and dairy through the 1930s. Today the home is called Sutherland. The lands have now been platted and sold. (BH.)

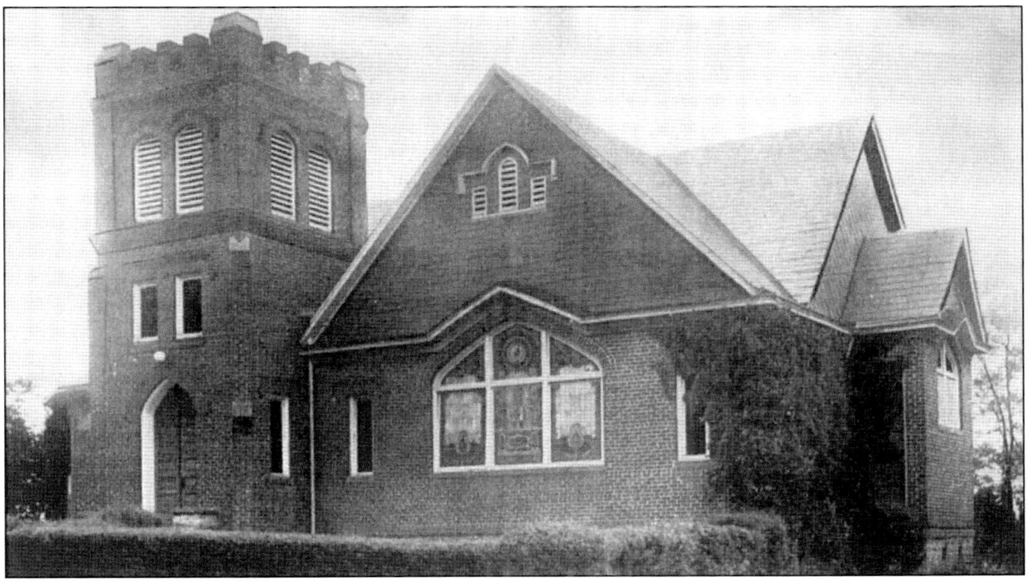

Jamieson Memorial Methodist Church, with its first recorded minister a Dr. Wealthy, was torn down and a new church built across the street in 1901. It was begun by members of the Greenwood family, and ministers from Randolph-Macon College occupied the pulpit for 35 years. The church was named for James Jamieson, a pastor there from 1876 until his death in 1880. His son, William, was a member of the congregation in 1871, when he joined C. H. Russell with the Mechanics Building and Loan Association until he was elected clerk of the county from 1888 to 1905. (Rebecca Cary.)

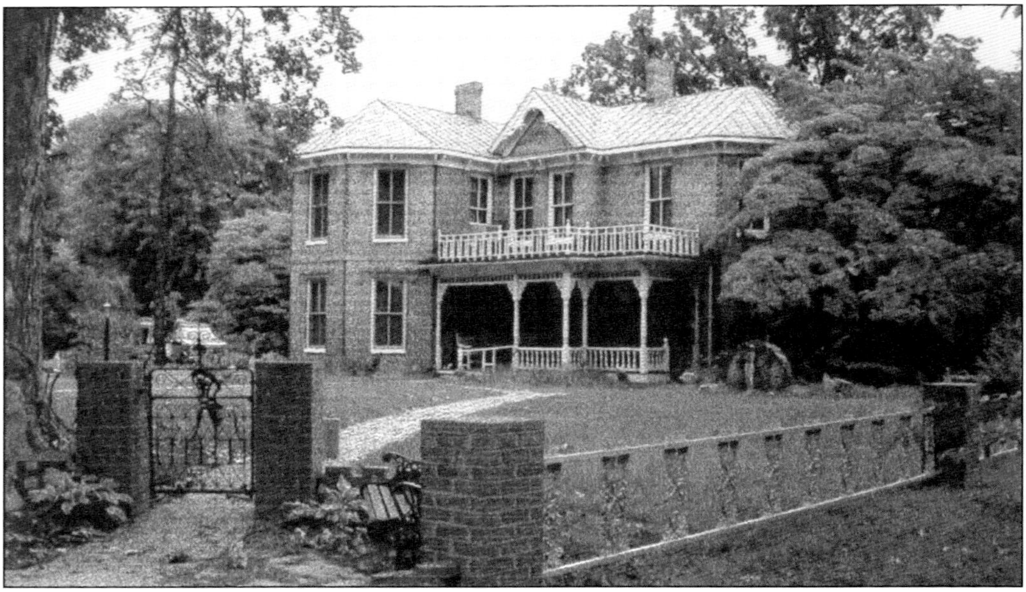

This home, part of the William Vowell tract, is referred to as the Judge Henry Wood house, but it was built by Dr. David Shelton of Buffalo Springs, who was keeping books for the Roanoke River Navigation Company. With many owners, the most prominent is Maj. Gen. William Mahone of Petersburg, who brought his family to Clarksville in 1862 for safety during the war. He was at the surrender with General Lee at Appomattox. Mahone did not make payments on the house from 1866 through 1868, and it was foreclosed. (Lacy C. Smith and Donald and Rebecca Hall.)

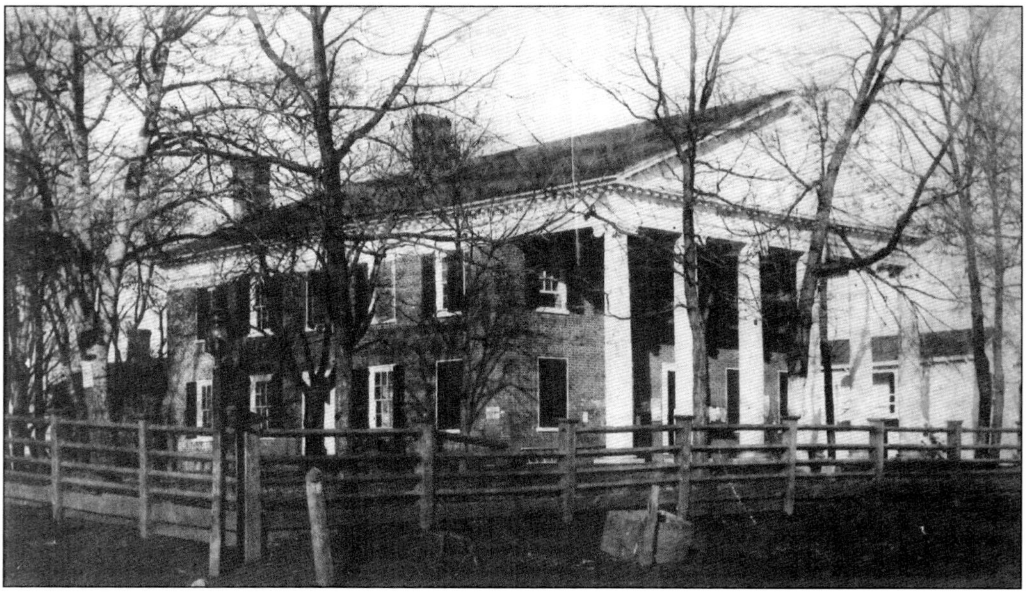

With so much growth and prosperity in the western part of the county, a new courthouse was commissioned, and it was completed in 1841. The bricks from the foundations of the old courthouse were to be used for walkways. Wooden fencing around the courthouse was to keep the animals of town off the lawn. In 1851, there was a need for a jail, shown here to the right of the courthouse. The jailer from 1868 until 1892, when he was shot during a jail break, was James Bugg. (REC.)

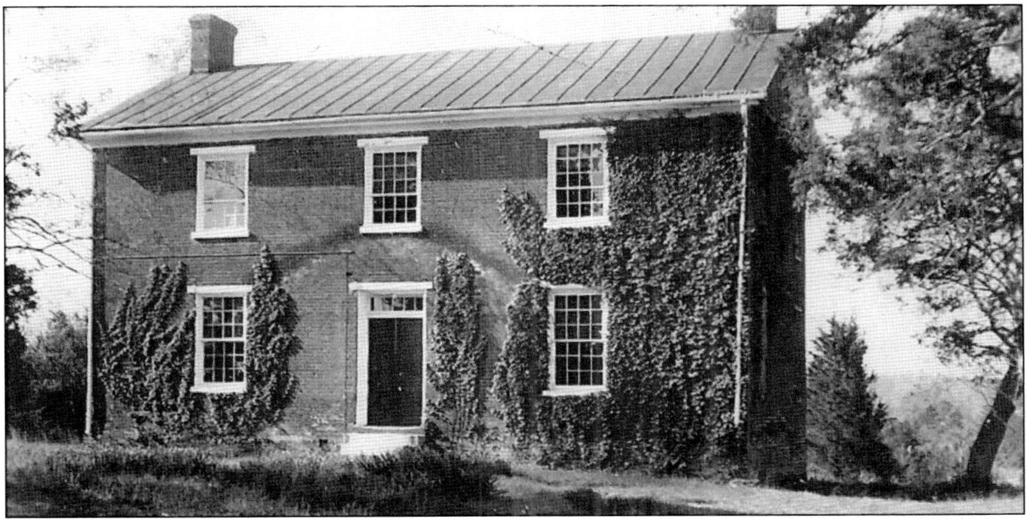

Within a year, Randolph-Macon College had grown to the extent that a Preparatory Department had to be added in 1833. This hall, located next to the president's house, contained two large recitation rooms capable of seating 50 to 75 students and also served as the social center of campus, but since dancing was not allowed, promenading events were held. In 1878, when it became the National Bible Training Institute owned by Dr. Charles Cullis of Boston, this building became Teacher's Hall. However, some folklore states that during the war, Randolph-Macon was used as a school to teach Confederate soldiers communication and other skills necessary to serve as spies. (Mary Ann Boyd Ottinger.)

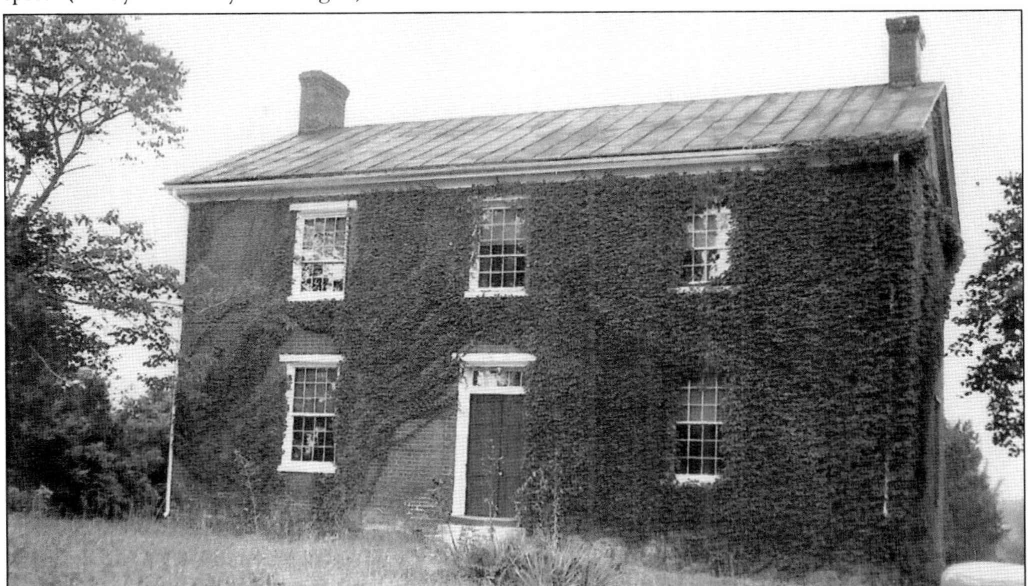

As the college and town of Boydton began to grow, so did travel and tourism. The college owned slaves and had several servants. Ministers graduating from the college were readily hired throughout the region and country. In 1834, Boydton had four stores, two hotels, two churches, a coach factory, a confectionery, and the Randolph-Macon Lodge, pictured here. (Mary Ann Boyd Ottinger.)

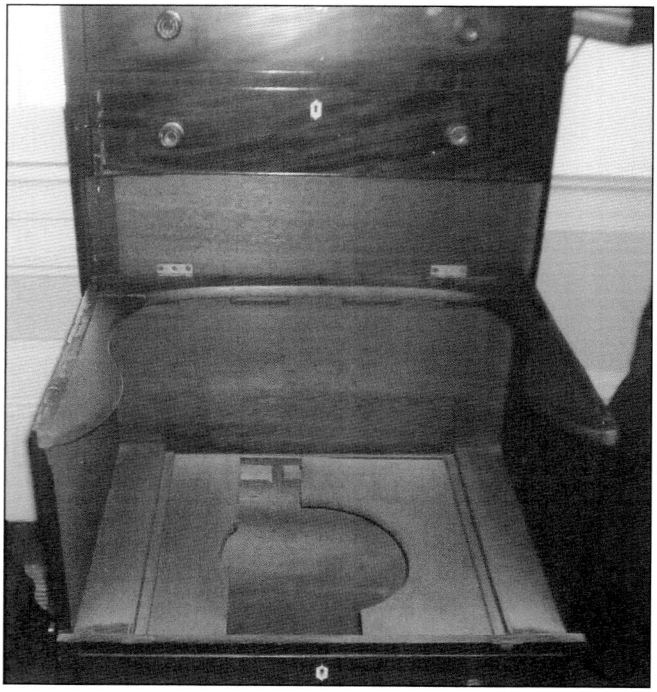

Until the dawn of the 20th century, most hotels did not have indoor plumbing. To accommodate guests' needs during the hours of darkness, most hotels had special commode tables, nightstands, or another socially graceful manner for guests to go to the toilet (pots). Each day, the pots would be collected and dumped outside. One such example is this Victorian nightstand from the Boyd Tavern, a very elegant-looking piece of furniture with a lid that includes the fake drawer facings, which lifts and folds back for a guest to sit on the pot and relax, then replace when done. Maybe that's why men have to learn to put the lid down. (Boyd Tavern Foundation.)

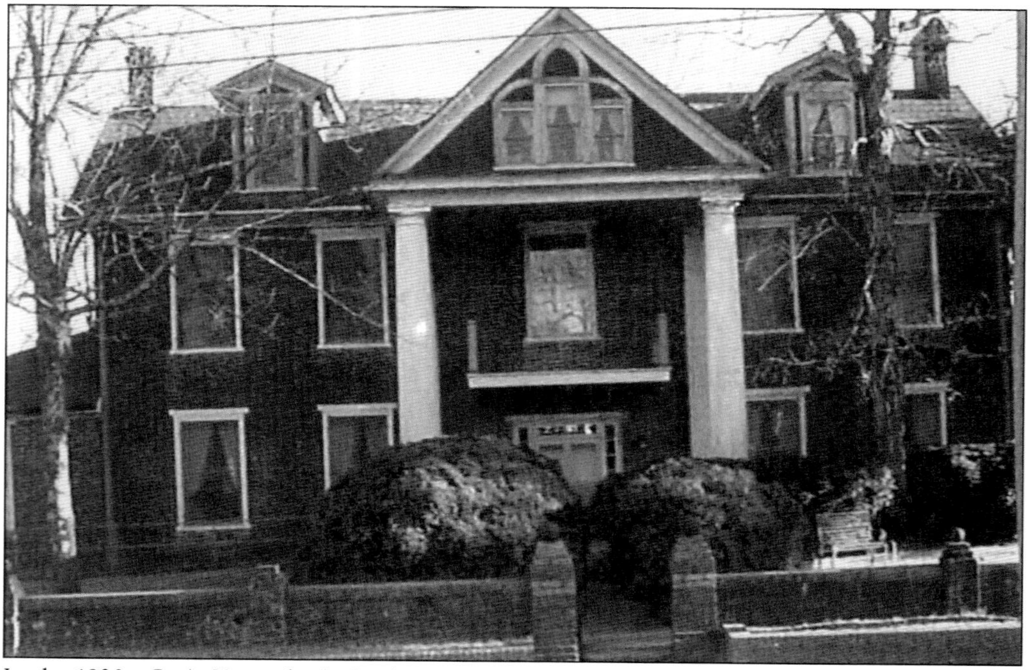

In the 1830s, G. A. Young built this home for his family. Purchased by Philo Alcott and his new wife, it was updated in the 1870s. Alcott came with his parents from New York to Clarksville before the war in 1858, and his father was a contractor. In 1878, Alcott was serving on the new Clarksville school board. The home was purchased in 1918 by Robert H. Easley Jr., owner of the Grace Hotel. (BH.)

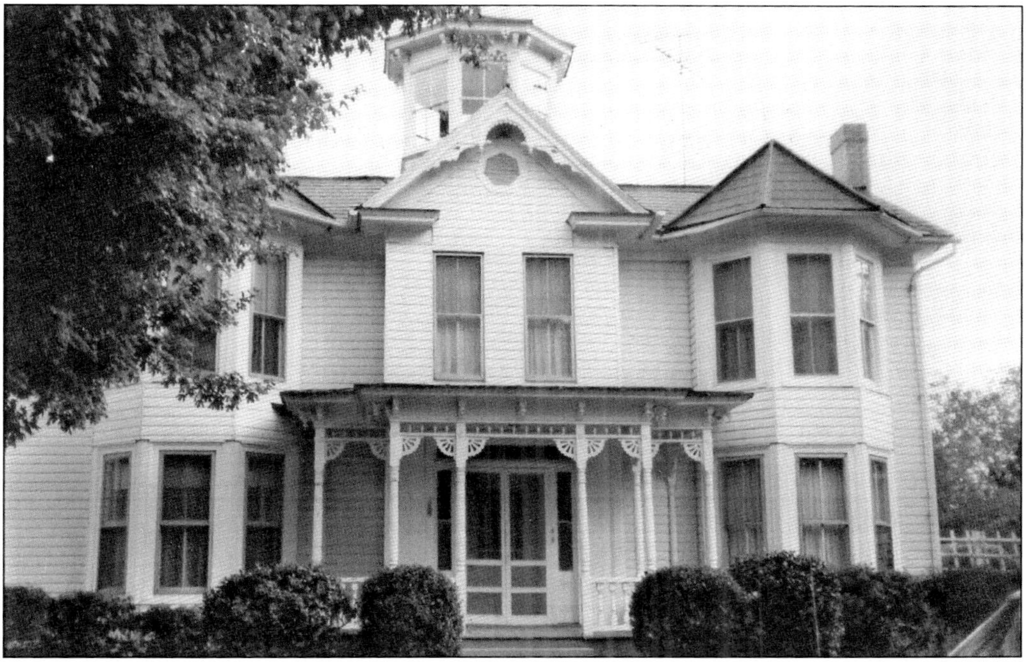

In 1843, William H. Gee, cashier for the Exchange Bank of Virginia, built this home while the bank was being built. In the backyard, he built a small shop, which his wife, Rebecca, used as a dressmaking shop. Gee remained with the bank until it closed in 1866, and in the 1870s, he was operating a "Confectioner" store in the Exchange Hotel near the bank. The bank reopened in 1871 as the Bank of Clarksville using the former Exchange building. (Jeanne P. Morgan.)

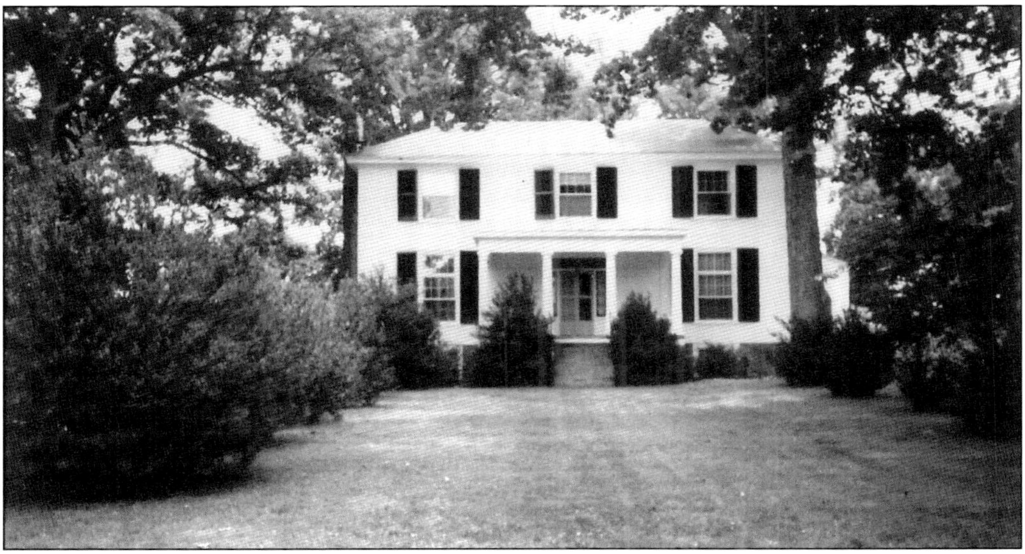

The southeasternmost plantation in western Mecklenburg north of the river, and one of the last to be developed, is Cuscowilla. It was built in 1857 by the acclaimed 25 slave master builders and 5 slave master brick masons of Col. William Townes for his only son, Dr. William Townes Jr., and included 2,000 acres as a gift for his new daughter-in-law, Emmett Barksdale of Charlotte County. The grounds included stables, kitchen, and smokehouse. (Lorene C. Lessing.)

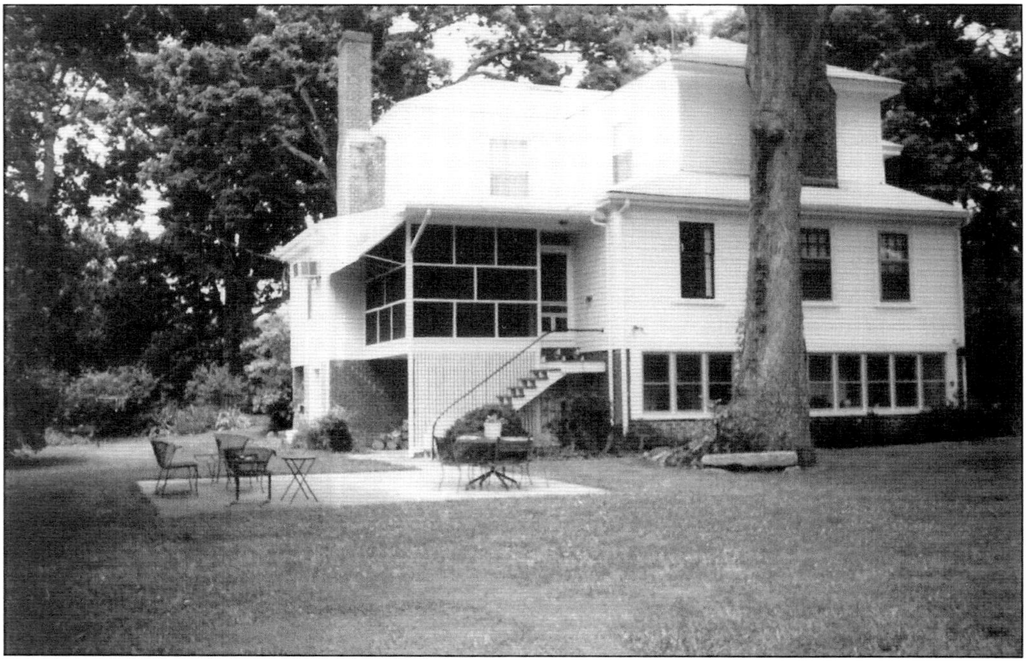

Cuscowilla Post Office opened in November 1875 with the first postmaster being Henry F. Jester. In this photograph of the back of the house, the first room to the right was the post office. As with a typical plantation village, icehouse, cooper shop, blacksmith shop, sawmill, store houses, servants and overseers quarters, slave quarters, gristmill, outdoor toilets, and sometimes a bathhouse could be found. (Lorene C. Lessing.)

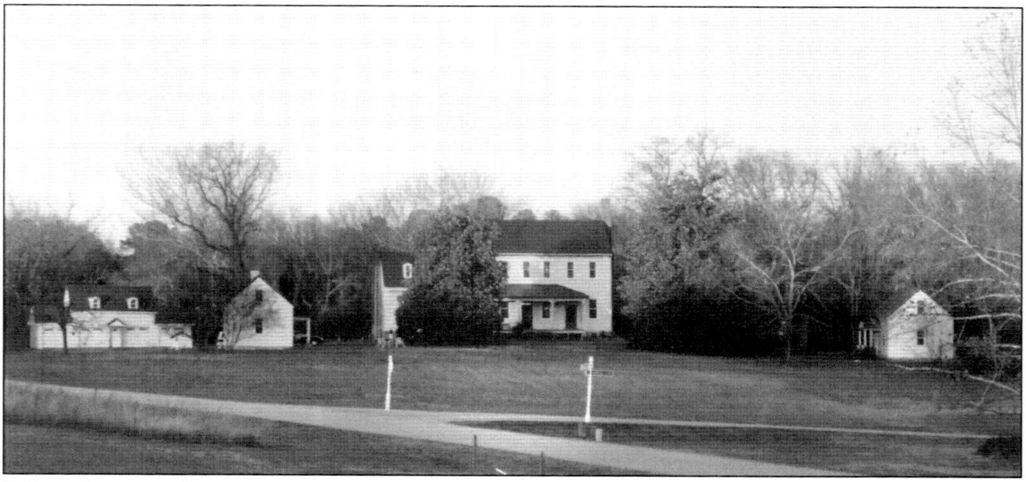

Below the river, the southeast corner of western Mecklenburg was called Eppes Fork. As was true of antebellum plantation life, each plantation was a self-sufficient village. The largest was this plantation, Berry Hill, 2,564 acres south of the Roanoke River. A ferry system to the north shore was established nearby—Taylor's Ferry—which became strategic during the war as a supply depot, magazine and commissary, and guard house for the river. (Irwin Garskof.)

Two

Civil War and Reconstruction

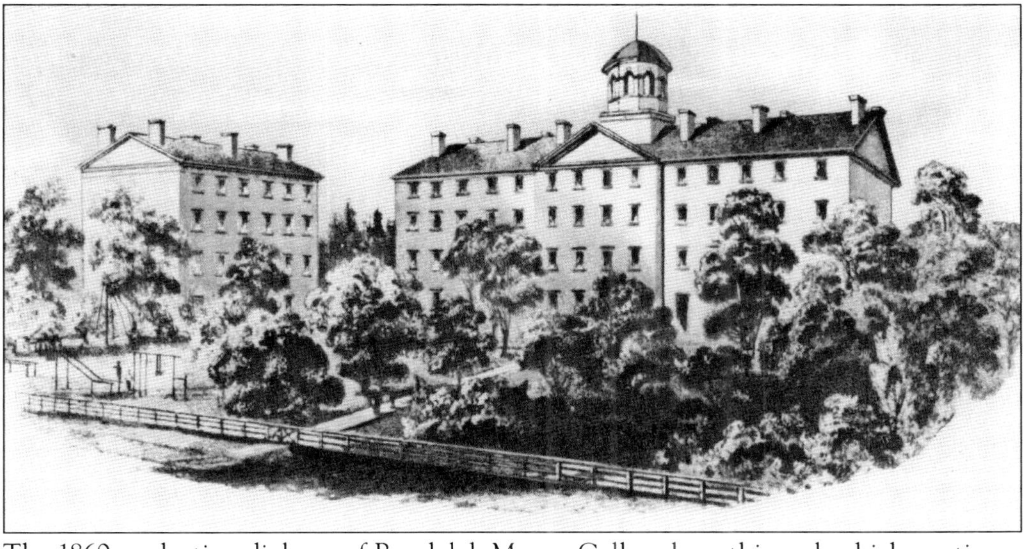

The 1860 graduation diploma of Randolph-Macon College bore this seal, which continues today. Little could have been known about the fate of the area for the next five years, but there was speculation. Dr. William Smith had been openly lecturing proslavery since at least 1858. Local congressman Thomas F. Goode was adamant about Virginia seceding from the union and received the nickname "The Bulldog of the Virginia Convention" for secession. (Southside Regional Library.)

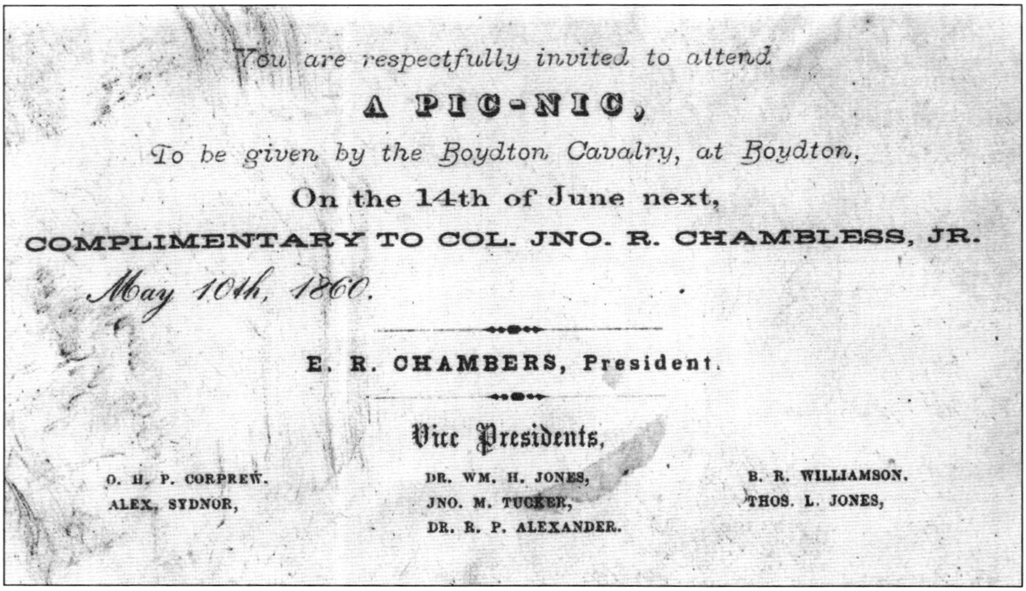

You are respectfully invited to attend

A PIC-NIC,

To be given by the Boydton Cavalry, at Boydton,

On the 14th of June next,

COMPLIMENTARY TO COL. JNO. R. CHAMBLESS, JR.

May 10th, 1860.

E. R. CHAMBERS, President.

Vice Presidents,

O. H. P. CORPREW.	DR. WM. H. JONES,	B. R. WILLIAMSON.
ALEX. SYDNOR,	JNO. M. TUCKER,	THOS. L. JONES,
	DR. R. P. ALEXANDER.	

With this invitation dated May 10, 1860, it is evident that Boydton military was in preparation of what was to come. The "pic-nic" was not only social but served as a fund-raiser and recruitment campaign, probably held on the campus grounds of the college. It is of note that though western Mecklenburg County was the horse capital of Virginia, only one company of cavalry left from the county. (RB.)

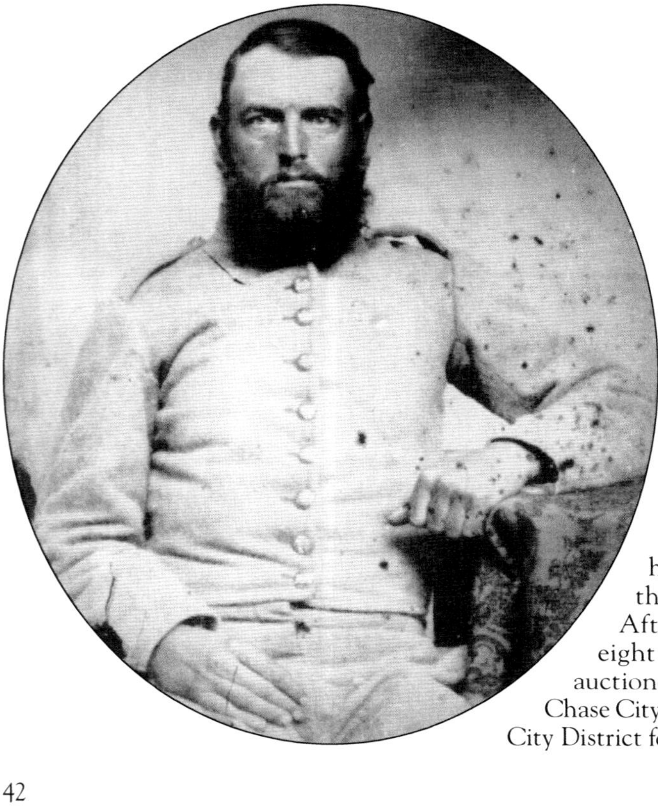

Home on leave in 1862, John Wesley Bugg had this portrait taken. He was a private in Company G, 38th Virginia Infantry Regiment, of Boydton. In 1865, he was captured and interned as a prisoner of war in Norfolk until his release on July 1, 1865, almost three months after the war ended. After the war, he married, fathered eight children, became an esteemed auctioneer in Clarksville, Boydton, and Chase City, and was a magistrate of the Chase City District for over 15 years. (RB.)

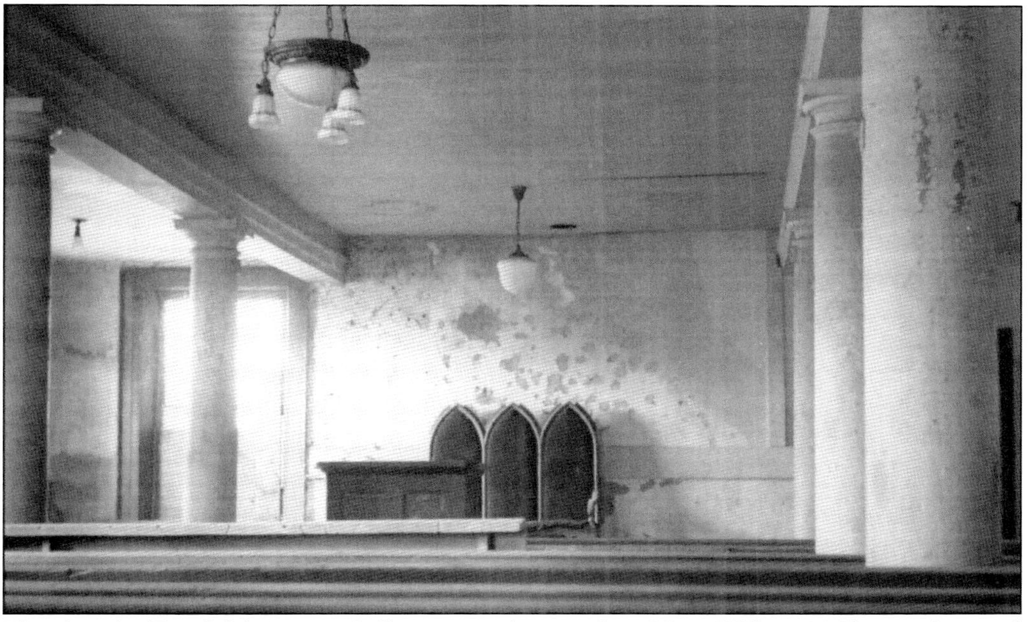

The chapel of Randolph-Macon College is a stark reminder of Gen. William T. Sherman's arrival in town in May 4, 1865, when this became his headquarters, where a detachment stayed for about three months. The fall 1865 semester began, but without faculty and with buildings having been ransacked by the invaders and in need of extensive repairs, the college closed in 1866 for the Freedmen's Bureau. (Mary Ann Boyd Ottinger.)

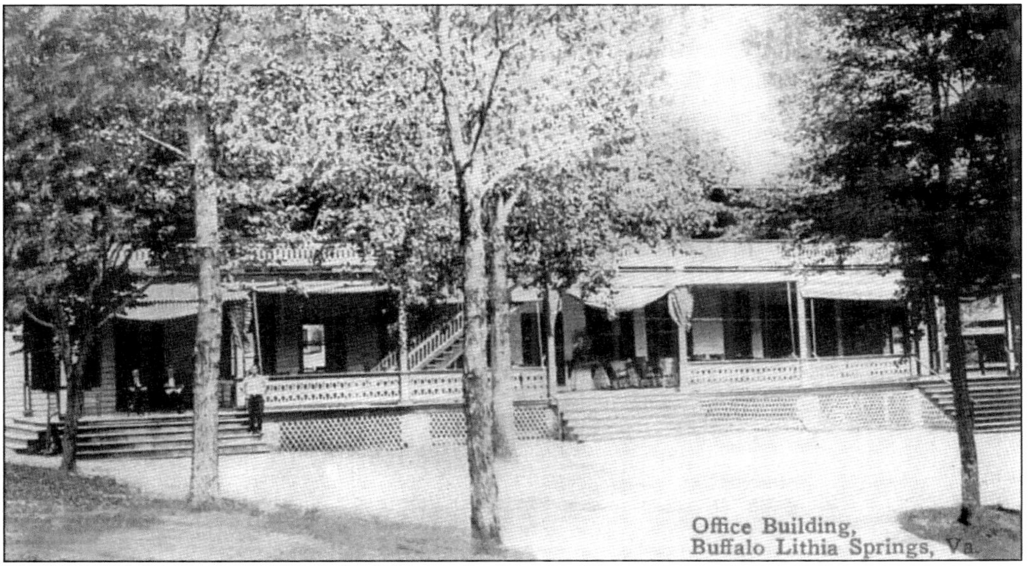

Charles Russell of southern Maryland resigned from the Washington Naval Yard and the Washington Light Infantry Company on April 21, 1861, and walked to Alexandria, Virginia. As a skilled blacksmith, he was sent to an ordinance depot in Richmond then to establish an ordinance company in Clarksville. This is the office built in nearby Buffalo Springs in 1864 that contained a meeting room, where he spent much time with Timothy Paxton, the new owner from Maryland. (WCG.)

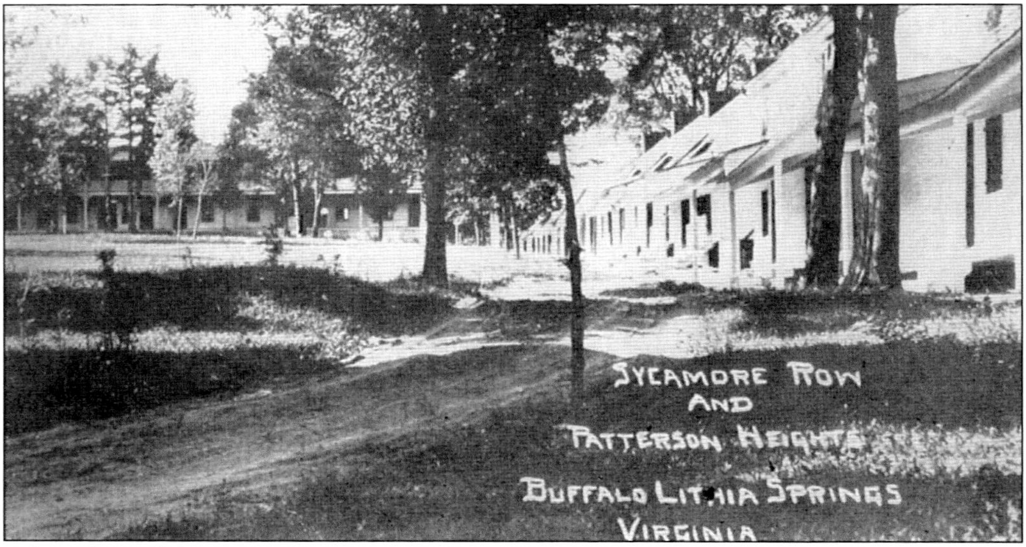

When the Buffalo Springs resort reopened in 1867, there was a new office and "Bachelor's Row" of cabins. In 1864, guests were recorded as Colonel Hicks, CSA, and his family, who stayed for three months to deliver their second child. Also staying were Confederate soldiers Charles and James Wilburn, who stayed at the resort even with it being (supposedly) closed. (CRM.)

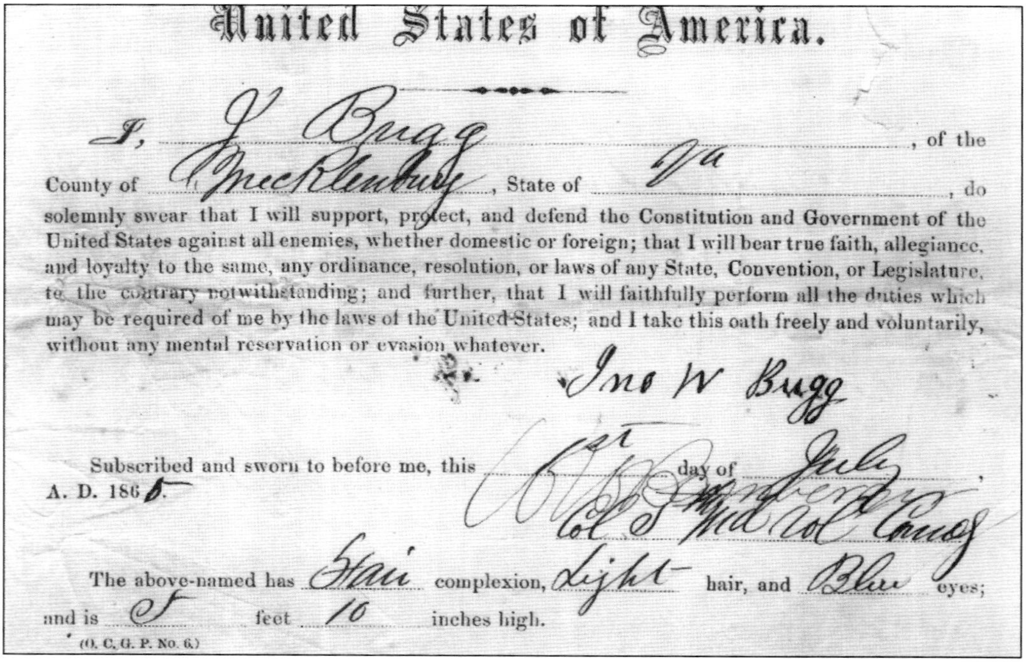

United States of America.

I, J. Bugg, of the County of Mecklenburg, State of Va, do solemnly swear that I will support, protect, and defend the Constitution and Government of the United States against all enemies, whether domestic or foreign; that I will bear true faith, allegiance, and loyalty to the same, any ordinance, resolution, or laws of any State, Convention, or Legislature, to the contrary notwithstanding; and further, that I will faithfully perform all the duties which may be required of me by the laws of the United States; and I take this oath freely and voluntarily, without any mental reservation or evasion whatever.

Jno W Bugg

Subscribed and sworn to before me, this 1st day of July, A. D. 1865.

[illegible]
Col. [illegible]

The above-named has Fair complexion, Light hair, and Blue eyes; and is 5 feet 10 inches high.

(O. C. G. P. No. 6.)

After the war's end, prisoners were released. Each had to swear an oath of allegiance to the U.S. Constitution and government. These oath certificates became their safe passage home. When John W. Bugg returned home, he would quickly learn of Generals James Wilson and August Kuntz's raid and defeat at Stanton River. The robbing, looting, and raping were so severe that General Wilson was contacted by a group of citizens who filed charges. Several men were brought to trial. All charges were dismissed by General Grant. (RB.)

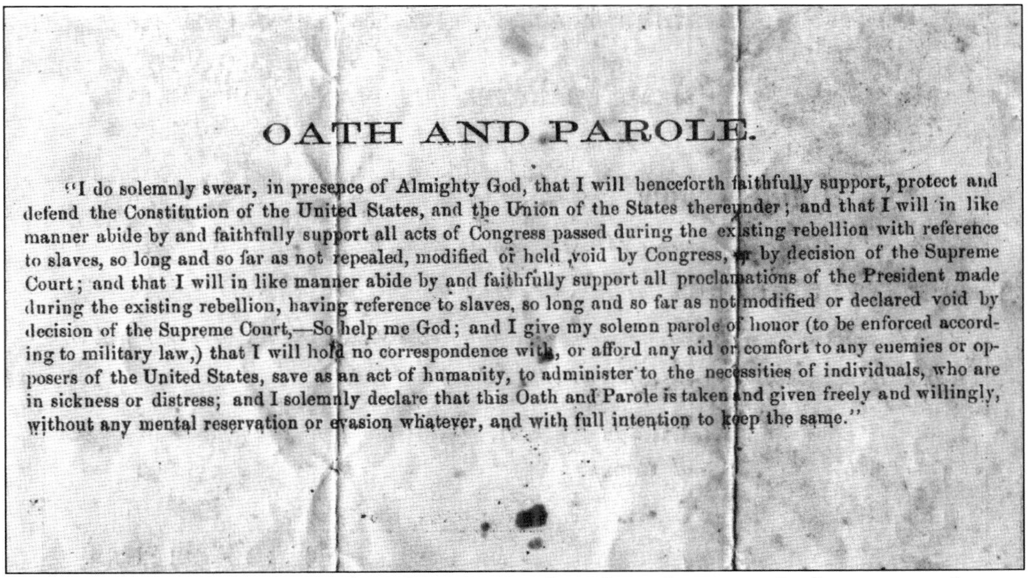

OATH AND PAROLE.

"I do solemnly swear, in presence of Almighty God, that I will henceforth faithfully support, protect and defend the Constitution of the United States, and the Union of the States thereunder; and that I will in like manner abide by and faithfully support all acts of Congress passed during the existing rebellion with reference to slaves, so long and so far as not repealed, modified or held void by Congress, or by decision of the Supreme Court; and that I will in like manner abide by and faithfully support all proclamations of the President made during the existing rebellion, having reference to slaves, so long and so far as not modified or declared void by decision of the Supreme Court,—So help me God; and I give my solemn parole of honour (to be enforced according to military law,) that I will hold no correspondence with, or afford any aid or comfort to any enemies or opposers of the United States, save as an act of humanity, to administer to the necessities of individuals, who are in sickness or distress; and I solemnly declare that this Oath and Parole is taken and given freely and willingly, without any mental reservation or evasion whatever, and with full intention to keep the same."

Page two of the oath was the oath and statement of parole each prisoner had to recite and swear to. This served as a reminder of their defeat. This oath and declaration had to be done by all enlisted men, non-commissioned officers, and commissioned officers up to a certain level of command. On June 24, 1864, most men and teenagers from the county went upstream to help defend the Stanton River bridge. The Union soldiers were commanded by Brigadier Generals Wilson and Kautz, who led 3,000 men and runaway slaves against 200 Confederate soldiers and 600 farmers. (RB.)

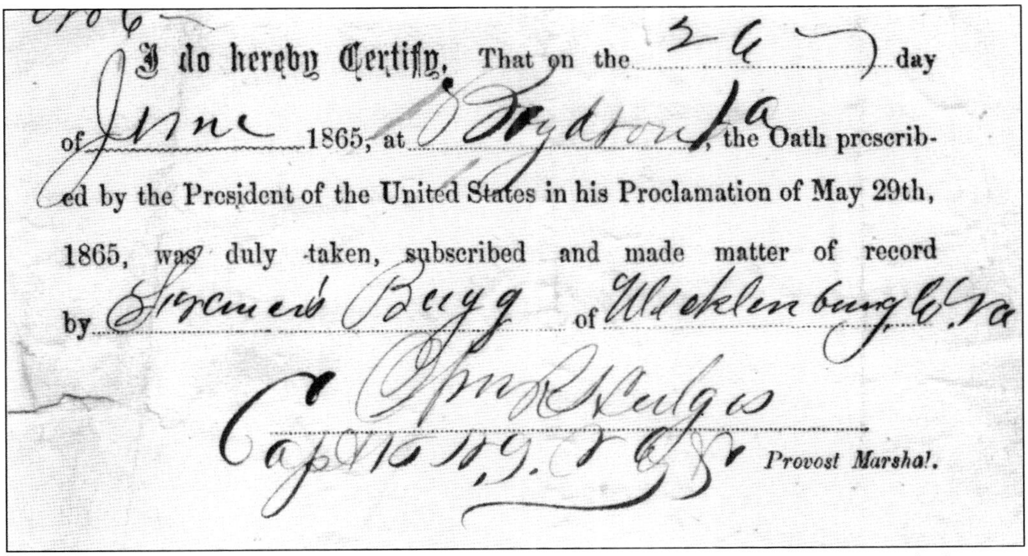

I do hereby Certify, That on the 26 day of June 1865, at Boydton Va, the Oath prescribed by the President of the United States in his Proclamation of May 29th, 1865, was duly taken, subscribed and made matter of record by [illegible] Bugg of Mecklenburg Co. Va

[illegible]

Provost Marshal.

This is the property owner's oath that Nancy Hatsell Bugg, a seamstress, had to sign before one of Sherman's officers on June 26, 1865, for her 3-acre parcel in the town of Boydton near the college. It is not known how many residents had to sign these, but the command was in Boydton for three months, with stragglers continuing to loot their way north until winter. One job of the provost was to ensure a Freedman's Bureau was created for assisting freed slaves with their rights and resettlement. (RB.)

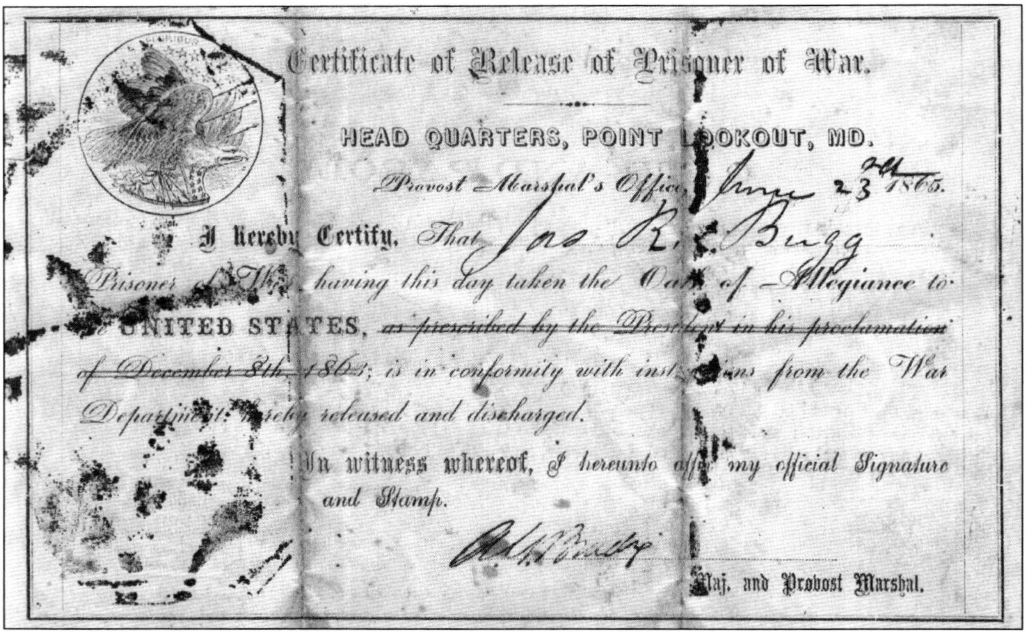

Certificate of Release of Prisoner of War.

HEAD QUARTERS, POINT LOOKOUT, MD.

Provost Marshal's Office, June 23rd 1865.

I Hereby Certify, That Jas R. Bugg Prisoner of War, having this day taken the Oath of Allegiance to the UNITED STATES, ~~as prescribed by the President in his proclamation of December 8th, 1863~~; is in conformity with instructions from the War Department hereby released and discharged.

In witness whereof, I hereunto affix my official Signature and Stamp.

[illegible] Brady

Maj. and Provost Marshal.

The non-commissioned officers release for James R. Bugg is pictured here. Most non-commissioned officers captured in Virginia and north were sent to Point Lookout, Maryland. Their release was somewhat delayed because of the assassination of President Lincoln. This release is signed by a Major Brady, provost marshal for headquarters of Point Lookout, and dated June 23, 1865. (RB.)

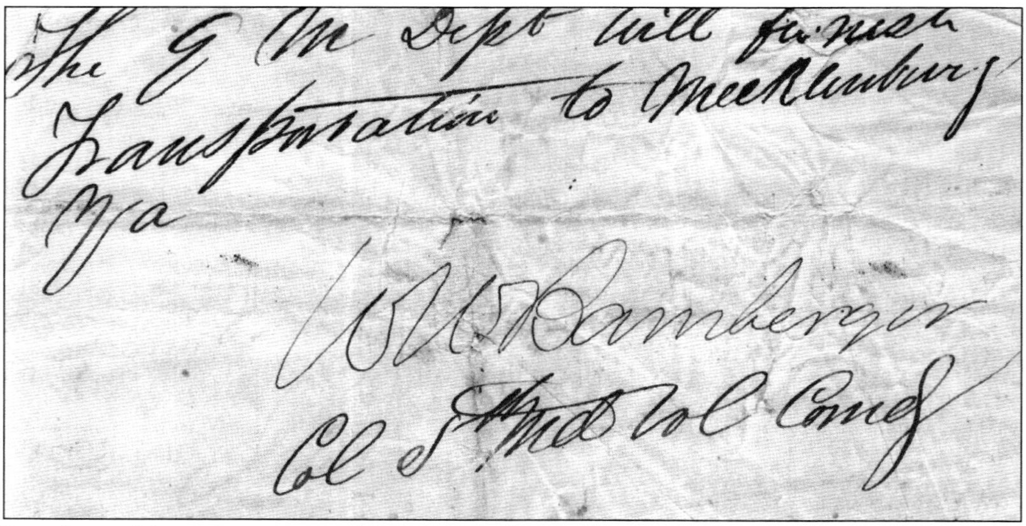

The Q M Dept will furnish Transportation to Mecklenburg Va

W U Ramberger

Col [illegible] Vol Comd

Page three of the oath was reserved for any special instructions or orders. James Bugg's oath includes an order by Col. W. U. Ramberger for the Quartermaster Department to furnish transportation for Bugg to Mecklenburg County, Virginia. This may have been a horse, a horse and wagon for several soldiers released to destinations in close proximity, or a train or ship's pass, if a train or ship was available. (RB.)

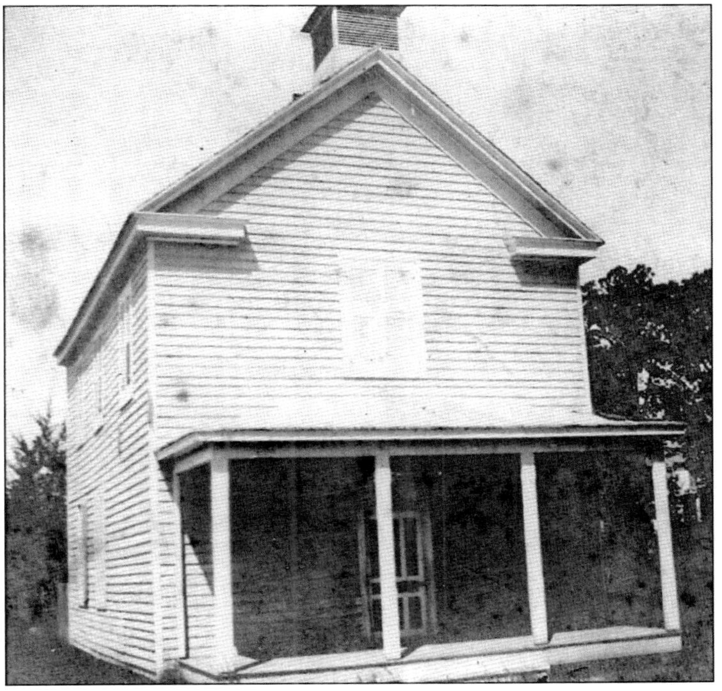

Col. George Rogers owned the Boydton Hotel from 1836 to 1846, when he sold it. His new home became the Mecklenburg Female College in Boydton around 1850. The college, having secured loans and garnered financial support, failed on November 27, 1874. It was sold at auction to C. N. Williams, treasurer of the Boydton Baptist Church. This *c.* 1890 photograph shows the east wing after having been moved about 100 yards to its new location. Around 1920, it became a rental until purchased for the law office of Walter R. Beales III. (Walter R. Beales III.)

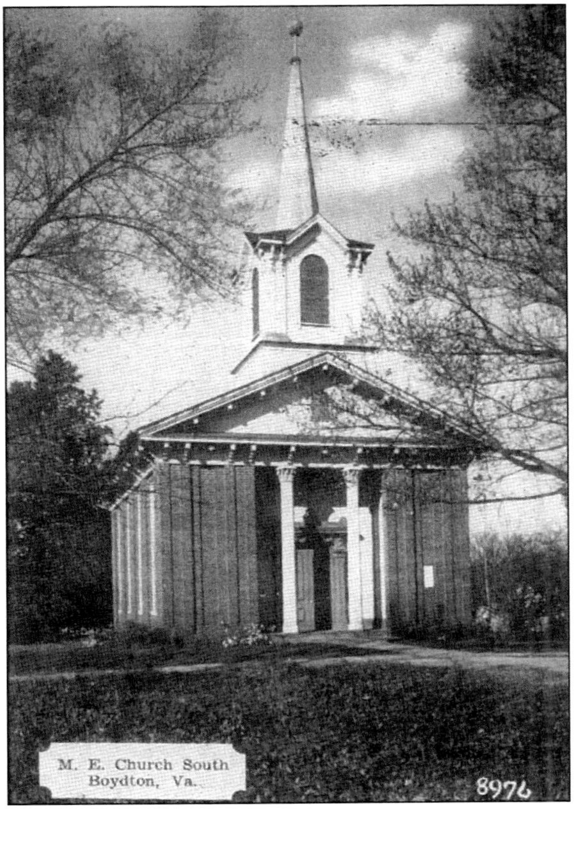

With the closing of Randolph-Macon College and relocation to a campus in Ashland, members of the Boydton United Methodist Church needed a building. In 1871, Jacob Holt was contracted to build the new church, completed in 1873 and located on Bank Street. The bell in the church is said to be from Randolph-Macon College, and the stained-glass windows were a gift from Col. and Mrs. Thomas F. Goode from an old church in Norfolk, Virginia. In 1953, the church added a basement, which housed restrooms, kitchen, furnace room, and fellowship rooms. The small house in the background on Monroe Street was the home of Willie Burton. (WCG.)

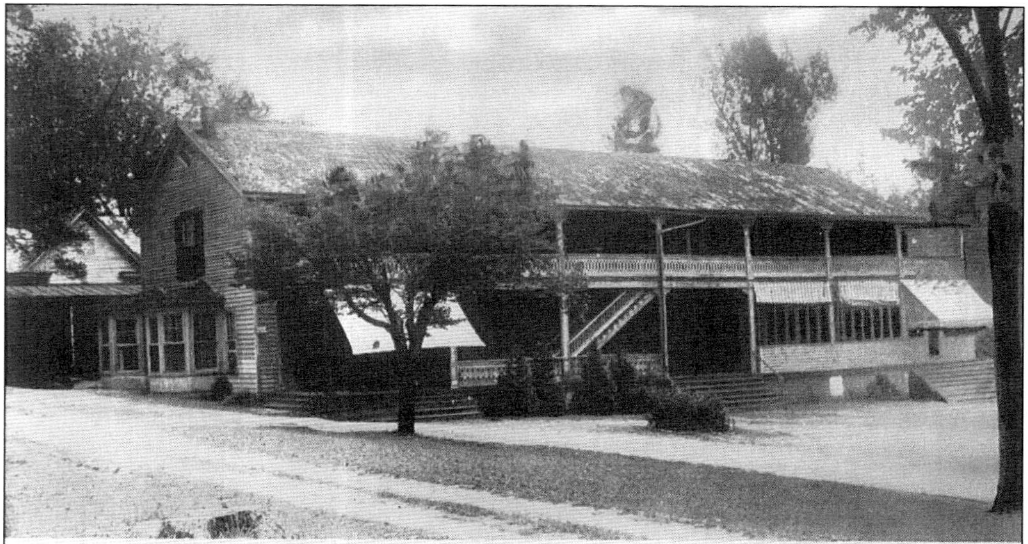

Buffalo Mineral Springs Hotel, Clarksville, Virginia

The Reconstruction years included financial devastation: Clarksville filed bankruptcy and lost its charter. The 50 plantations of western Mecklenburg were being divided and sold as farms and new communities—the most successful was Chase City. One local businessman made a valiant attempt at protecting past traditions—Col. Thomas F. Goode. Goode, a statesman, military hero, and attorney in Boydton, represented Paxton of Buffalo Springs in an estate suit brought by the family of Dr. David Shelton. Goode purchased the resort and built this new hotel in 1874. (WCG.)

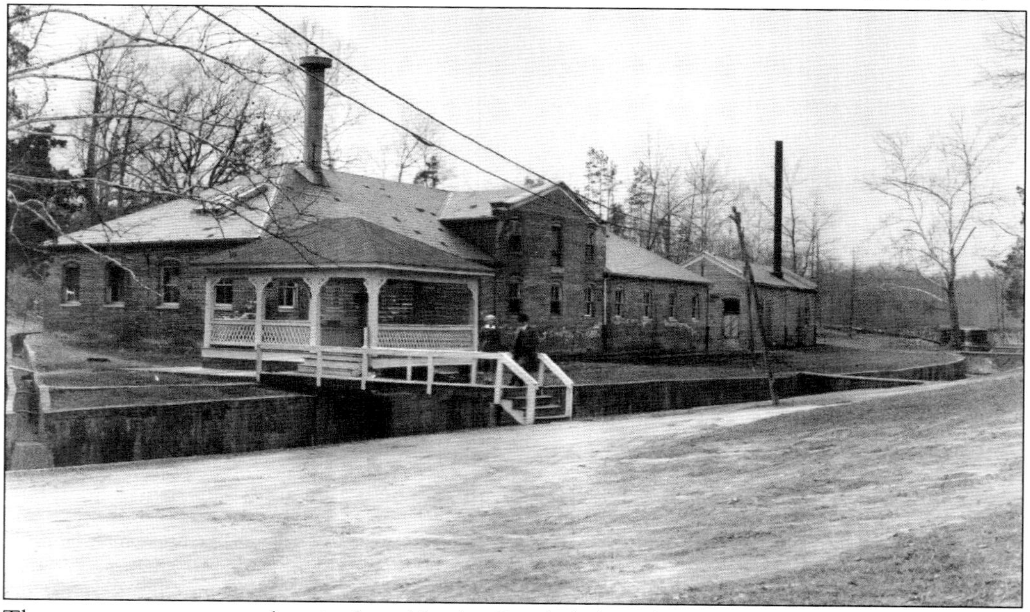

The new management advertised worldwide. Goode believed people needed a place for respite. Alcohol was no longer served; instead, the healing waters were served liberally and this bottling facility was added to bottle and ship the water worldwide to drugstores and pharmacy wholesalers. The water was originally bottled in large containers for druggist dispensing but later bottled in half- and 1-gallon bottles and shipped in wooden crates. (WCG.)

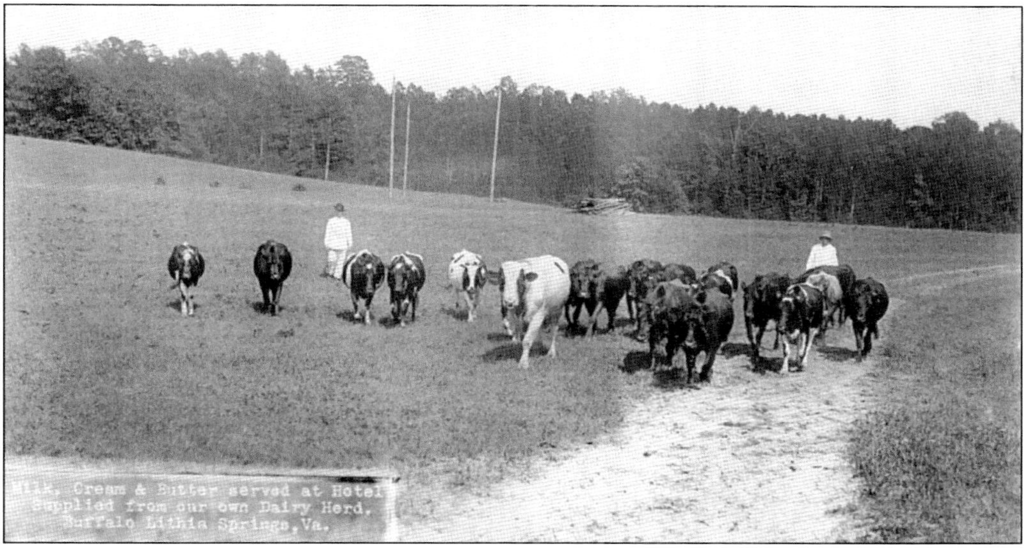

Not wanting to leave the springs, Timothy Paxton purchased and developed the John Newton farm and two smaller farms to the extent that it became self-sufficient, with produce and products available for sale to guests and the local community from its new larger store. He joined with the two farms Goode owned and two large farms that were already supporting the springs. All foods and beverages on the menu were from the farms. By 1877, the repeat guest list was reaching full capacity, with many guests staying the entire season, including Mrs. Stonewall Jackson (Mary Ann). (WCG.)

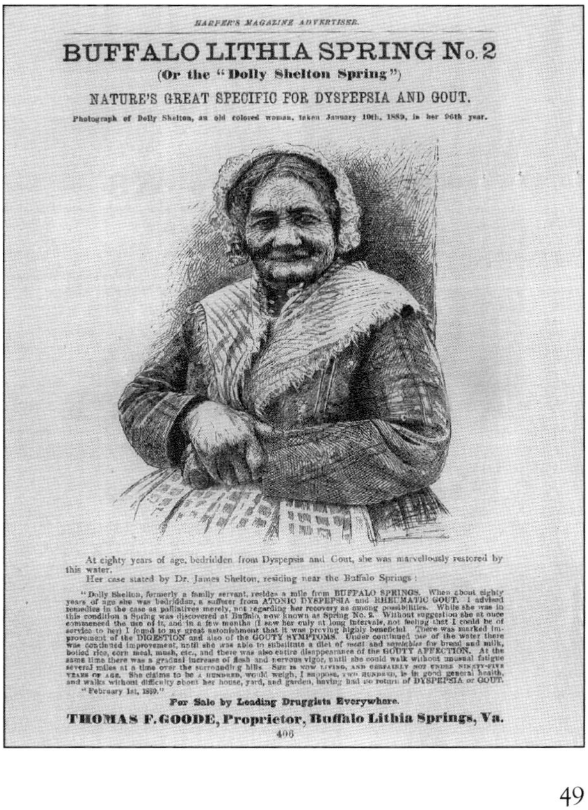

HARPER'S MAGAZINE ADVERTISER.

BUFFALO LITHIA SPRING No. 2

(Or the "Dolly Shelton Spring")

NATURE'S GREAT SPECIFIC FOR DYSPEPSIA AND GOUT.

Photograph of Dolly Shelton, an old colored woman, taken January 10th, 1889, in her 96th year.

At eighty years of age, bedridden from Dyspepsia and Gout, she was marvellously restored by this water.

Her case stated by Dr. James Shelton, residing near the Buffalo Springs:

"Dolly Shelton, formerly a family servant, resides a mile from BUFFALO SPRINGS. When about eighty years of age she was bedridden, a sufferer from ATONIC DYSPEPSIA and RHEUMATIC GOUT. I advised remedies in the case as palliatives merely, not regarding her recovery as among possibilities. While she was in this condition a Spring was discovered at Buffalo, now known as Spring No. 2. Without suggestion she at once commenced the use of it, and in a few months (I saw her only at long intervals, not feeling that I could be of service to her) I found to my great astonishment that it was proving highly beneficial. There was marked improvement of the DIGESTION and also of the GOUTY SYMPTOMS. Under continued use of the water there was continued improvement, until she was able to substitute a diet of *meat* and *vegetables* for bread and milk, boiled rice, corn meal, mush, etc., and there was also entire disappearance of the GOUTY AFFECTION. At the same time there was a gradual increase of flesh and nervous vigor, until she could walk without unusual fatigue several miles at a time over the surrounding hills. SHE IS NOW LIVING, AND CERTAINLY NOT UNDER NINETY-FIVE YEARS OF AGE. She claims to be A HUNDRED, would weigh, I suppose, TWO HUNDRED, is in good general health, and walks without difficulty about her house, yard, and garden, having had no return of DYSPEPSIA or GOUT.

"February 1st, 1889."

For Sale by Leading Druggists Everywhere.

THOMAS F. GOODE, Proprietor, Buffalo Lithia Springs, Va.

406

About this time, an old black lady living on the farm told Goode about Spring No. 2, which had been closed and overgrown for almost 15 years. After testing the water and discovering it was the richest of the six springs, he cleared and reopened it, and a new bottling plant was built next to it. Goode was so impressed with the lady he named the spring after her; this famous advertisement was developed in her honor and appeared in several magazines and pharmaceutical publications in 1889 and for years later around the world. This is from *Harpers* magazine of May 1889. (Adam Glasscock.)

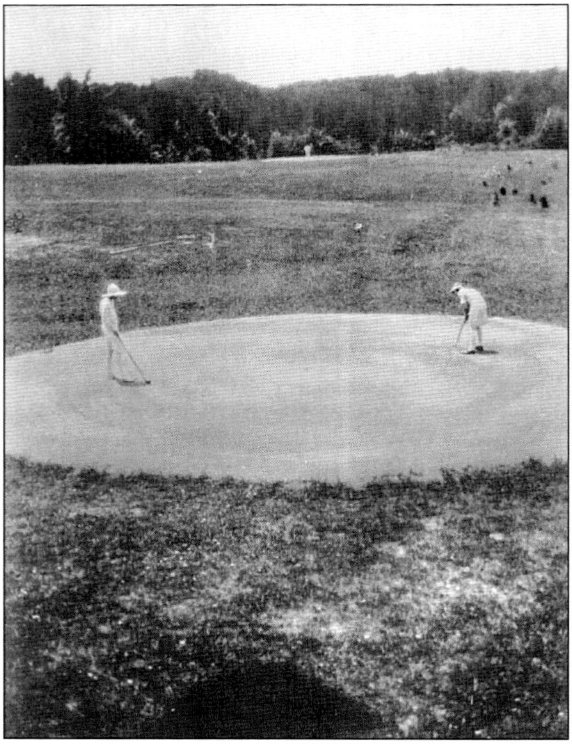

By 1880, Goode had rehabilitated the nine-hole golf course with sand greens, two new grass tennis courts, a barbershop, horseback riding trails, an icehouse, a small 5-acre lake, and a baseball field. Boating, fishing, hunting, shooting tournaments, horseback riding instruction, and swimming were added activities for the guests. In the late 1880s, mining had resumed in the area and the water was delivered to the mining sites. (CRM.)

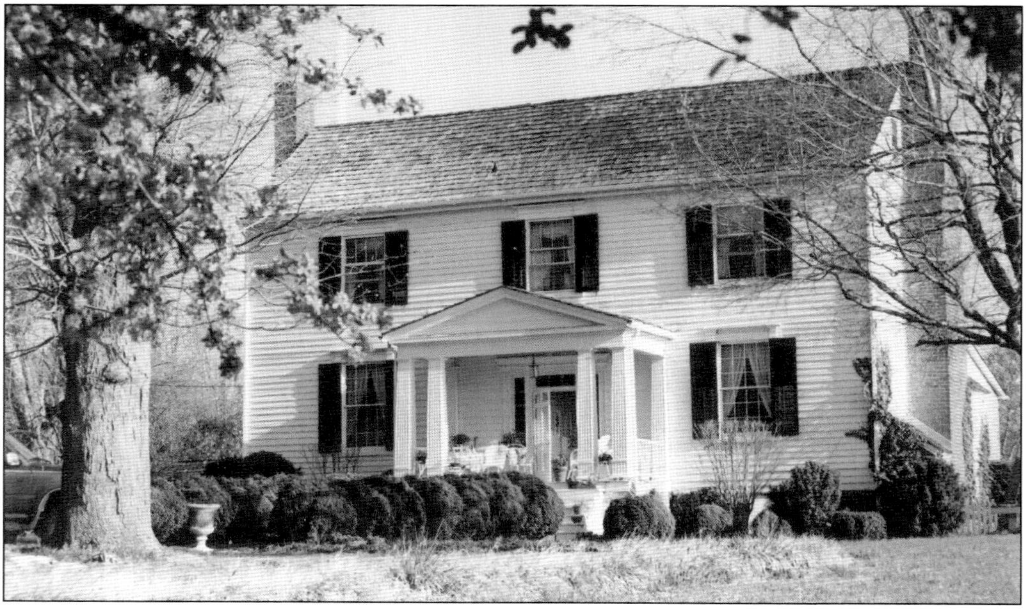

Near the springs was the Charles Baskerville Watkins farm, which had partnered with Goode for produce and dairy. When Watkins's wife became ill, her sister Ella moved in to take care of her and teach the four children. Shortly after she died in 1881, Charles married Ella. They lived across the pasture from Timothy Paxton and became business associates. (Gerhard and Margarette Raquot.)

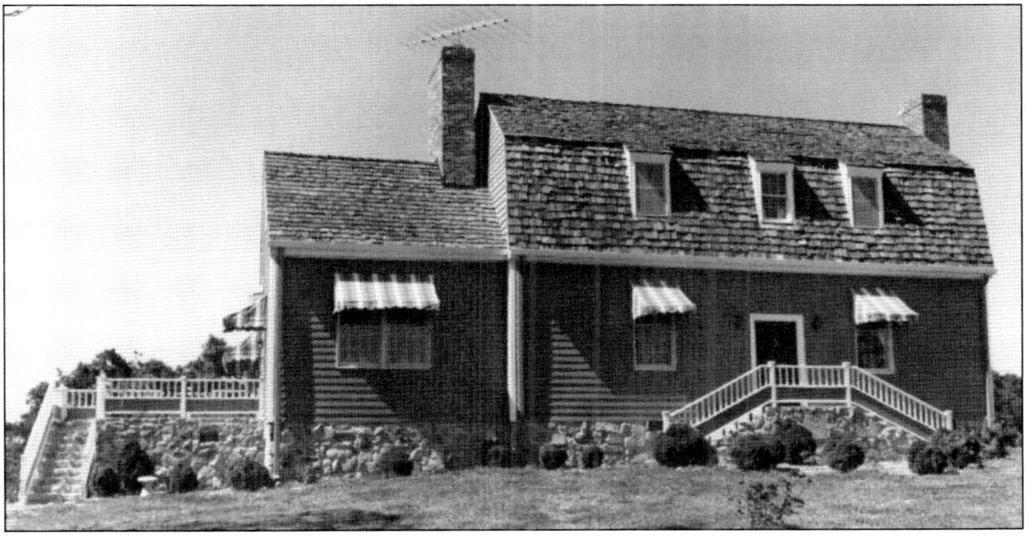

Across the river, near Abbeyville, was the Adcock tract of 1,000 acres, which became the community of Oakley. From 1794, when Alexander Boyd Sr. purchased the Boyd Tavern, until Boyd Sr.'s death in 1801, his elder son, Richard, was the manager. Alex Jr. purchased Richard's share of the estate, and he moved his family to the Adcock tract and built a family home. In 1831, Richard's elder son, Robert, remodeled and expanded the home, Oakley, to accommodate a large and growing family. Robert's son Richard graduated from Randolph-Macon College, attended Virginia Military Institute, and was appointed a first sergeant and aide to Gen. Robert Lee until the end of the war. (Beth Boyd Baker.)

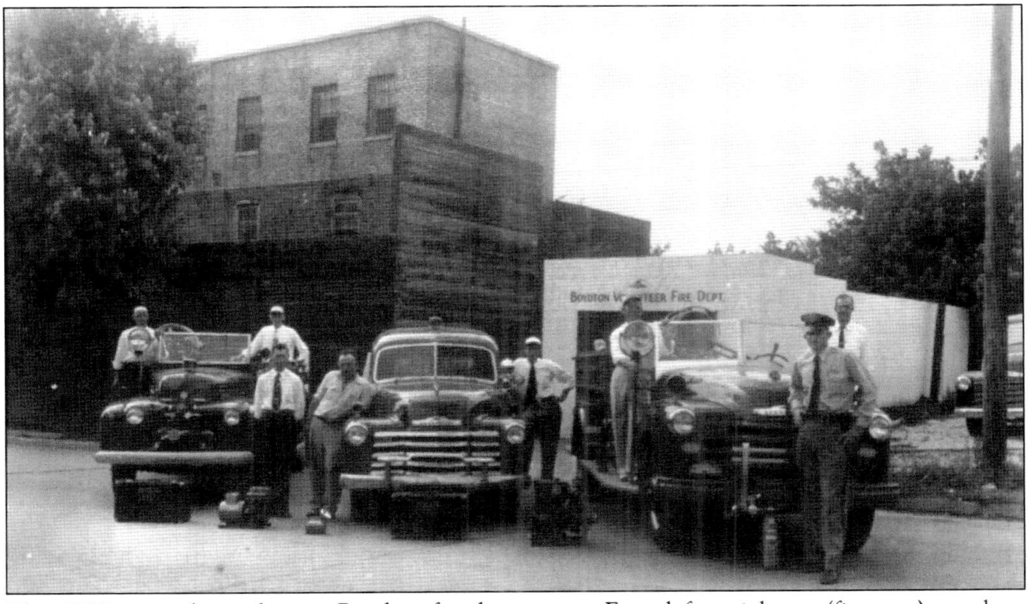

This 1950 image shows the new Boydton fire department. From left to right are (first row) members Norfleet Wright, Tommy Gregory Jr., and Robert Evans in uniform; (second row) W. E. Lambert, Landon H. Carter, Willard Smith, unidentified, and R. H. Park Jr. The jail, built in 1871 by Jacob Holt, has closed and been remodeled and the fence removed; the building is the offices of the Commonwealth's Attorney. (Henry H. Gregory Jr.)

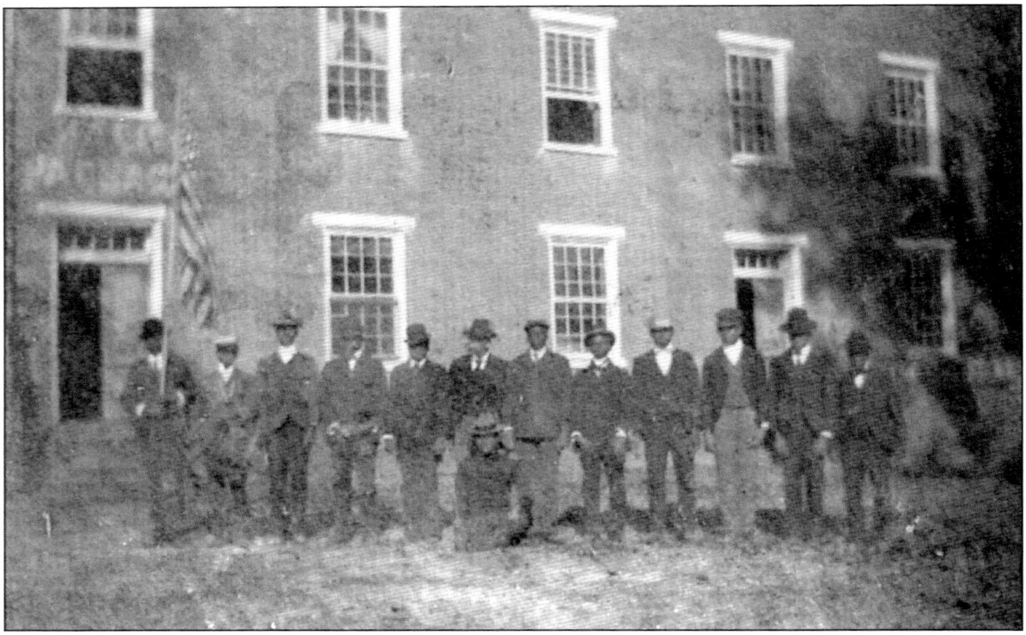

Boydton National Bible Training Institute operated from 1878 until 1916. It was purchased in 1871 by Dr. Henry McGonegal of New York and later sold to Dr. Charles Cullis to operate the Christian School for Negroes. This is a picture of a group of unidentified students gathered in front of the school in the 1890s. (REC.)

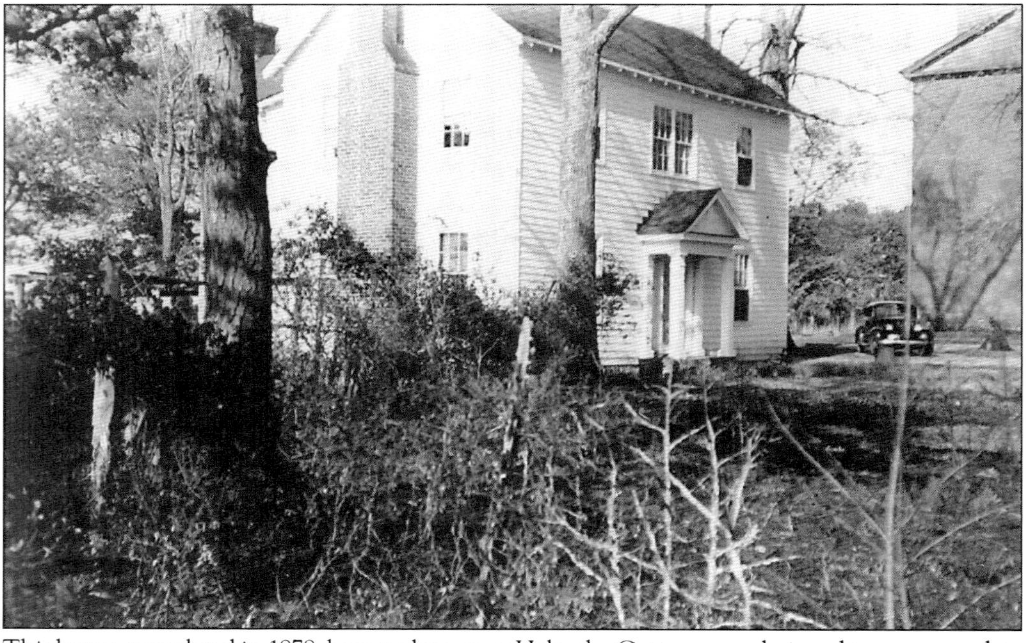

This house, completed in 1878, became known as Heleusha Cottage, was designed to accommodate the head officer of the school, and was located adjacent to the school. This house was utilized until the school closed during the Depression. The main building and several other buildings on campus faced the plank toll road. (Mary Ann Boyd Ottinger.)

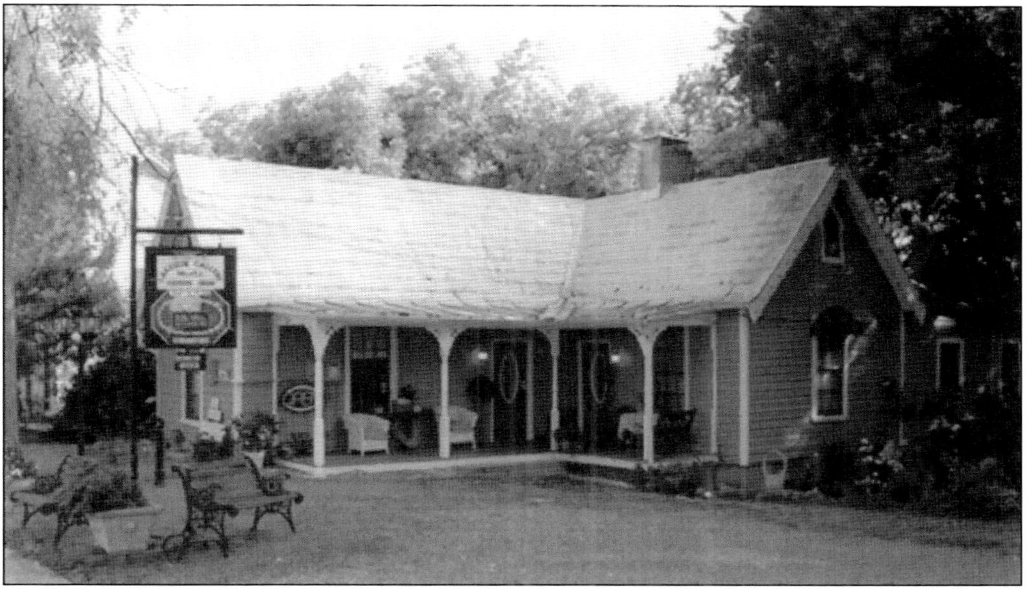

Frank J. Liipfort arrived in Clarksville from Saxony, Germany. Accomplished at his trade of carpentry, in March 1873, he purchased lot No. 24 from John Lewis under contract to build a home and business. He began building cabinets, furniture, and coffins. His estate was sold at auction in 1901. In 1936, Dr. Patrick Winston purchased the home, added a five-room basement and a large rear addition, and opened Clarksville Maternity Clinic. In 1942, Dr. Winston served as a psychiatrist at Walter Reed Army Hospital but returned to Clarksville in 1946 and reopened the clinic. It is said he delivered over 1,800 babies. (BH.)

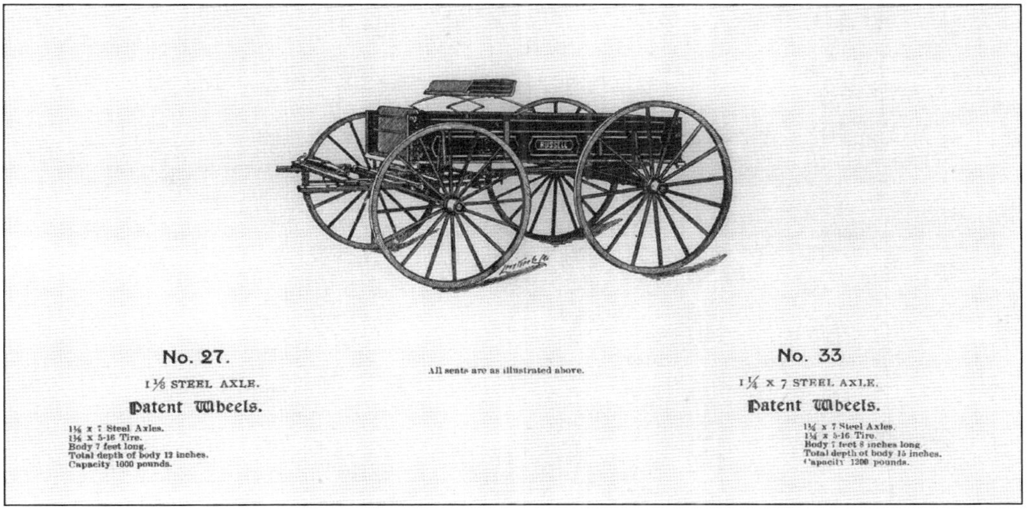

In 1871, C. H. Russell, G. N. Wells, William Jamieson, and others began the Mechanics Building and Loan Association. That same year, Russell married a second time to Virginia Price Moss of Clarksville. In 1872, his son William attended the Preston-Olin Institute (renamed the Virginia Polytechnic Institute or Virginia Tech). With the severe depression of the time, they quickly began to foreclose on tax-laden properties in the Clarksville area. Russell's factory began making a cheaper wagon to sell, and by 1873, the carriage and buggy company in town was out of business. (WCG.)

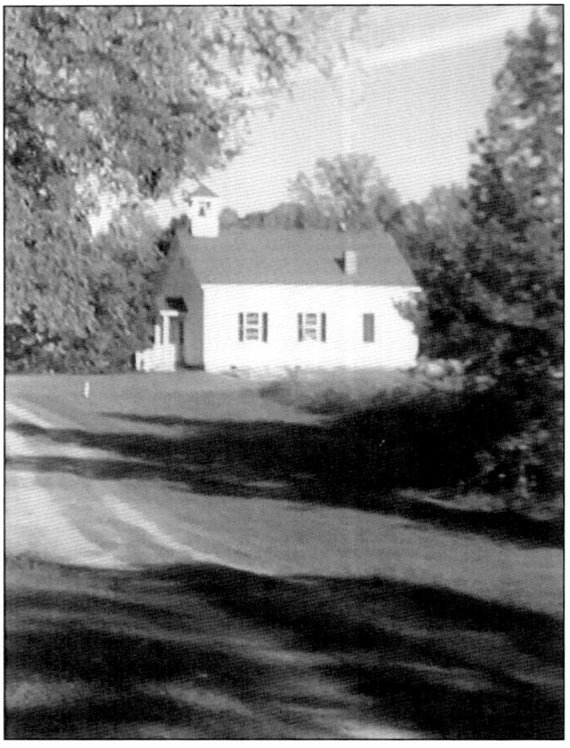

St. Ephesus Church served a community along the intersection of the Abbeyville Road to Christiansville and the Barnesville/Spanish Grove Road to Clarksville, called Trotter's Ridge Road. The church, built in 1876, was soon joined by a community store and post office, begun by Capt. Thomas Orgain. The community was given the name of Orgainsville. Leaving Orgainsville toward Clarksville, the road passed (David) Doggett's Mill, where a bridge has been built today. The post office closed in 1907. Early roads generally followed the high ground for year-round travel. The store is gone, the little church has been removed, and a new church has been built. (BMC.)

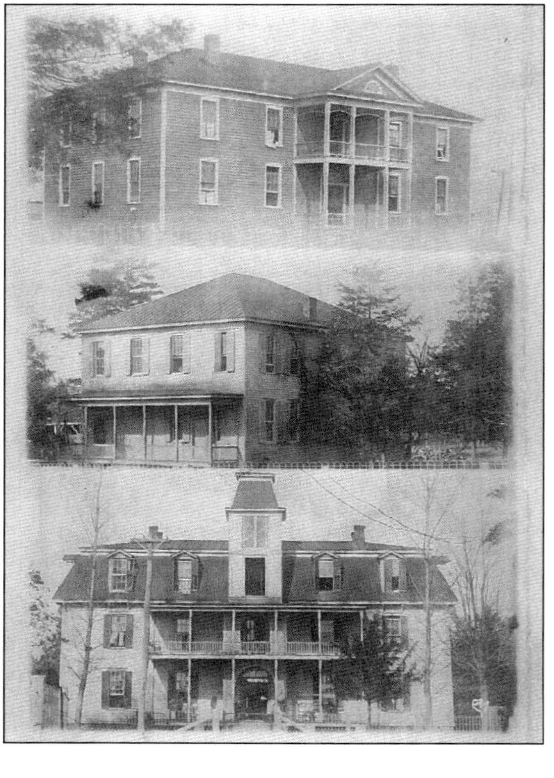

On June 3, 1872, William H. Dunlap, a contractor, sold 70 acres of the 172.5-acre farm of the Finch tract he owned to the Freedman's Bureau of Pittsburgh, Pennsylvania, and constructed a building for the bureau. Around 1874, John Thyne arrived in the area and was referred to as the "barefoot preacher" but always wore his full-length black coat. The first school building in the new community was completed in 1876 and was named Thyne Institute. It grew rapidly and by 1893 was the only black boarding school of its type in the state, with over 100 students. This turn-of-the-20th-century picture is of the original buildings. (WCG.)

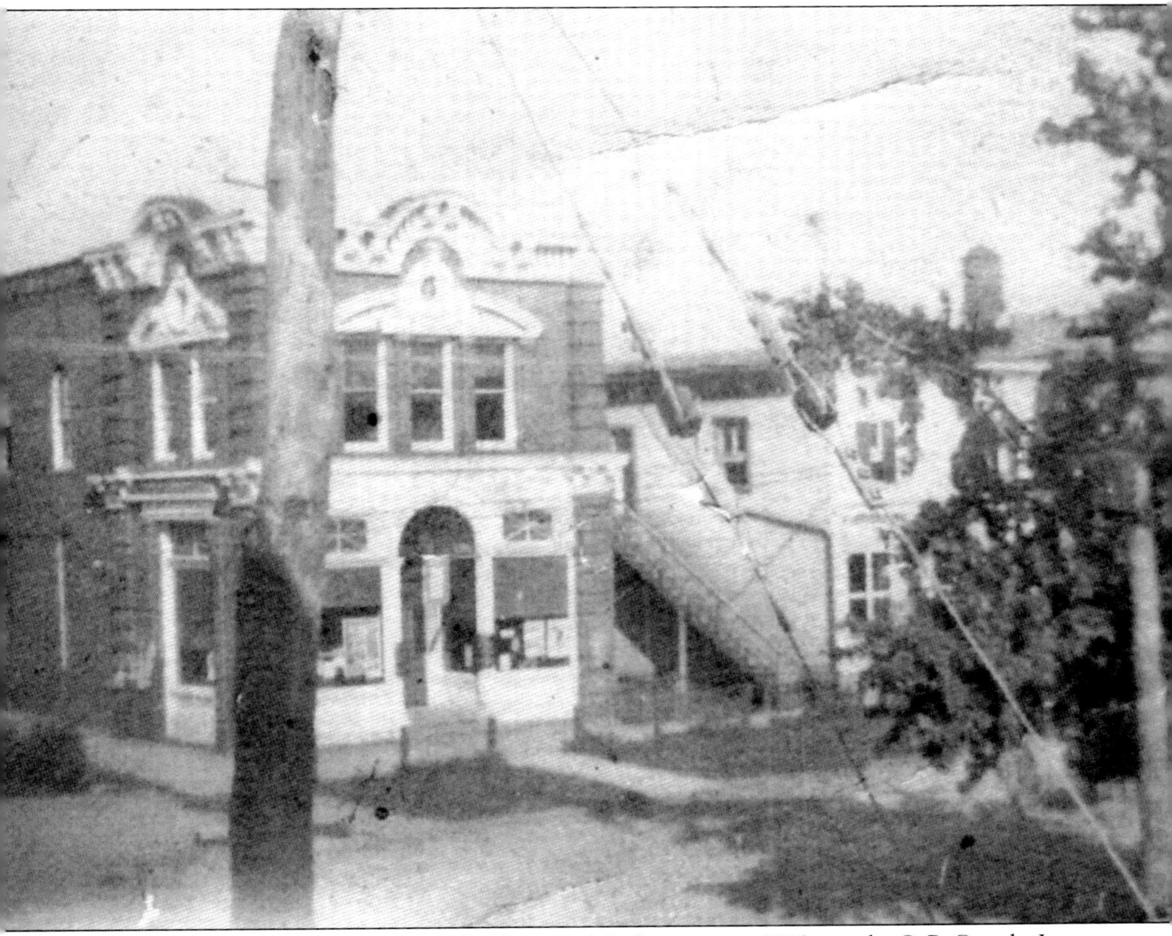

To greet the passengers, the new City Hotel opened for business in 1883, run by S. P. Couch. In 1888, the Bank of Chase City opened next door with its president, George A. Endly. The Bank of Chase City closed in 1907 and reopened under new management in 1909 but closed for good in 1929. The City Hotel, purchased and renamed the Barnett Hotel, was taken down in 1945 to make way for a miniature golf course. Between the Barnett and the bank, in 1902, was the armory building. The armory was sold and removed in the 1980s. (Thomas and Pat Gryder.)

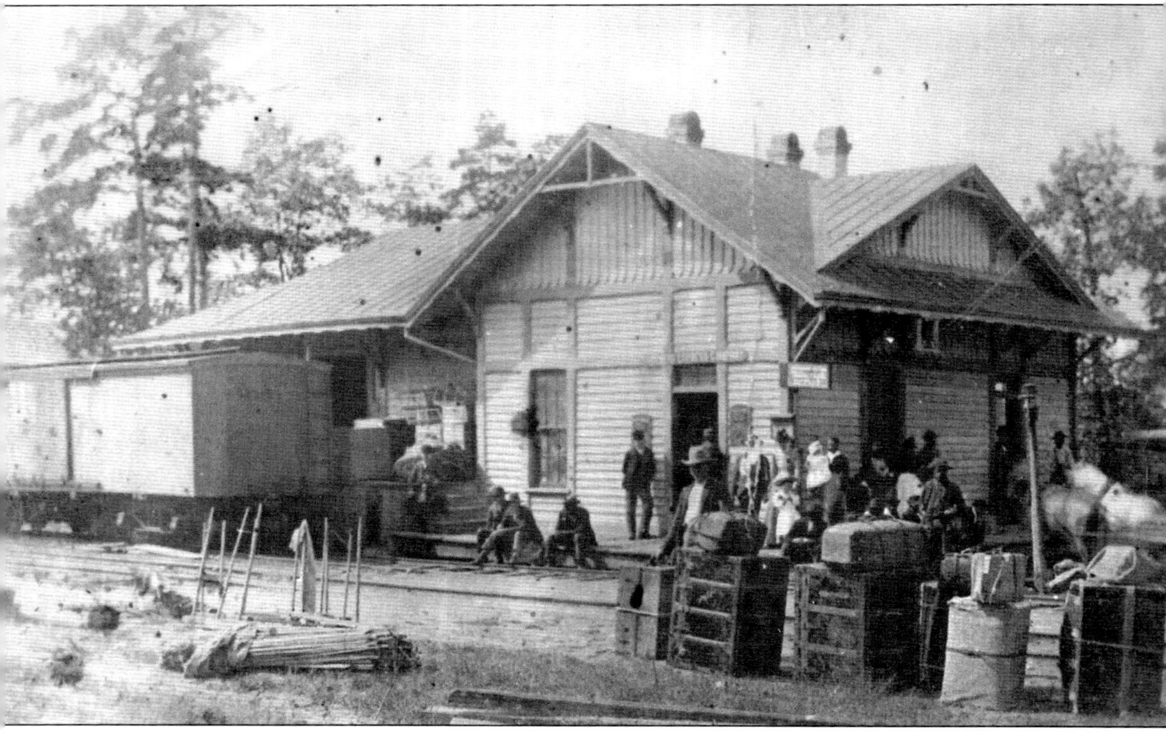

The railroad continued to extend south through Esnon, Gregory's Store, and on to Five Forks, where an ordinary had been operating since 1818. The lands for a depot and foreman's house were purchased from William and Lucy Ann Bowers with the stipulation the name be changed to "Skipwith." Across from the depot was a saloon, later a black grocery store and today the site of the new post office. Five additional stores were built along with a new church. (REC.)

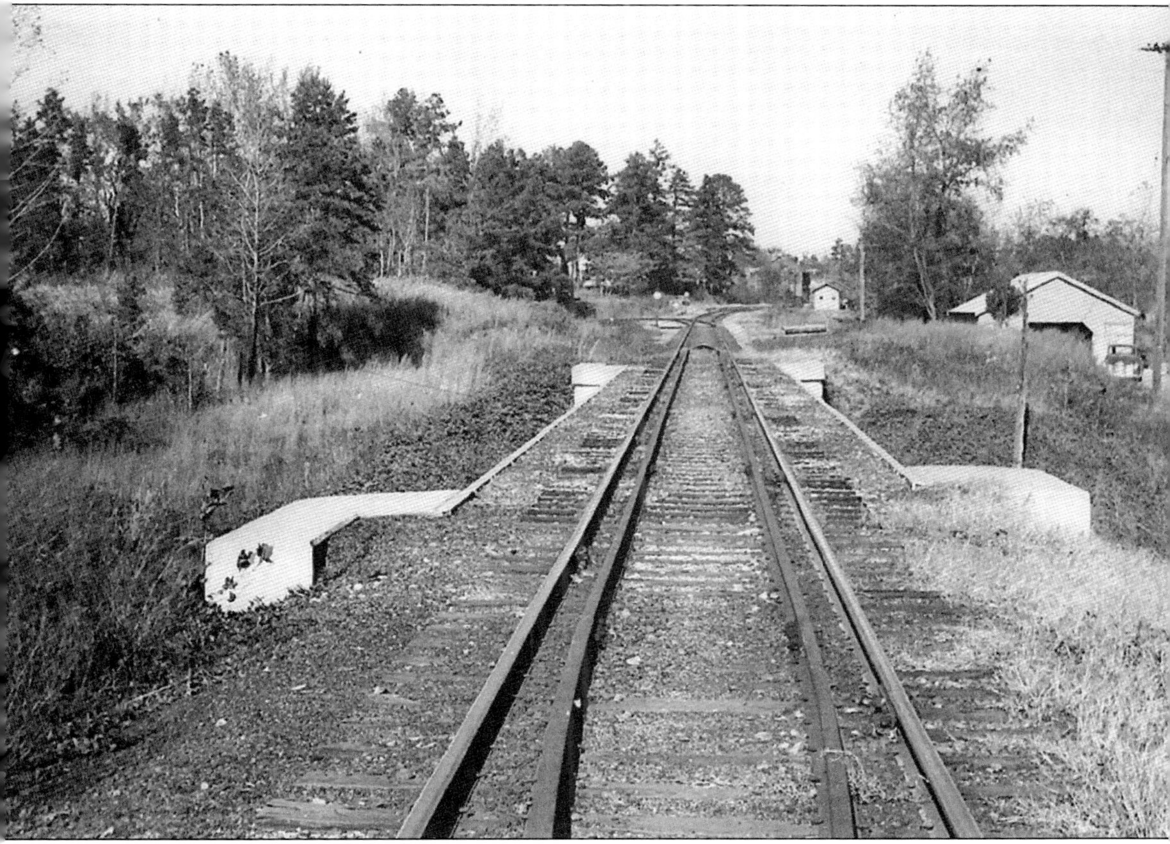

In 1892, with a new railroad terminal and warehouse, Cabin Point became Jeffress Junction. A Dr. Shadrich arrived and built a saloon to add to the several stores already in place. The saloon was purchased in 1912 by Capt. William Willis and was rebuilt as Jeffress Baptist Church. In 1930, the telegraph operator, a Mr. Mercer, was sent to Washington, D.C., and became the chief of White House Telegraph Operations. (COE.)

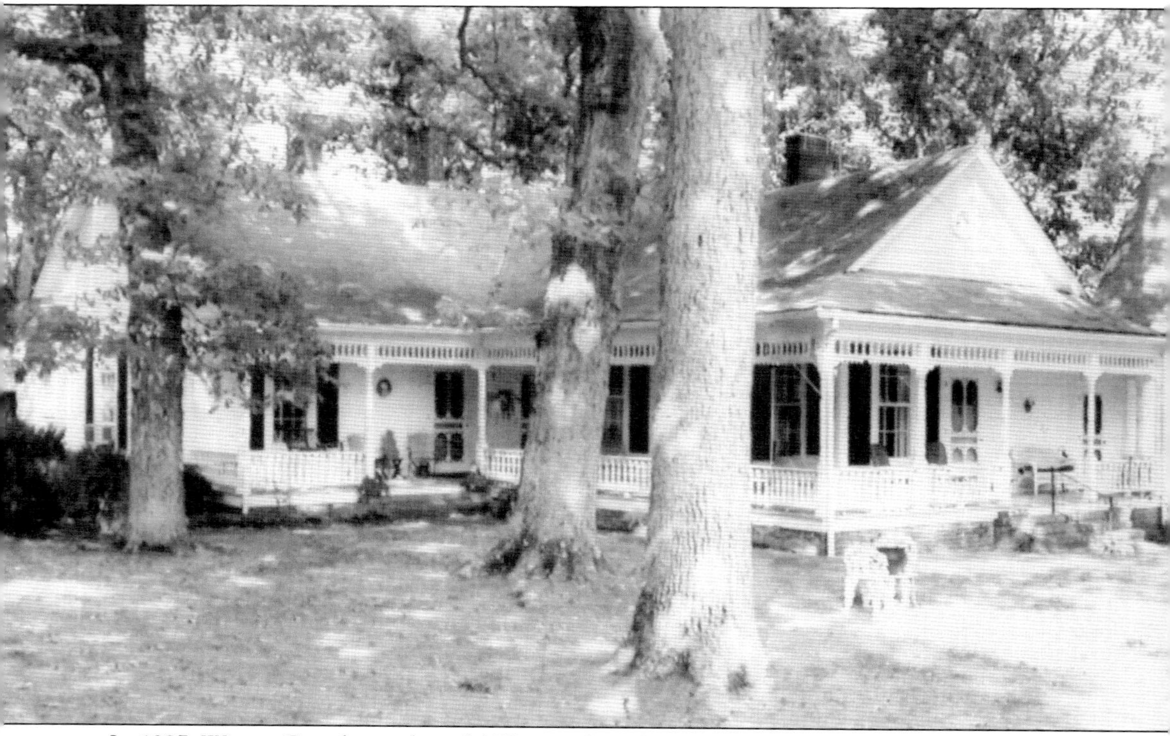

In 1897, Wayne Gooch purchased 137 acres from W. H. Ligon on the south side of the junction on the Clarksville–to–Chase City road. From the depot, he built a tavern, warehouse, distillery, and a new mansion home, although he only stayed there part-time and used it for entertaining clients and politicians. The home was occupied primarily by his mistress until her untimely death in 1904. After divorcing his wife and remarrying in 1915, Wayne Gooch was shot and killed while traveling through Texas by train with his bride and returning from the San Francisco World Exposition, leaving an estate with today's value of several million dollars. (Mary C. Horn.)

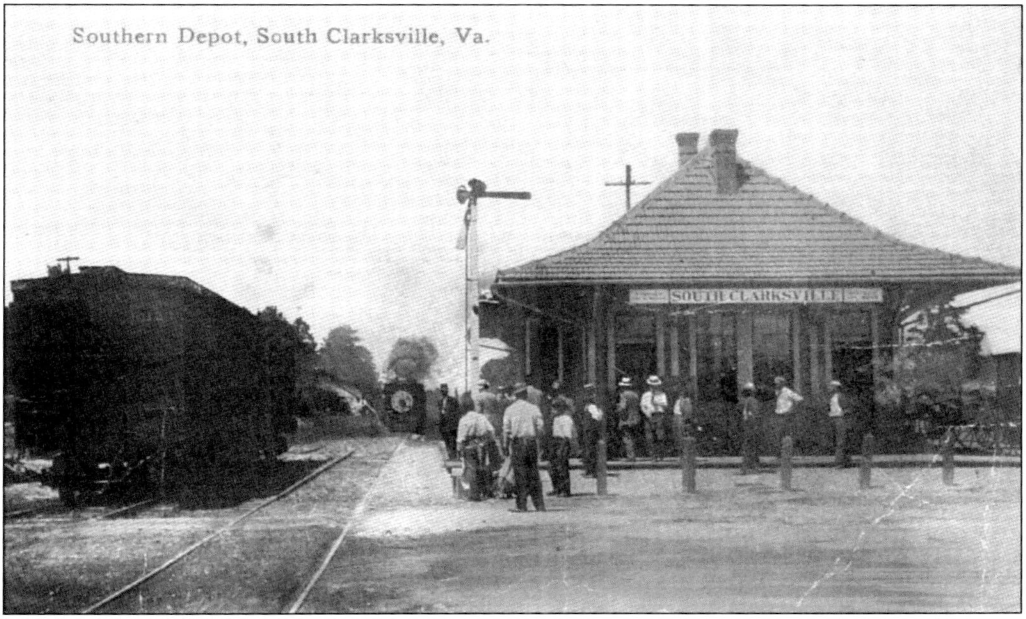

On January 1, 1888, a new spur line opened from Clarksville to Oxford, North Carolina. A passenger station was built on First Street in Clarksville, and next door, a new hotel was built. Behind the station was the Magee Warehouse, and across the street from the warehouse was the Magee Springs and bottling company. This postcard was taken about 1909. (CRM.)

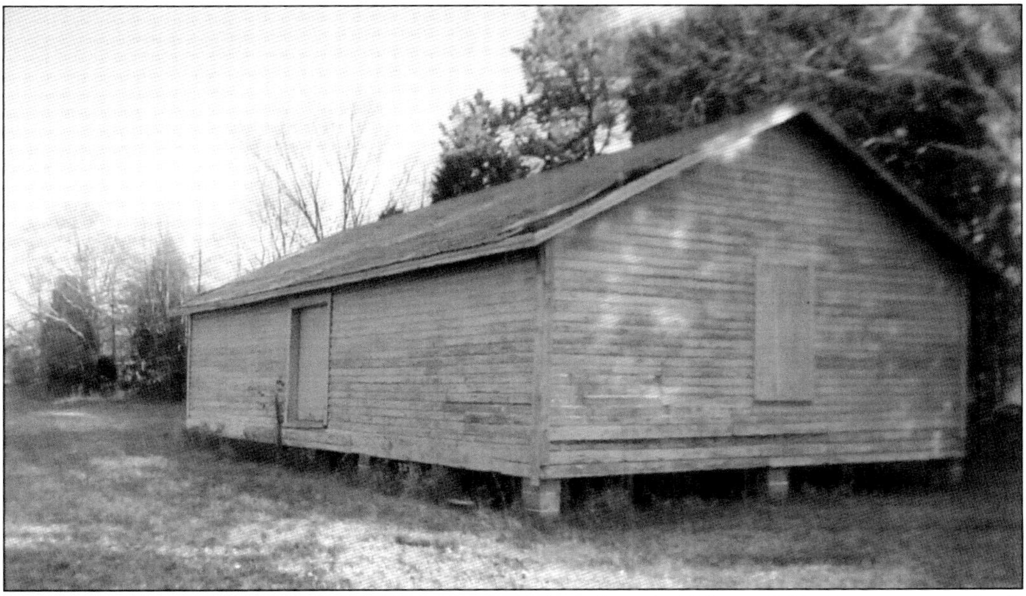

After completion to Clarksville, the line continued south to Buffalo in 1884. A station was built very quickly. Soon the passengers on the train would change to more and more miners and families as well as mine workers who were coming to southern Mecklenburg and Halifax Counties, where gold had been discovered by the Native Americans 400 years earlier. Real mining didn't start until 1843 in the remnants of mines used by the early Native Americans, but in 1848, they were abandoned for the California Gold Rush. (BMC.)

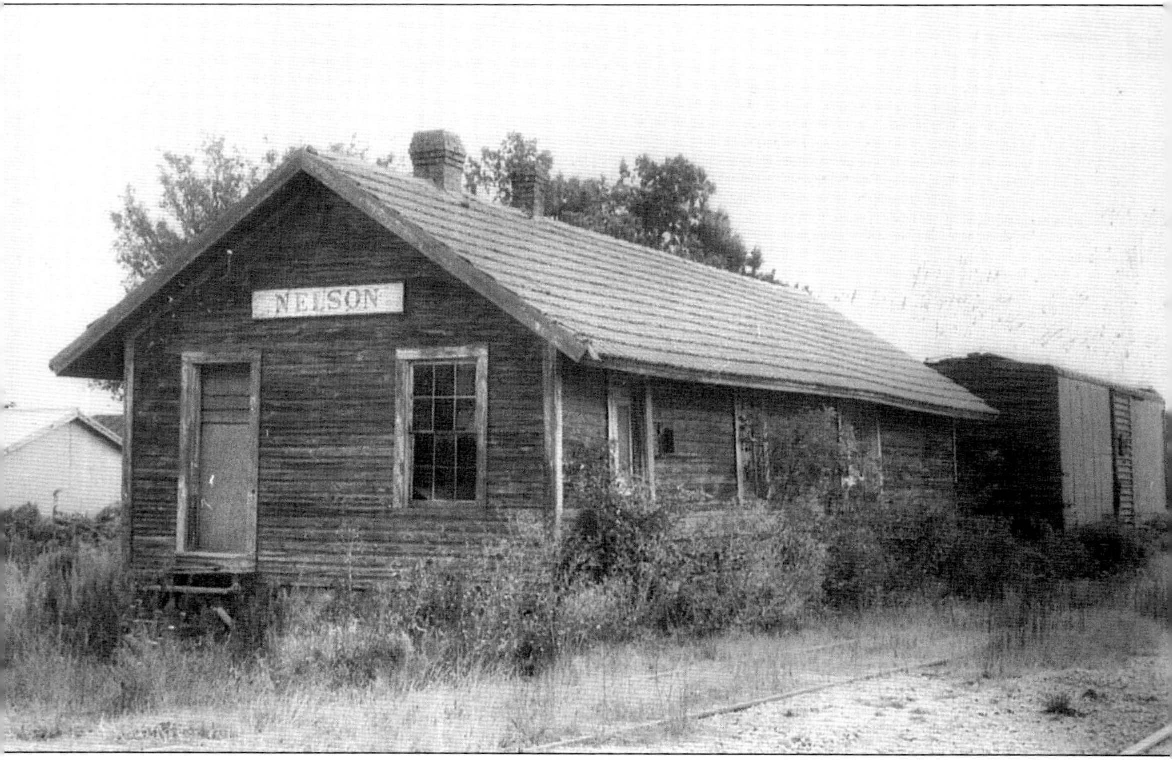

The train line continued on south to Nelson, in the heart of mining country. By 1890, there were 17 gold, 9 copper, and 3 tungsten mines in operation. Many of the surface gold veins ran out, but the veins seemed to open into a copper vein, so mining continued and expanded into northern North Carolina. The Nelson community did not benefit from this newfound wealth, as there is no record of a hotel or tavern, but at one time, there were two stores with a post office and a depot. (Southside Virginia Historical Press.)

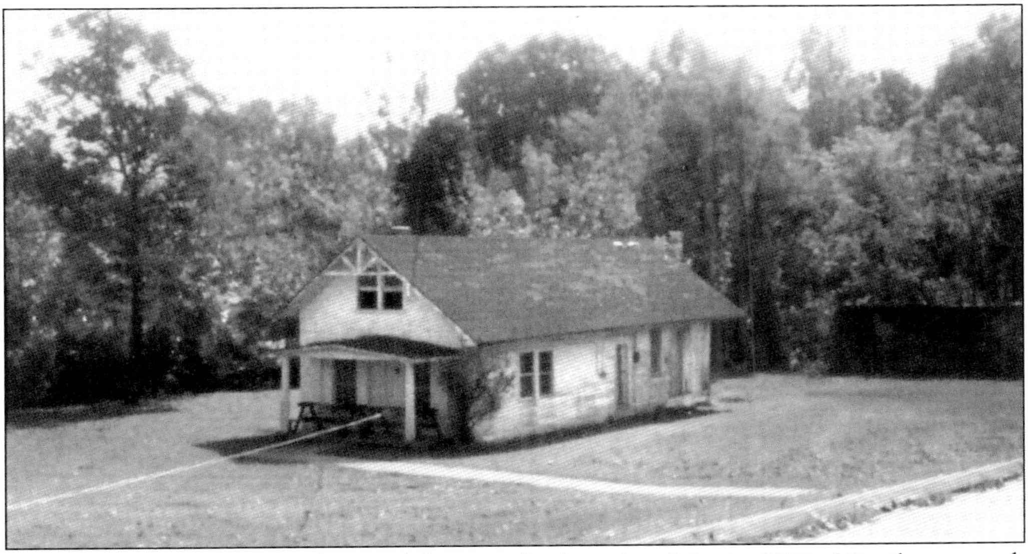

The mining activity generated so much business for the railroad that in 1890 a 3.9-mile spur track was laid from Buffalo to Buffalo Springs and a new station was built at Buffalo Springs, near the big store. This spur allowed for the freight cars to continue on their way while passengers and shipments were being off- and on-loaded at the springs station. In this photograph, the front of the station was for shipments of water bottles and supplies, and the back was for passengers, with a lounge area and refreshments. (Louis R. Hite.)

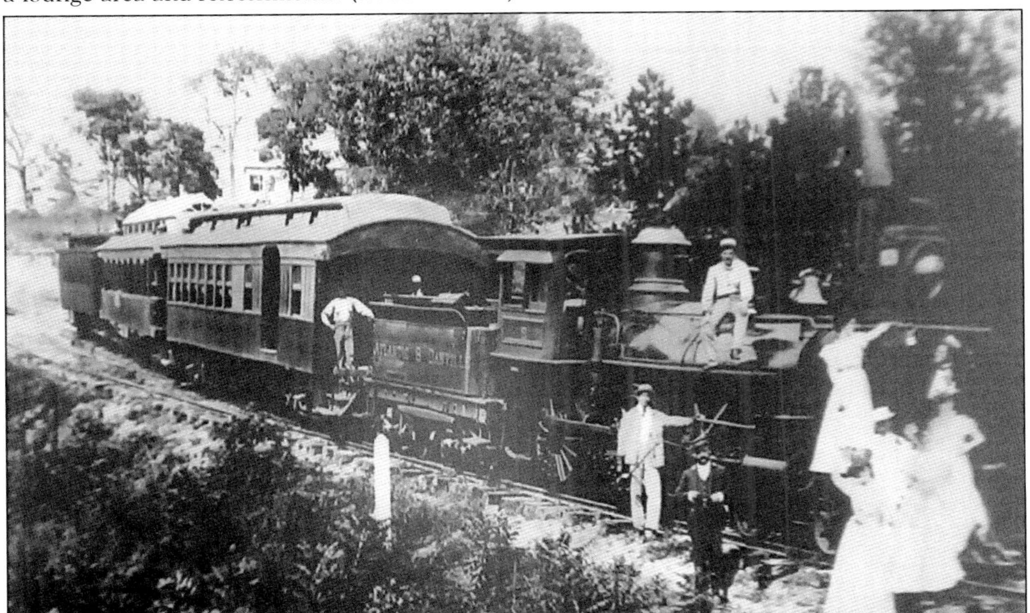

This locally famous photograph is of the grand arrival of a passenger train on July 4, 1895. With each arrival, there was a greeting party to escort guests to be checked in. Luggage would be loaded on wagons and taken to the guests' accommodations. Pictured from left to right are Harry Newton, engineer J. J. Ninman, conductor ? Vanderson, James A. Nunn, and ? Sampson; standing with the Wagstaff ladies is J. W. Baptist. (CRM.)

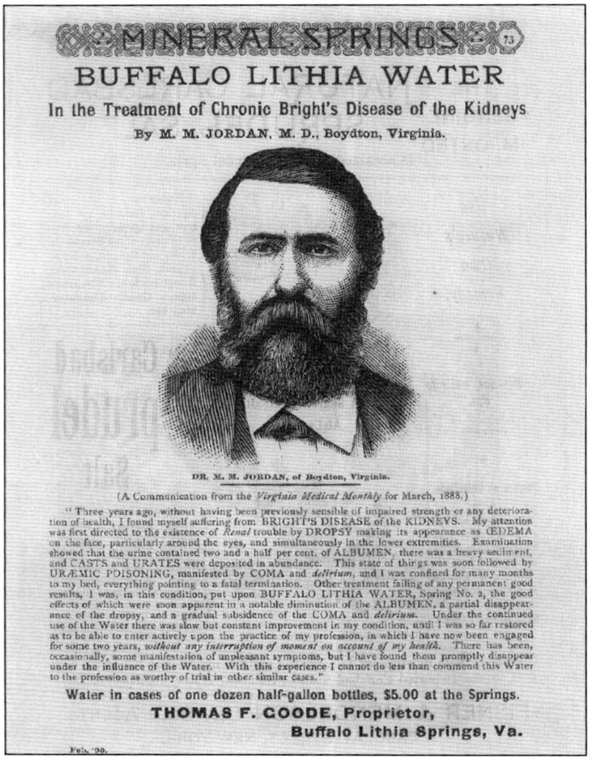
MINERAL SPRINGS 73

BUFFALO LITHIA WATER

In the Treatment of Chronic Bright's Disease of the Kidneys

By M. M. JORDAN, M. D., Boydton, Virginia.

DR. M. M. JORDAN, of Boydton, Virginia.

(A Communication from the *Virginia Medical Monthly* for March, 1888.)

"Three years ago, without having been previously sensible of impaired strength or any deterioration of health, I found myself suffering from BRIGHT'S DISEASE of the KIDNEYS. My attention was first directed to the existence of *Renal* trouble by DROPSY making its appearance as ŒDEMA on the face, particularly around the eyes, and simultaneously in the lower extremities. Examination showed that the urine contained two and a half per cent. of ALBUMEN, there was a heavy sediment, and CASTS and URATES were deposited in abundance. This state of things was soon followed by URÆMIC POISONING, manifested by COMA and *delirium*, and I was confined for many months to my bed, everything pointing to a fatal termination. Other treatment failing of any permanent good results, I was, in this condition, put upon BUFFALO LITHIA WATER, Spring No. 2, the good effects of which were soon apparent in a notable diminution of the ALBUMEN, a partial disappearance of the dropsy, and a gradual subsidence of the COMA and *delirium*. Under the continued use of the Water there was slow but constant improvement in my condition, until I was so far restored as to be able to enter actively upon the practice of my profession, in which I have now been engaged for some two years, *without any interruption of moment on account of my health.* There has been, occasionally, some manifestation of unpleasant symptoms, but I have found them promptly disappear under the influence of the Water. With this experience I cannot do less than commend this Water to the profession as worthy of trial in other similar cases."

Water in cases of one dozen half-gallon bottles, $5.00 at the Springs.

THOMAS F. GOODE, Proprietor,

Buffalo Lithia Springs, Va.

Feb. '90.

With the announcement of the railroad, Dr. M. M. Jordan of Boydton, then in poor health, sold the Jones and Jordan Drug Store to Arthur P. Snelling and moved to Buffalo Springs in 1888. At this time, Thomas Goode believed the resort needed to be remodeled to accommodate guests year-round, so fall, winter, and spring entertainment had to be structured. He expanded a 5-acre lake to 10 acres for boating, fishing, and swimming. Guests were encouraged to take cases of the water home with their baggage, and he designed and built wooden crates for shipping. (WCG.)

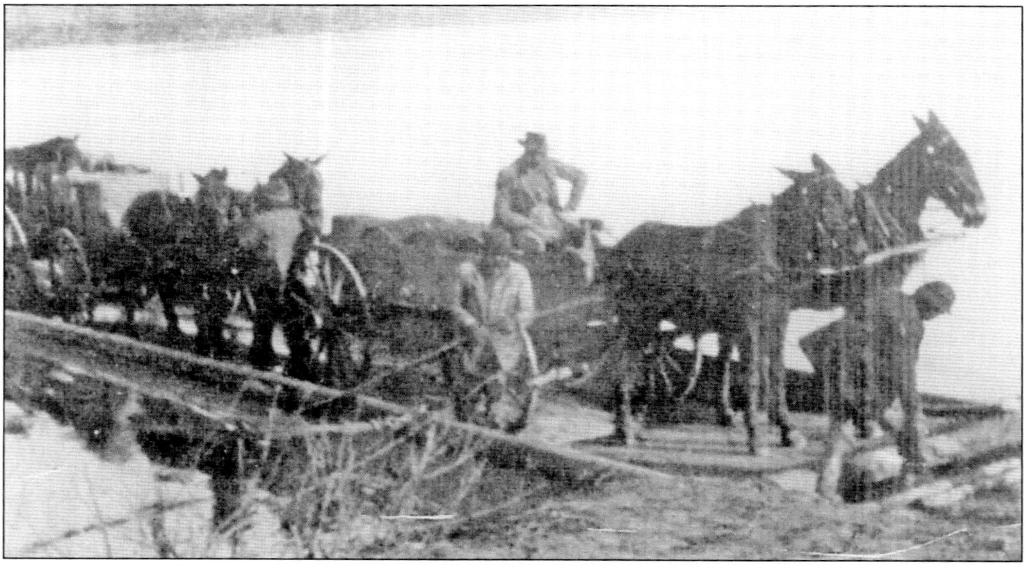

Clarksville steadily grew, the tobacco market was rebounding, and most of First Street to Fifth Street and Main Street were developed. There were five taverns in town with as many distilleries, and distilled spirits were a new economic base. The ferry system continued in use, and this 1890s photograph depicts a ferry load of distilled spirits being brought from Wayne Gooch's distillery in Jeffress to Clarksville. Gooch was the most prominent distiller in the area, with five stills and his own railroad car. All the other local distillers had one still. (CRM.)

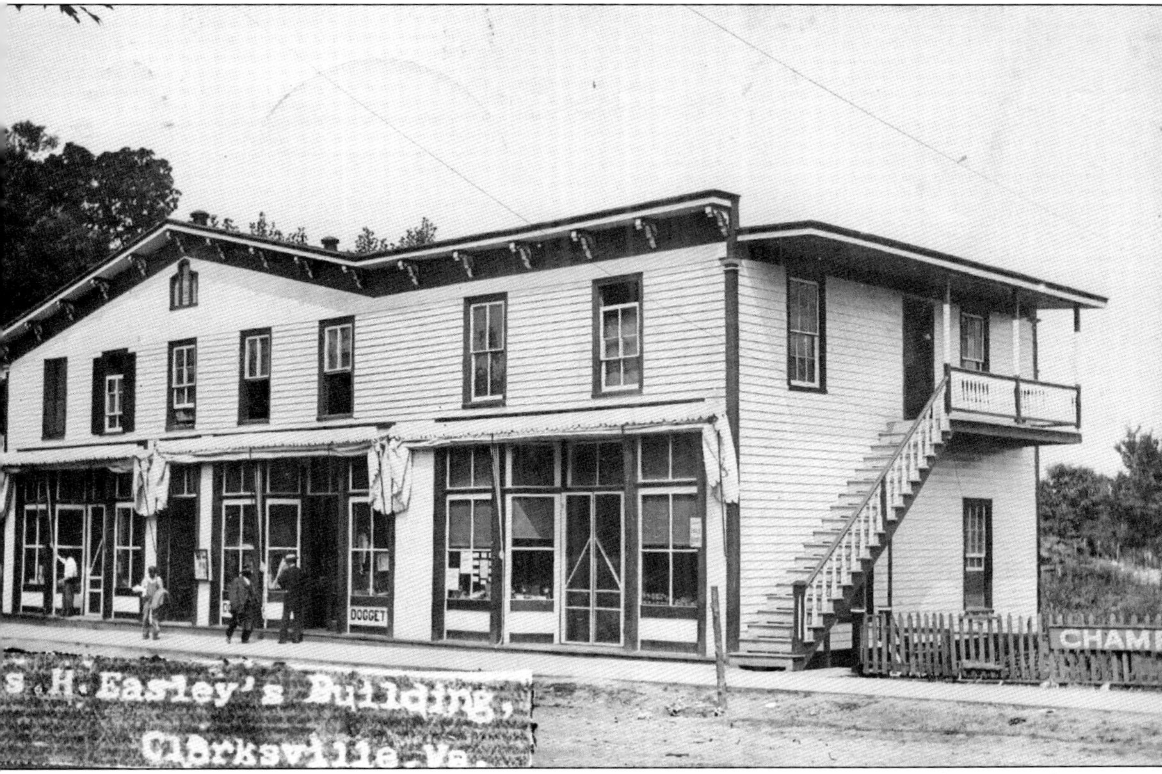

The entire western Mecklenburg community came to aid Clarksville in rebuilding homes and businesses after the great fire of 1893. This postcard is of the new Thomas H. Easley building on First Street, which housed a mercantile, dry goods store, pharmacy, and the Roanoke Hotel upstairs. (Kathryne B. Routt.)

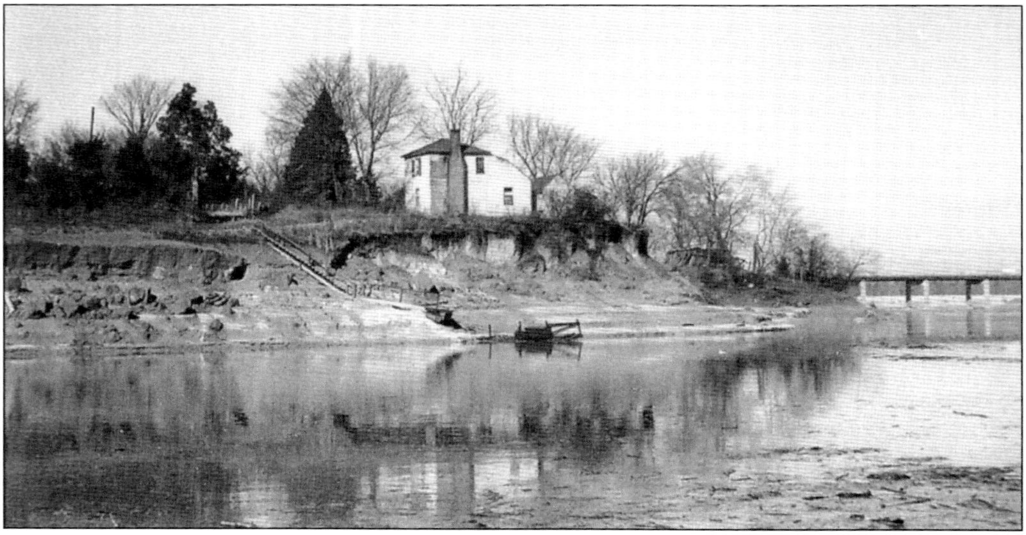

Next to the warehouse, on the bluff overlooking the Dan River and First Street, was the home of John A. Ligon. John brought his family downstream from Wolf Trap by bateaux in 1885. The home was built in 1859 for Lucy Royster, who lived there until her death, and it was then purchased for John by W. H. Ligon, a real estate dealer in the area. John was part of the original group of citizens responsible for Clarksville's charter being reinstated. (Betty Jack Ligon.)

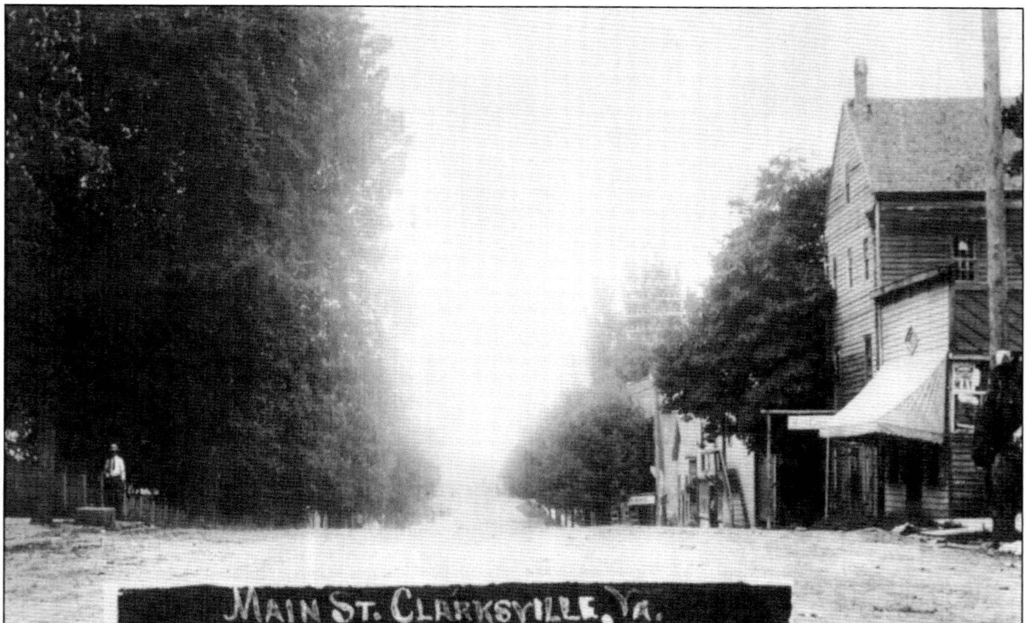

Wagons were extremely popular at the dawn of the 20th century. The old ordinance/wagon factory having burned, a new facility on Virginia Avenue was comprised of several buildings, all shown on the right of this 1908 photograph. The wagon factory relocated to a new location on Buffalo Road just south of town but experienced another fire in November 1941 in the lumber yard, delaying production for a short time. The factory continued to be operated by the Russell family until it closed in late 1954. (BH.)

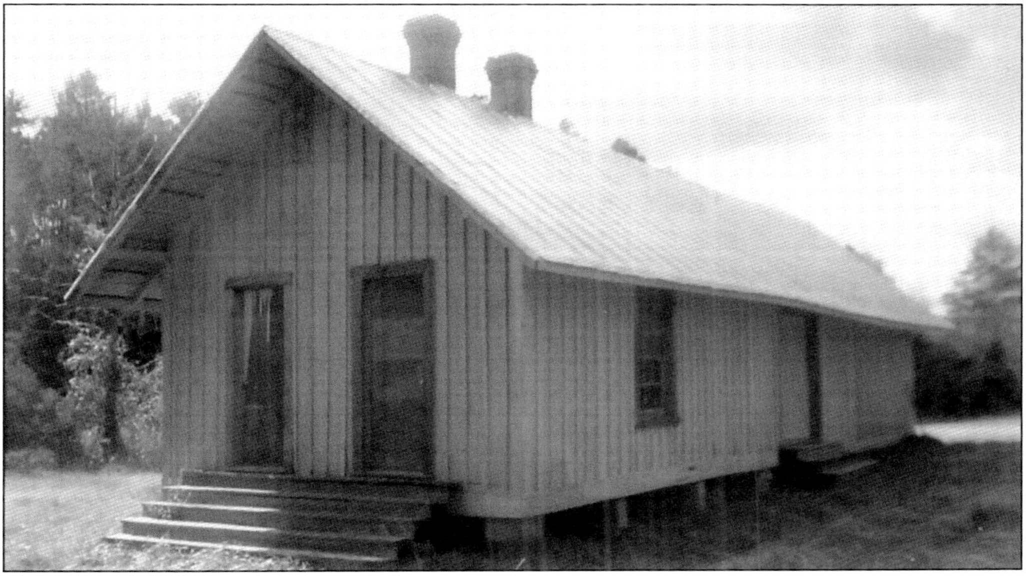

Entering western Mecklenburg County, the Atlantic and Danville Railroad had a station in Antlers in 1891. The community never flourished, although there was a boardinghouse there for a time and a community store. This area became strategic in the 1940s as it was the site of a spur track to Kerr Village, where construction was taking place for the new Kerr Dam. This is also the location of a civil suit against the Corps of Engineers, the only one to reach the U.S. Supreme Court. (BMC.)

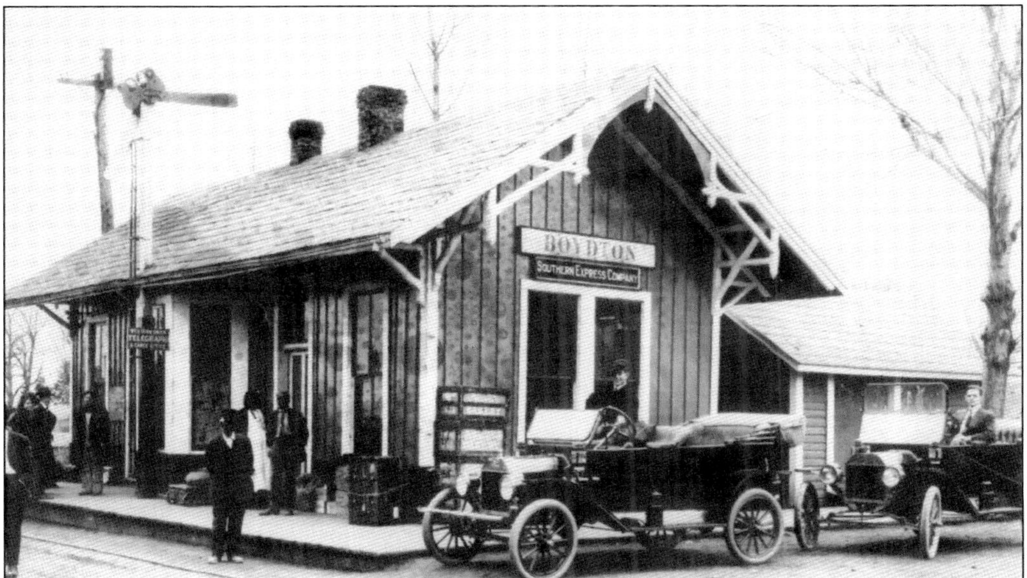

Leaving Antlers, the next station was Boydton. This 1920s photograph shows the passenger station, built in 1891. Many people in town would ride to Clarksville, shop during the day, and return on the evening train. To the left of the station on the other side of the tracks was a freight platform and station. The last passenger train came through town in 1969. The man in the second car is Arthur P. Snelling Jr. (HBR.)

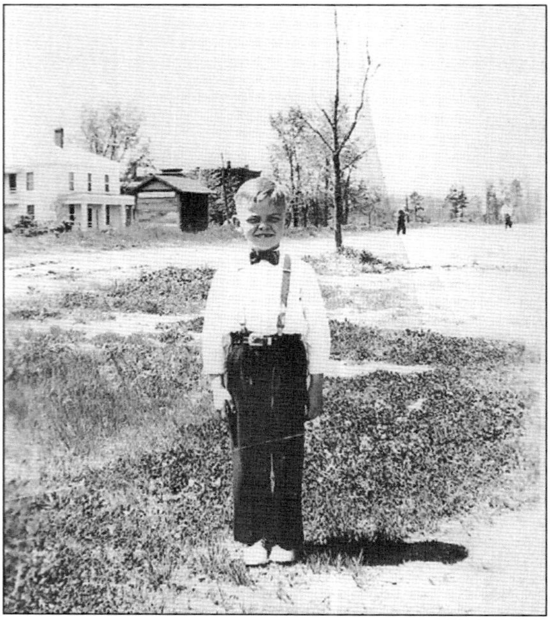

In 1881, Langston Finch lost the hotel he owned to foreclosure and moved halfway between Boydton and Clarksville, where he opened a tavern/ordinary. When the train came to the area, he sold to S. O. Barnett, who became the postmaster and station master of the new Finchley in 1890. The tiny passenger house is over the right shoulder of Vince Hudson. (Barbara Carter Royal.)

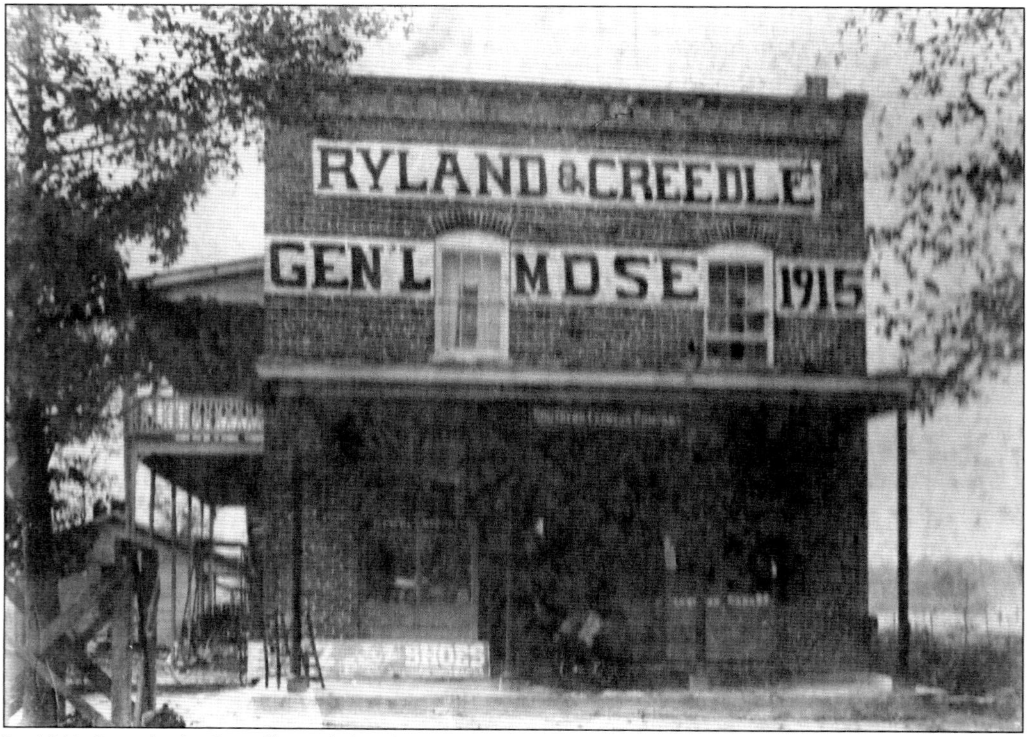

In 1914, Joseph A. Creedle and family came to Finchley to have access to the railroad to supply their store. Having sold their store in Smith's Crossroads, Creedle became the new postmaster and purchased the store from Barnett. In the early 1920s, with the new highway in front of the store, Creedle added a gas pump and oil tank. This 1915 photograph of the store shows respect to Creedle's wife's family by naming the store after them: Ryland and Creedle. (Claire Puryear Martin.)

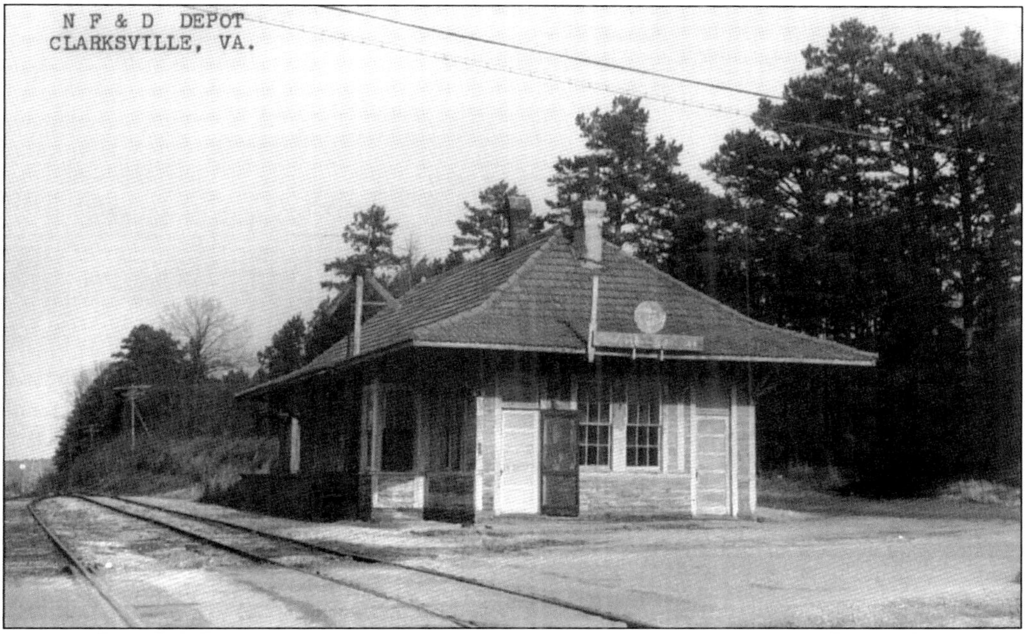

After the Jeffress Junction connection was completed, a new Atlantic and Danville station was built in south Clarksville at Buffalo Road. This station opened in 1892 and served both freight and passengers. This became an important freight station around 1919, with Russell Wagon Factory locating across the tracks. (CRM.)

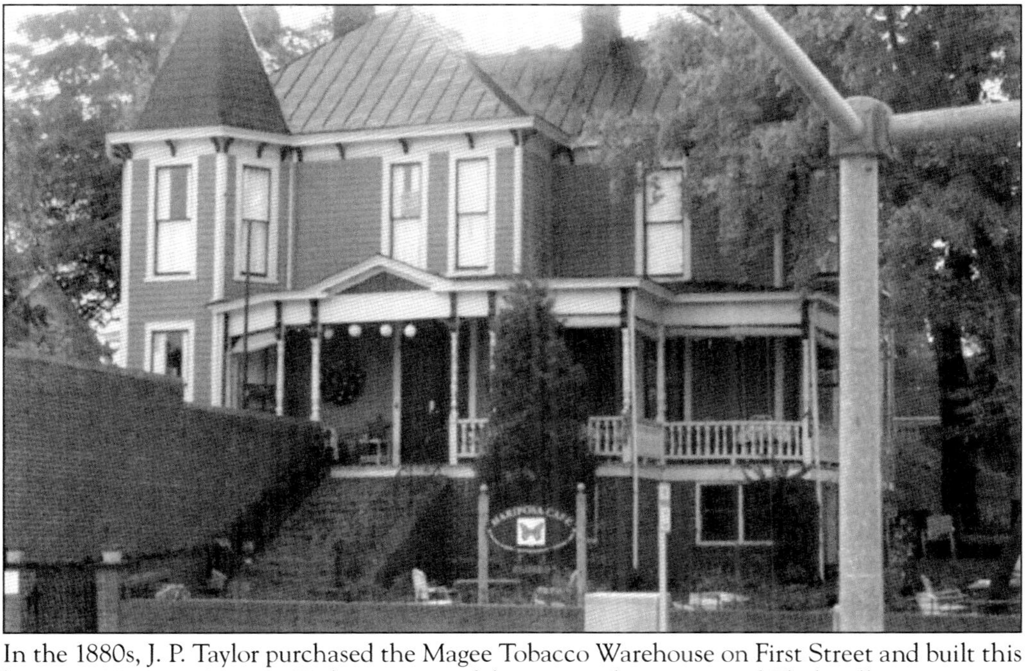

In the 1880s, J. P. Taylor purchased the Magee Tobacco Warehouse on First Street and built this home on Virginia Avenue. Taylor was one of the principal organizers of Clarksville regaining its charter and was the first citizen elected mayor. He sold the warehouse and opened an insurance agency in a small brick building he constructed in front of his home. (CRM.)

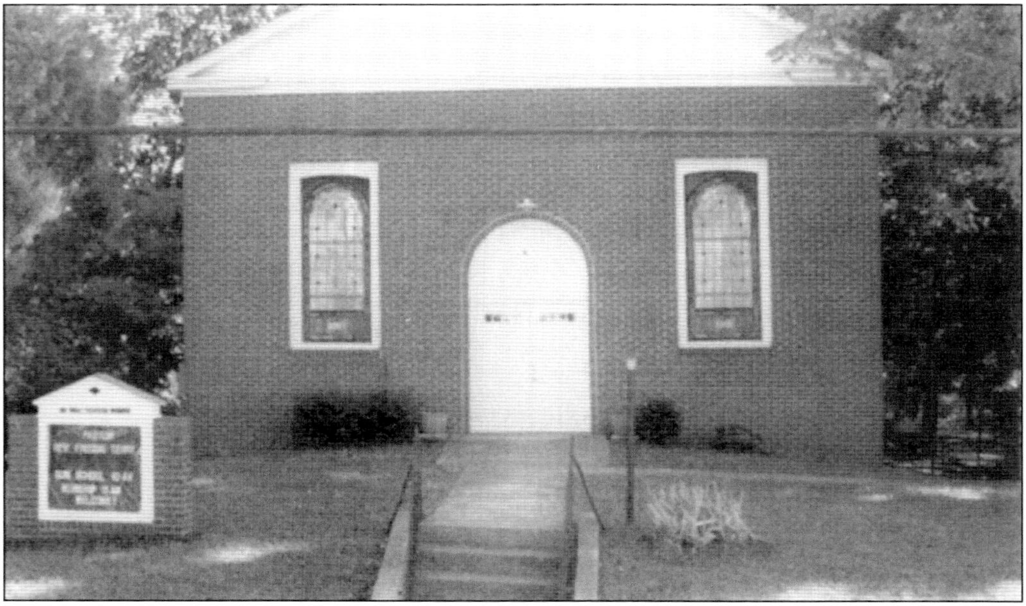

In 1871, Mount Zion Baptist Church was organized as one of the first churches for freedmen in Clarksville. Located on Market Street at Second Street, it was in harm's way and a frame structure during the fire of 1893 but survived. Dedicated in 1875, this church was host to Frederick Douglass when he came to visit the area and continues to serve the African American community of Clarksville. (BH.)

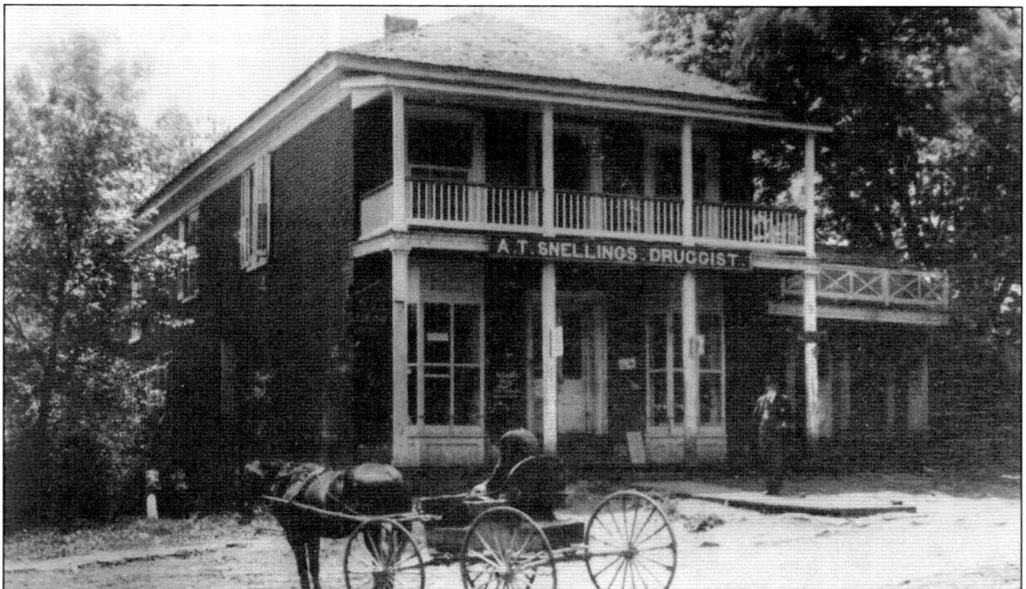

The A. P. Snelling Drug Store served the Boydton community from at least 1845, changing owners but serving in the same capacity. His son, Arthur P. Snelling Jr., having recently completed pharmacy school, the two built a new pharmacy after the fire of 1909 nearly destroyed most of Boydtown. Also with various owners, the Boydton Pharmacy served the town for many years. (REC.)

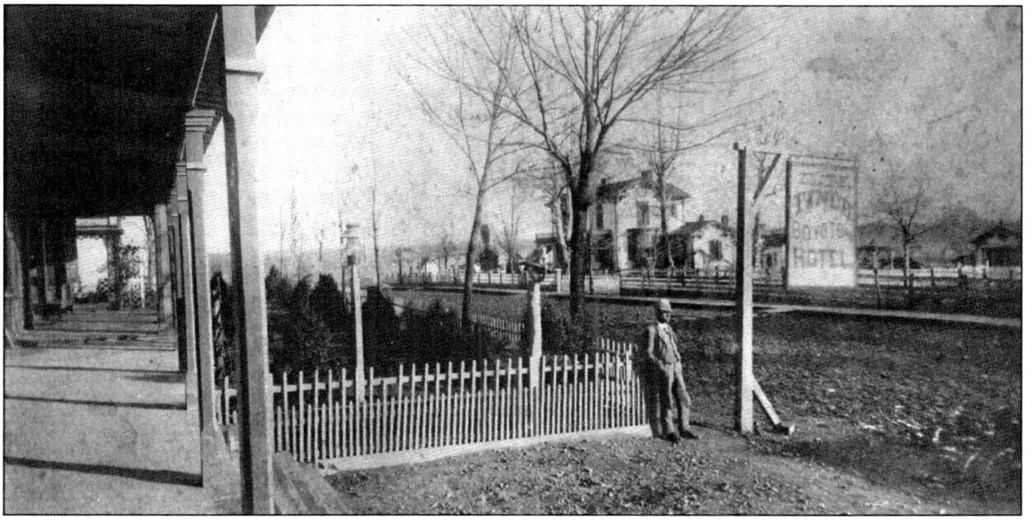

Aiken's Hotel was across the street from the Finch Hotel and next to the railroad station. It was later sold to Elizabeth Toone, who turned it into her personal residence. Next door, in the photograph, is the small house that was the Boyd cabinet and furniture shop of 1820. Edwin and Ruth Crowder purchased the cabinet shop and used it as the center entrance to their home, which also included two wings of the former Kensington, across from Rose Hill in Boydton. The individual is unidentified. (REC.)

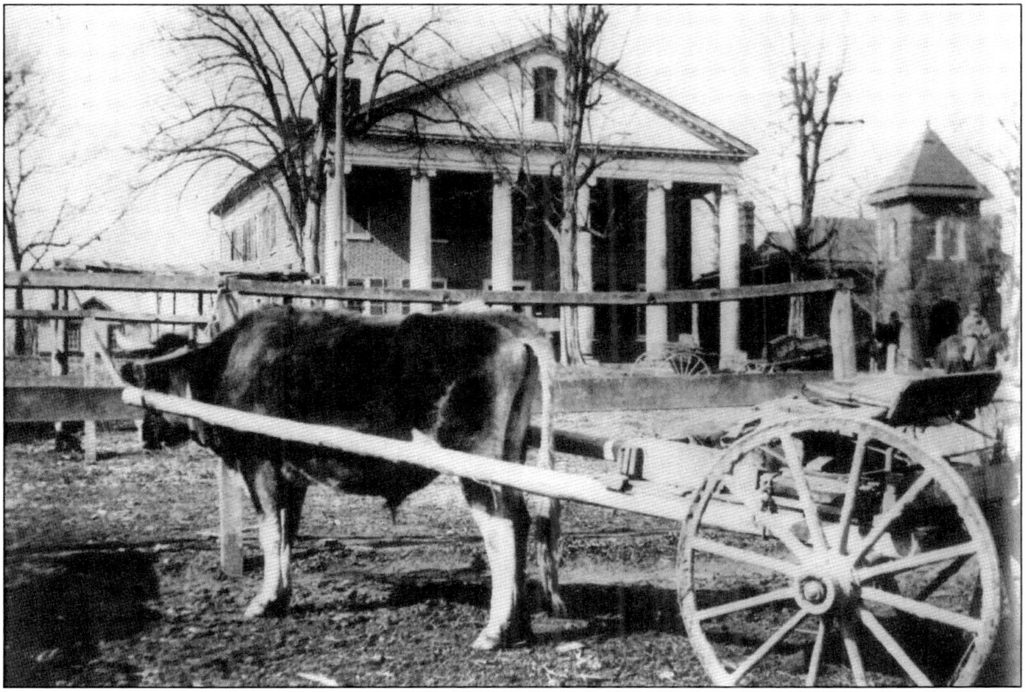

The jail was removed, and around 1890, a new clerk's office was built next to the courthouse with a bell tower. To the rear of the courthouse on Bank Street is a law office, the Bank of Mecklenburg, a café, and a tobacco warehouse. The old wooden fence is being removed to install the new wrought-iron fence. (REC.)

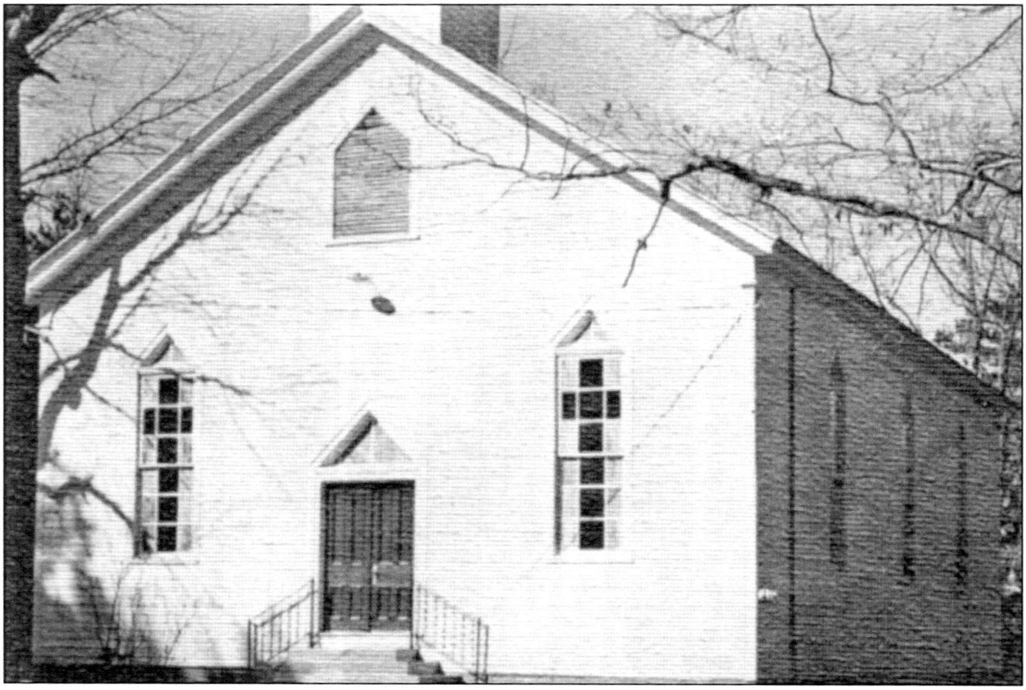

St. Paul's Baptist Church was built in 1880 to serve the black community of Boydton. When Clarksville had their great fire, St. Paul's congregation was one of the first groups to respond, with a fund-raiser dispatched within two days. One of the early visiting preachers was William Smalley, a graduate of Thyne Institute in Chase City. He became the first supervisor of black public schools in the county. (Henry H. Gregory Jr.)

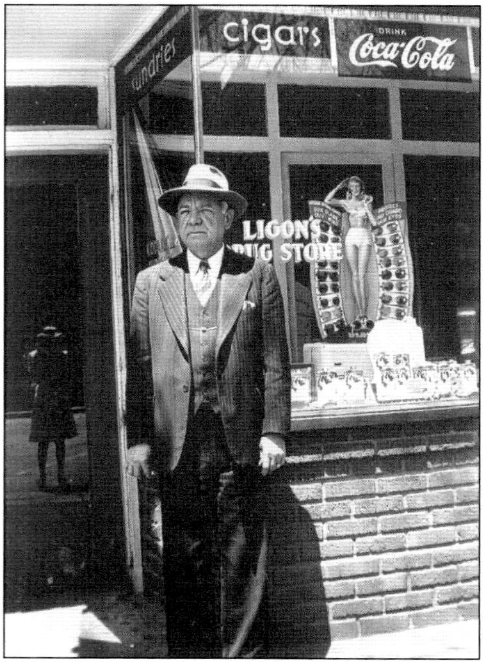

In 1895, Dr. J. A. Drake, a former physician with the Confederacy, moved from his farm in Palmer Springs to Clarksville, opening a new drugstore on Virginia Avenue. The slogan on his pharmacy bottles was "Dr. Drake, shake and take." By 1915, the store was being run by J. J. Harris and was also selling school books and supplies. Dr. Drake died in 1926, and the store was purchased by Dell Newcomb Pharmacy, with Dutchie's beauty shop upstairs. After World War II, it was purchased by John A. Ligon Jr. (standing in front), who operated it until 1960. (Betty Jack Ligon.)

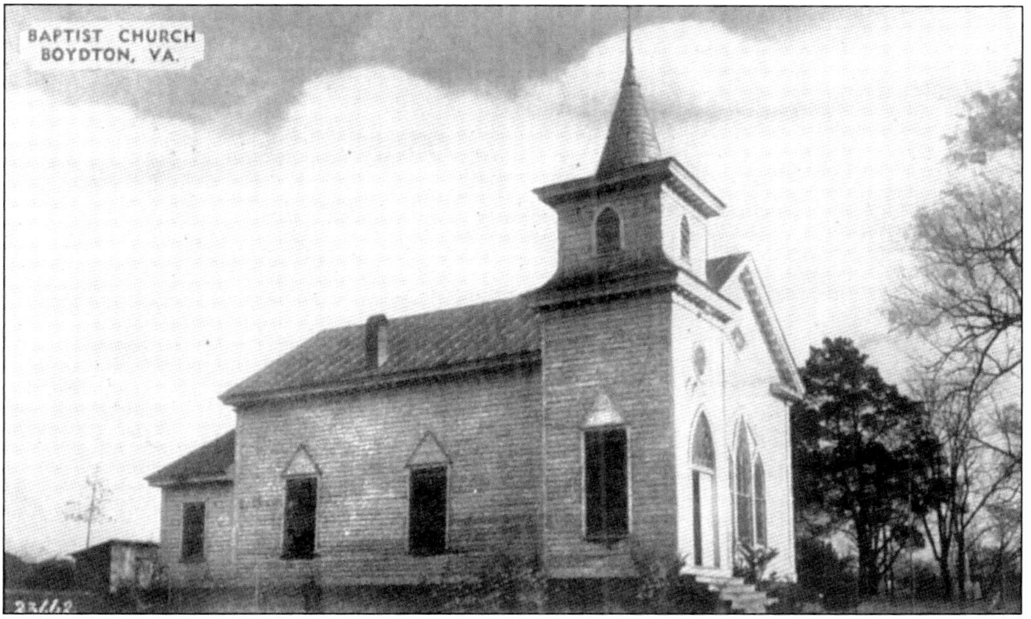

For $2,000, the Boydton Baptist Church trustees, Rev. E. L. Baptist and C. N. Williams, purchased at public auction the Female Academy with 14 acres in 1879. The church, having begun in 1877, used the west wing of the school for their meetings until it could be moved to its present location in December 1881. (WCG.)

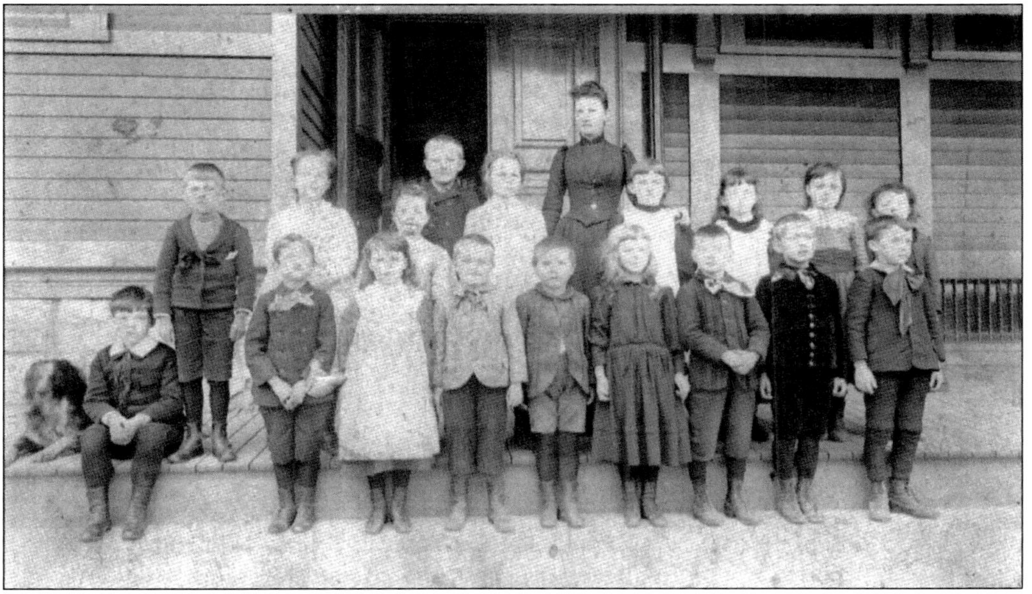

Prior to the Civil War, Clarksville had a male academy on Buffalo Road and a girls' on Fifth and Commerce Streets. After the fire, the girls were consolidated with the boys. This photograph is believed to be of the first class of students of the new school, Jubilee, around 1894. With the age of the picture, some of the students have been identified with reluctant speculation, thus no names are listed. (Richard Burnett/Mac Crowder.)

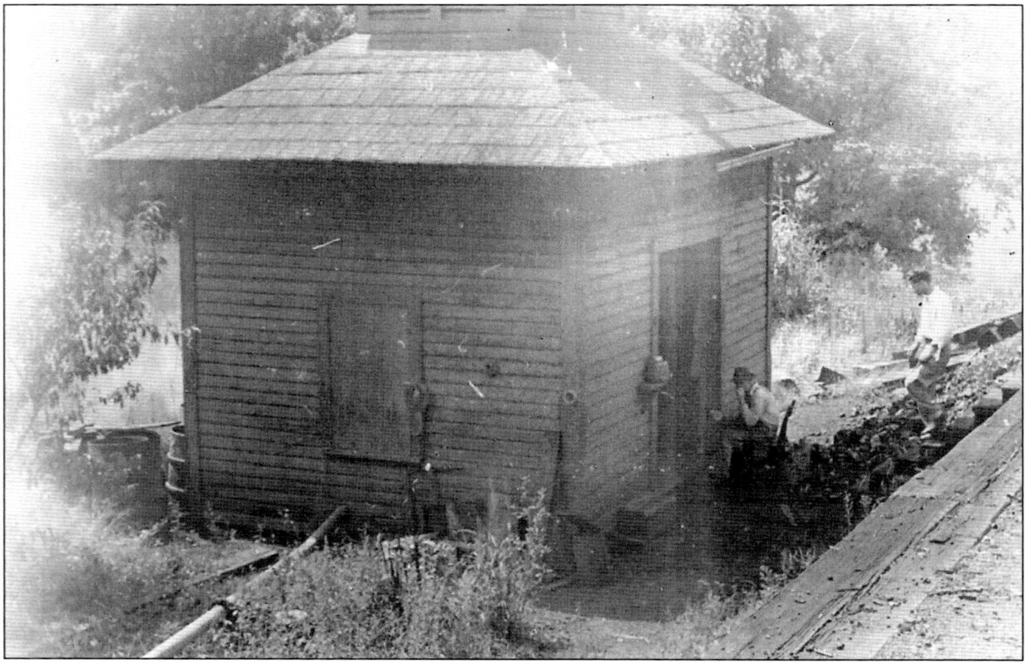

By 1894, the Atlantic and Danville Railroad was in foreclosure and sold. In 1899, Southern Railroad leased the lines, eventually agreeing to a 50-year lease, and in 1952, all was sold to the Norfolk and Western Railway Company. This is an old pumphouse next to the Dan River to be used for the steam engines. (COE.)

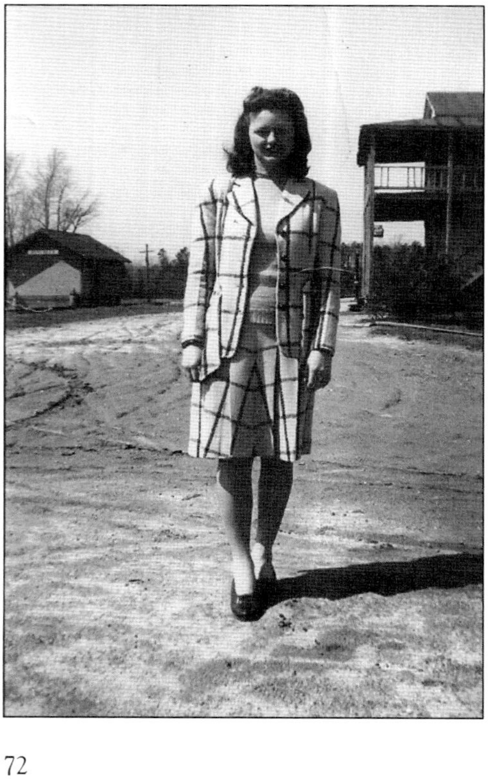

In the background (left) is the new Southern Railway freight station of Finchley, built around 1892. The station was sold and moved when the rail line was removed in the 1970s. In this 1940s picture is Frances Carter Schridde, a resident born in Finchley, standing near the J. A. Creedle store. When Highway 58 came through Finchley in the late 1930s, there were four other stores in the village (with one located on either side of the highway), a public white and a black school, Creedle's holdings, a church, and a brand-new airport. (Barbara Carter Royal.)

Three

The Clarksville Bridge to Prosperity

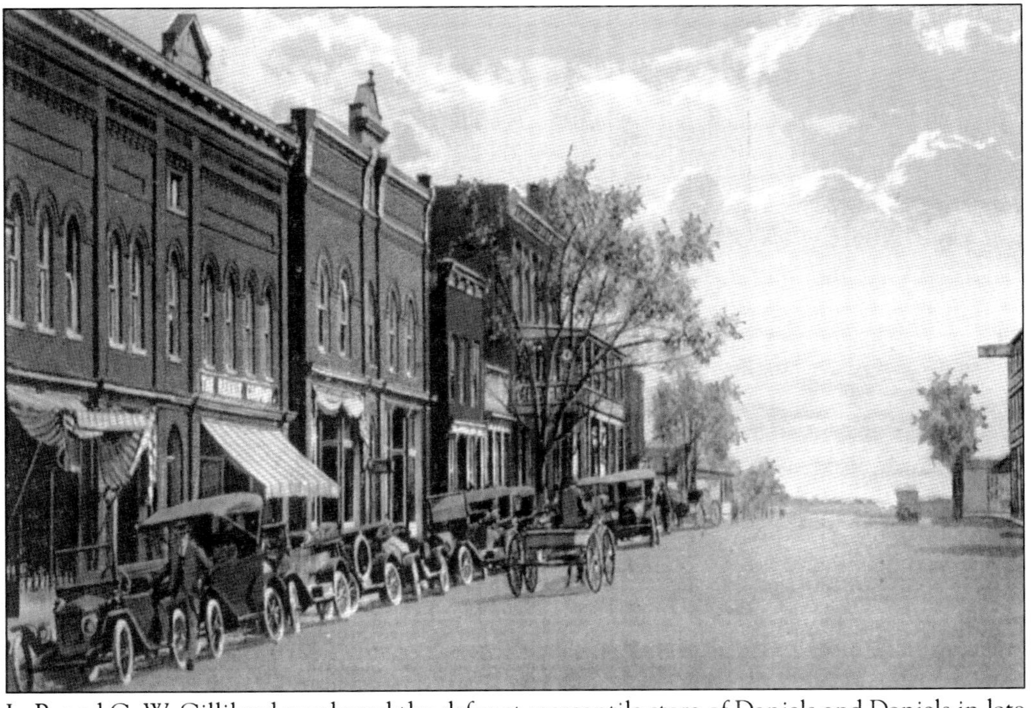

L. B. and G. W. Gilliland purchased the defunct mercantile store of Daniels and Daniels in late 1868, but the store burned in 1893. A month later, G. W. died. Reorganizing the business, L. B. and his wife, Mary Liipfort, built a new hotel in 1897 on the site, with stables in the back. Next door, the Rennie Company opened in 1913. (Southside Virginia Historical Press.)

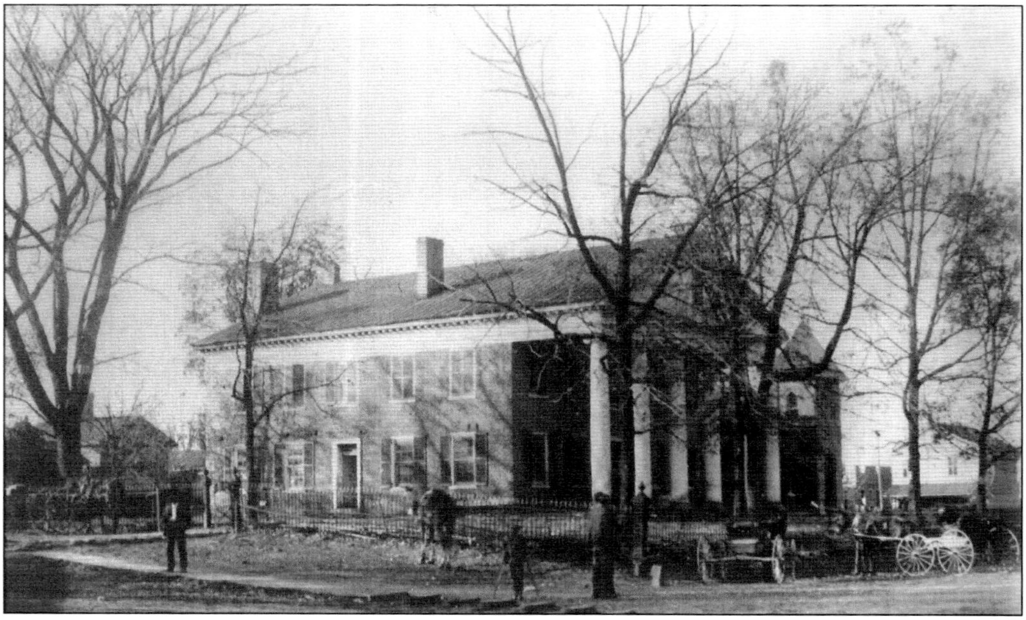

In August 1899, the L. A. Armistead Camp, Confederate Veterans, held their reunion at the Grace Hotel but set aside one day for a dedication. During the dedication, John Bowen of the 3rd Virginia Cavalry used a ladder to climb atop the monument, posing with an empty sleeve and holding a musket for the artist in attendance to photograph and sketch him for a soldier to be placed on top in future years. The people are unidentified. (REC.)

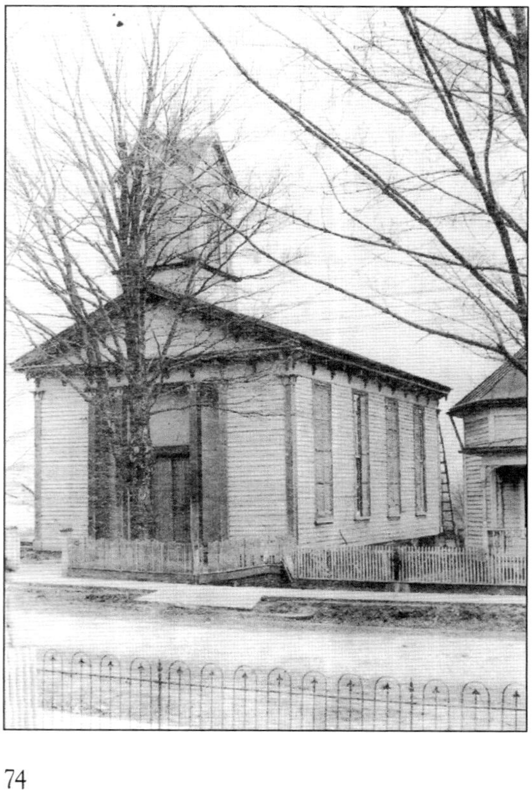

Clarksville Baptist Church was established in 1833 but has no known records until 1889. Pastors changed every two to four years, except for Rev. R. E. Peele. During World War I and the flu epidemic, Reverend Peele is said to have gone about the community ministering to the sick and shut-in, cutting wood when needed and arranging Red Cross assistance for others. (BH.)

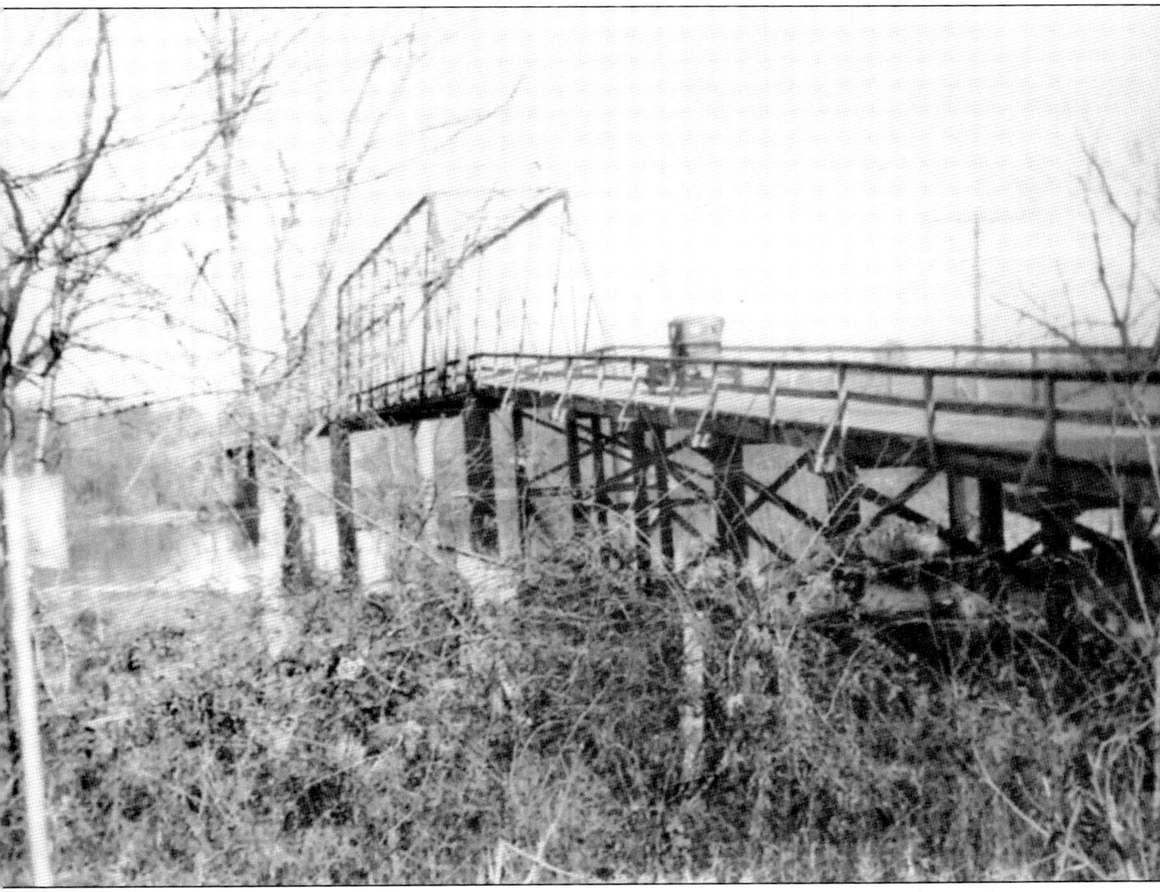

On July 8, 1905, the new Clarksville plank bridge opened crossing the Stanton and Dan Rivers. The town was excited at the new opportunities, and the first bridge keeper was J. A. Ligon. The bridge keepers were deputized for bonding purposes and enforcement of bridge regulations. (Richard Burnett.)

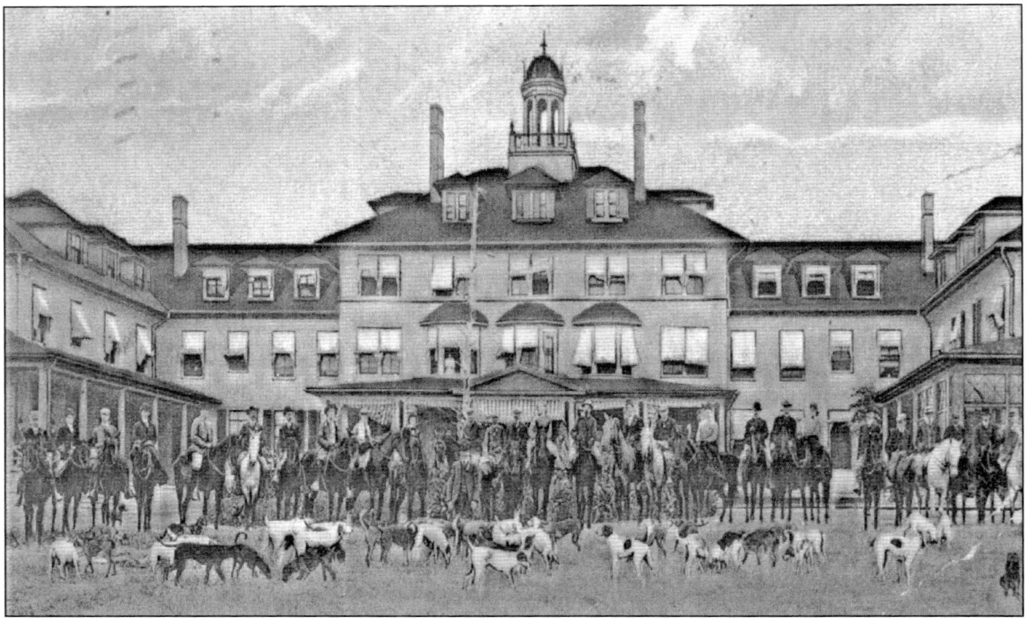

In 1903, the Mecklenburg Mineral Springs Hotel and Sanitarium opened in Chase City. The hotel has received much notoriety through the years. This image is a close-up of the front, showing the hydro spa and wings on either side of the first hospital located in southside Virginia. This photograph shows the Virginia Medical Society convention or the governor's party in 1905, standing in front of the hospital after a long day of fox hunting. (HBR.)

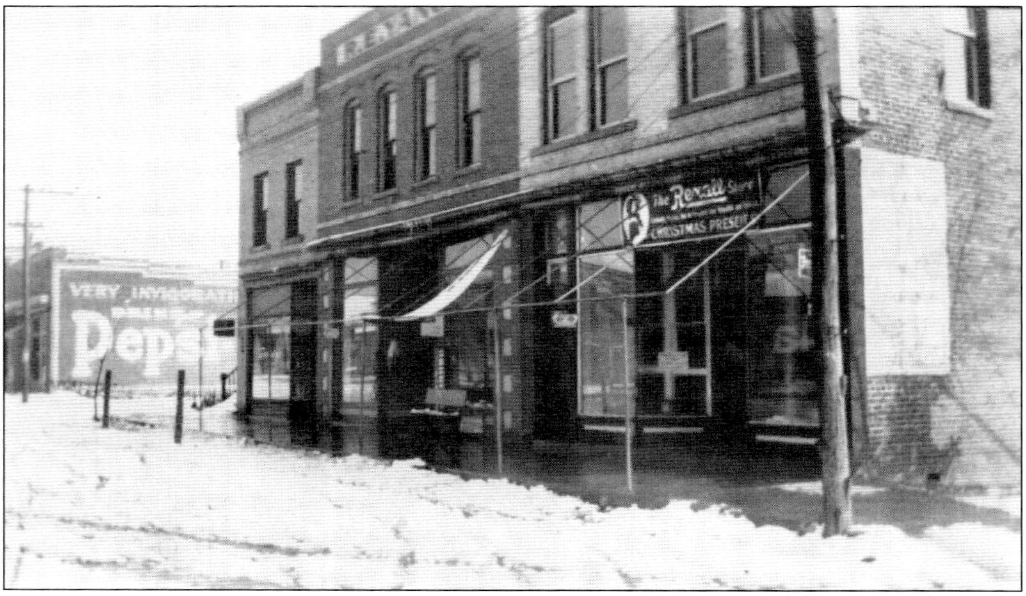

Graduating medical school in 1888, Dr. Adam Finch returned to Chase City. Enticing Dr. Henry L. Burwell and P. H. Maddox, he helped build a pharmacy in 1889 with his practice in back. Dr. Finch organized the National Guard of Chase City and trained them on his family's farm. Next door is the R. E. Yancy mercantile and Gregory's Millinery. In the distance is Bigger's Grocery and dry goods (founded 1898). (James Lewter.)

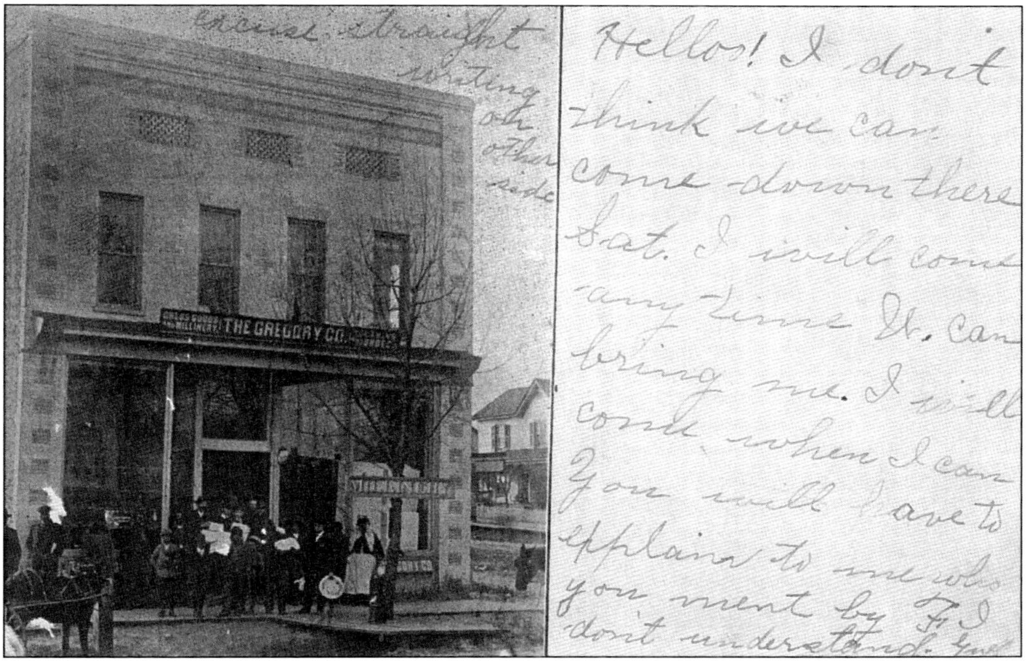

The former 1885 store of J. F. Brown dry goods was purchased in 1905 by Myrtle Gregory and expanded with a new millinery shop, hosting a grand celebration on April 2 and 3, 1907. The shop was run by Gregory with her seamstress, Etta Annig, her niece from North Carolina. The house in the background is that of R. M. Jeffreys; it was built by October 1901 on Fourth Street. As this is the grand reopening, the people in front are the local merchants and city council. (WCG.)

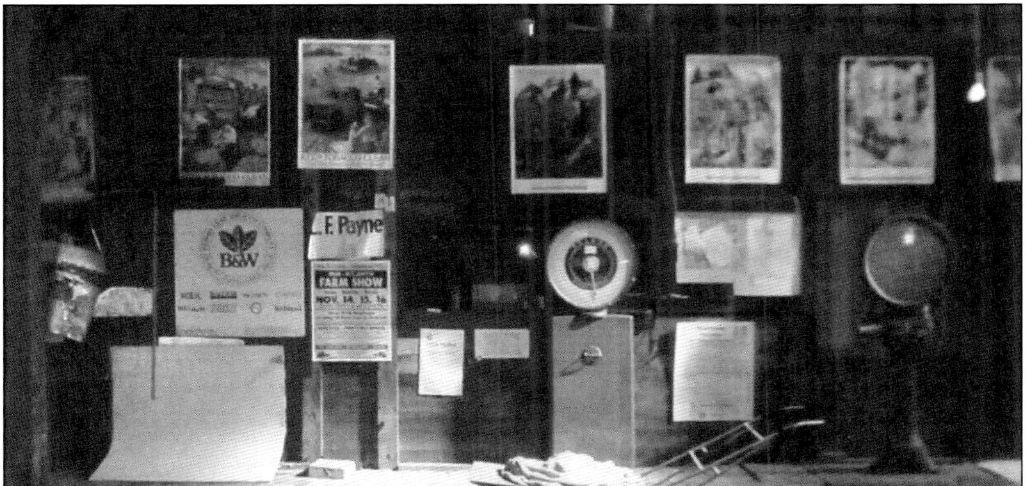

The Advance Warehouse was built and operated in 1883 by A. F. Thomas and H. E. Edmonds. Still standing as a majestic reminder of the glory days of tobacco, this warehouse was chosen for its interior character to be used in filming the movie *Sommersby*, starring Jodi Foster and Richard Gere, in 1992. Mac Burnett, the world champion auctioneer from Clarksville, was a consultant and voiceover in the auction scene. This warehouse was used by the Chase City High School basketball team and others, as a skating ring, and for revival meetings and dances. (Garnett E. Clark.)

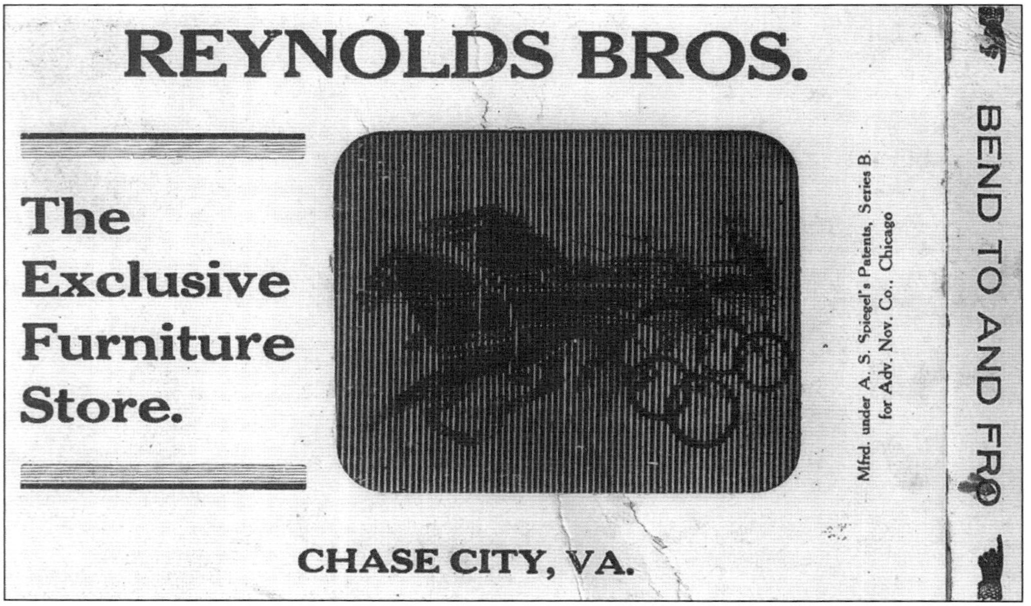

Reynold's furniture was the original outlet store for Nichols' Furniture Factory of Chase City and for Liifport coffins from Clarksville, opening around 1895. Nichol's Furniture introduced a new line of Chase City dining tables and chairs, as well as schoolroom tables. This introduction card was a sign of the times; bending the tab up and down shows the moving image of a horse race. (Lucille Tisdale Campbell.)

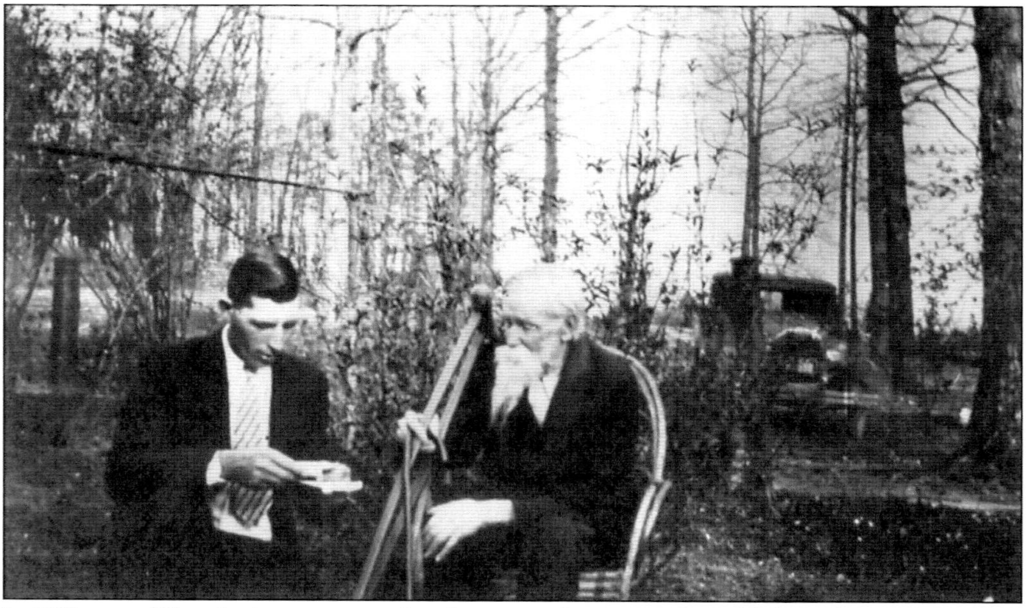

In 1870, one of Sheridan's men returned to the area—Cummings C. Reddick. He began to purchase land and build homes and businesses. When the railroad came through town, along the rail line 6 miles south of Chase City, he built and developed the community of Esnon with a store, gristmill, sawmill, and freight platform. In this photograph, taken around 1930, Reddick, being visited by his grandson Lloyd Gryder, is 100 years old. (Thomas and Pat Gryder.)

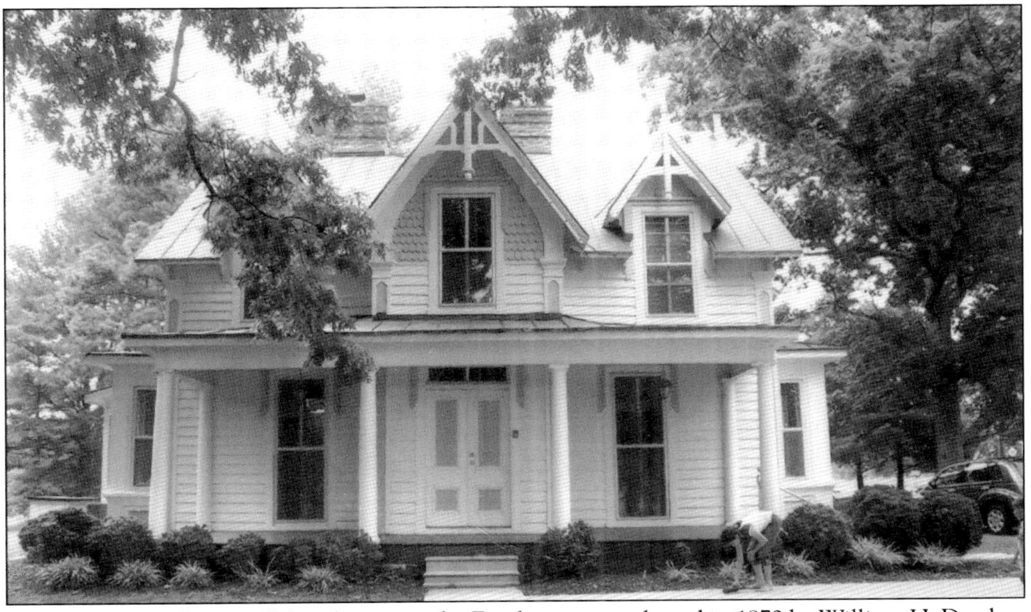

This was originally a small farmhouse on the Finch tract, purchased in 1872 by William H. Dunlap, a contractor. He had the home extensively remodeled for himself and his four children facing the old Keysville–to–"Virginia City" road. He was the principal builder of the Thyne Institute from 1872, completing the principal's house in 1895, when he died. In 1897, the house was purchased by J. L. Woodyard and became a boardinghouse. (John and Denise Russell.)

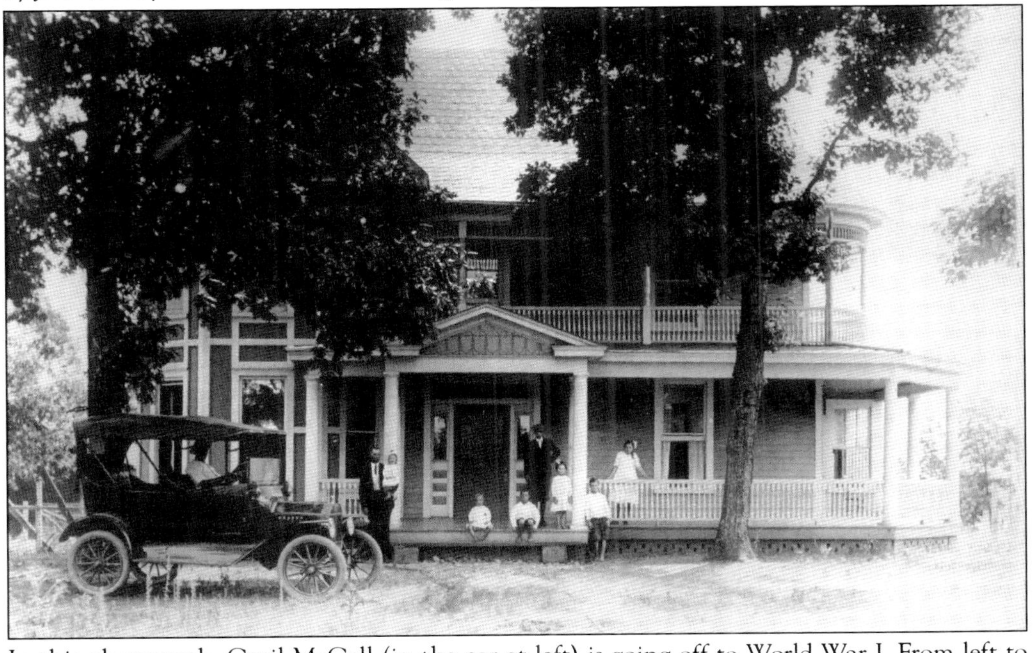

In this photograph, Cecil McCall (in the car at left) is going off to World War I. From left to right are Cecil's father, Robert S. McCall, holding Lula; Joe McCall; Bill McCall; Louie McCall; Edna McCall; Robert McCall; and Nellie McCall. Not in the picture is Cecil's grandma Myrna McCall, who was living in the home. (Judy McCall Mathis.)

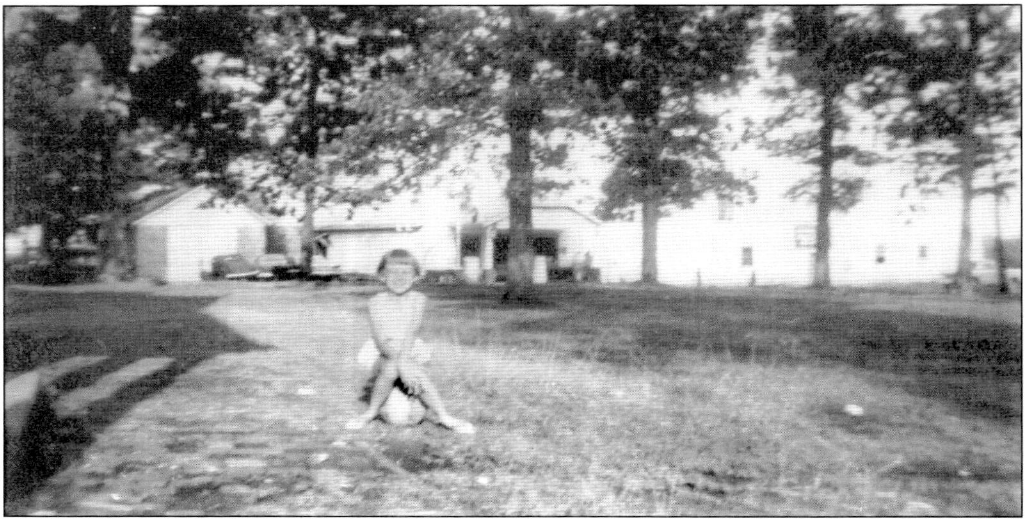

Shortly after McCall moved into his new home, around 1908, J. C. Collis moved into the Woodyard house with his family from North Carolina. At the bend of the Keysville Road, Collis proceeded to build his family home with a dry goods and produce store next door. This 1963 photograph shows Collis's home garage, his store with car repair station, and his expansive wholesale warehouse. (BMC.)

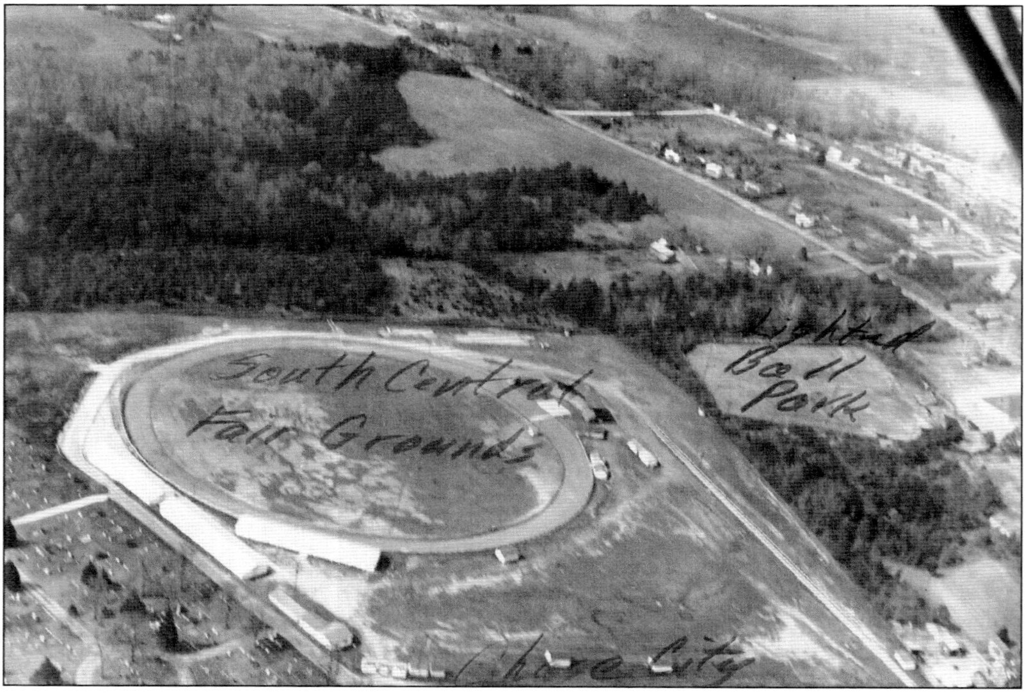

In 1911, following the tragic fire of the Mecklenburg Mineral Springs Hotel, the Mecklenburg Agricultural Fair was held on the old hotel grounds. In 1912, twenty-five acres were purchased next to the cemetery for the fairgrounds, and next door is Victory Field, which was equipped with lights in 1948, next to the American Legion Hall on the Boydton Road in the distance. (Bryan Queensberry.)

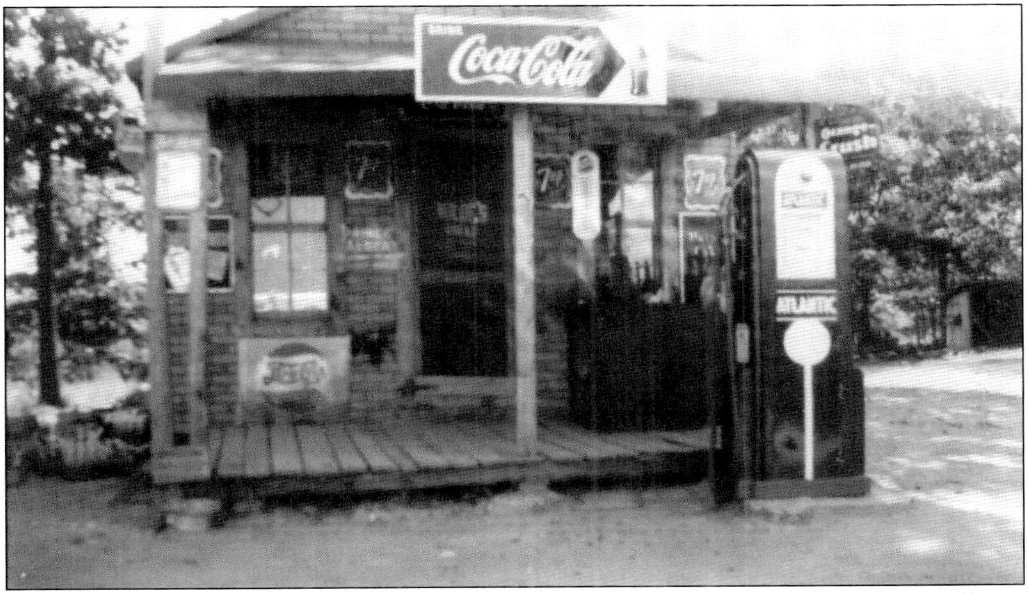

This was originally the Hanford Grocery and post office, near Cephus on the Barnesville-to-Clarksville Road. The first postmaster was John Y. Richards. The store sits on a hill overlooking the Trotter Plantation manor house, purchased by the Morgan family around 1900. The store and post office operated until November 1910, when Richards was no longer the postmaster. (Henry H. Gregory Jr.)

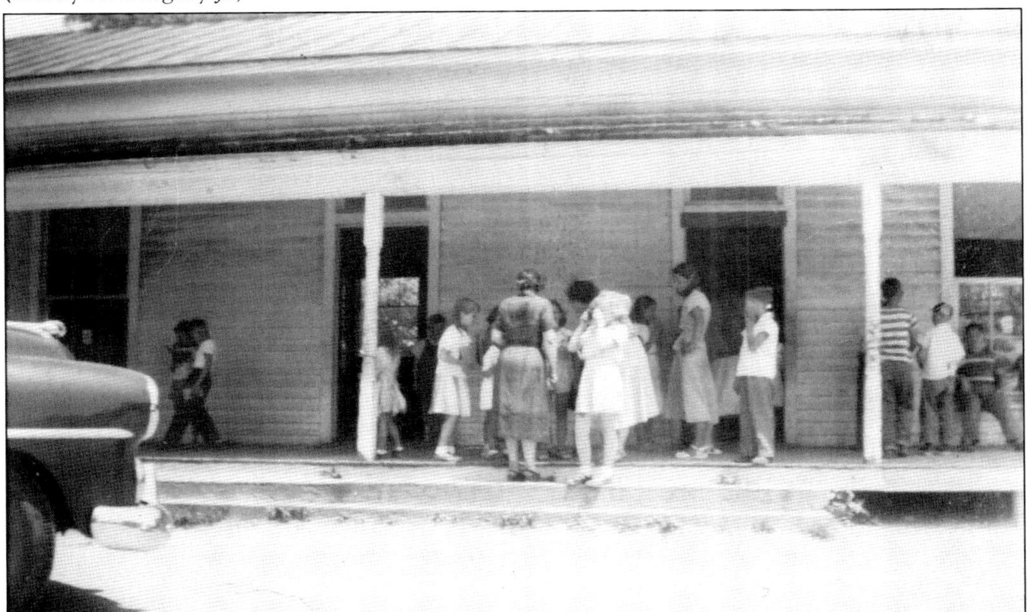

In protest of the bridge tolls into Clarksville, a group of residents from the Jeffress Junction and Doggett's Mill areas established a two-room school called Mooresville near the bend in the Clarksville–to–Chase City Road, across from the Gooch property. This is a photograph taken in 1953 of the last class in attendance. The teachers were Jeanie Hinson (left) and Alma Bullock (right). (Joyce Pharr.)

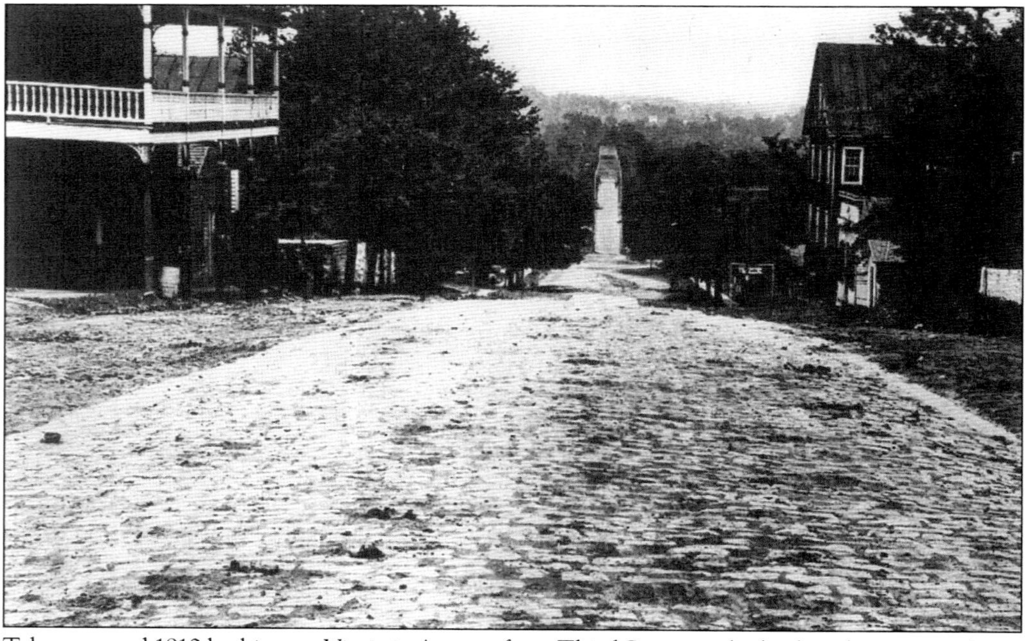

Taken around 1910 looking up Virginia Avenue from Third Street to the bridge, this picture shows the cobblestones on the hill. On the left is N. M. Harris "Outfitters to men and boys" store, with the Home Telephone and Telegraph Company upstairs. Behind and to the side of the store is the tin roof of the Gooch tavern and home, and the small white building is the old lock-up next to a town well and firehouse. (Jack Hite.)

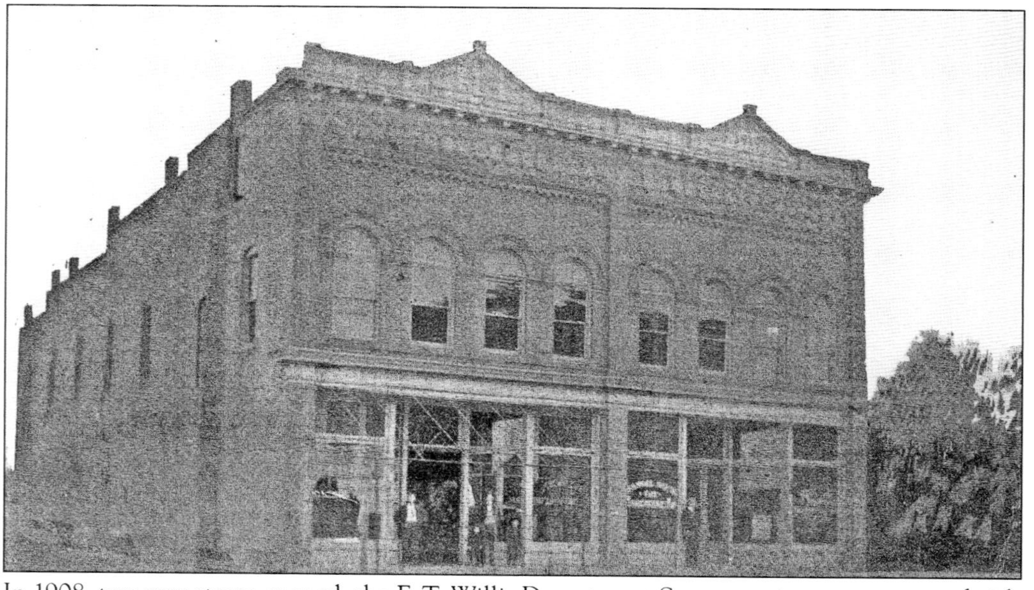

In 1908, two new stores opened: the F. T. Willis Department Store catering to women and girls and the new James S. Haskins Jr. Hardware store, run by Sam Davis. In this photograph are, from left to right, Finis Tyler Willis, his partner and son, Ralph Willis, and Sam Davis, who bought out Haskins in 1915 and built a larger store three doors down the street, which he opened in 1930. (Richard Burnett.)

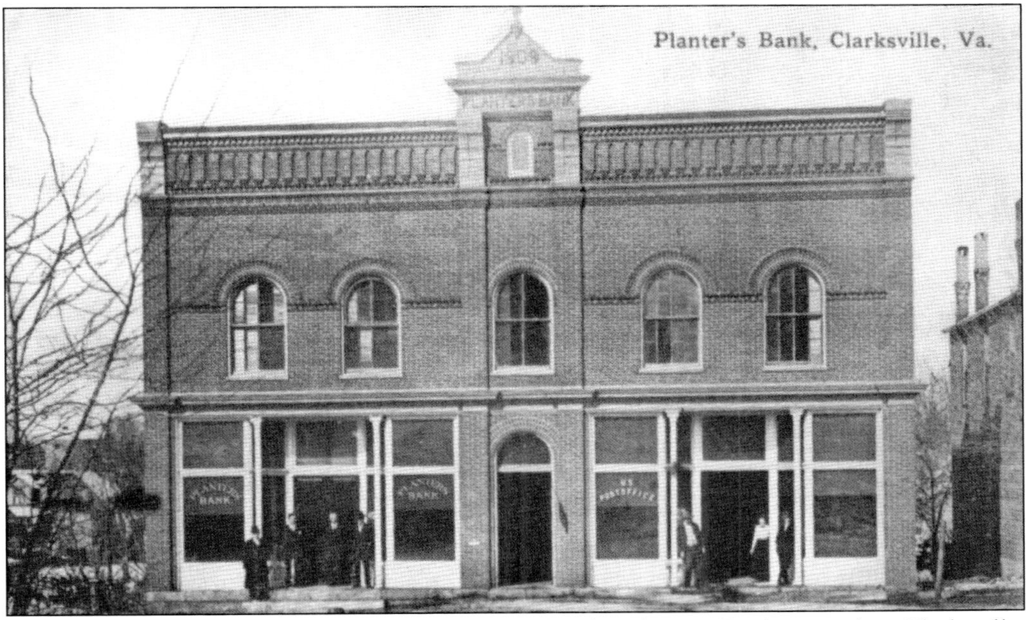

Begun in 1892 with its first president, W. D. Blanks, the Planters Bank opened in Clarksville. In 1898, it was a partner in the Mecklenburg Mineral Springs Corporation of Chase City. In this early photograph are, from left to right, Charles L. Doggett, Cabel Woods, Ben Blanks, and ? Blairs. The bank did not survive the Depression and closed in 1931. In front of the post office are ? Bell and an unidentified man. (Rebecca Cary.)

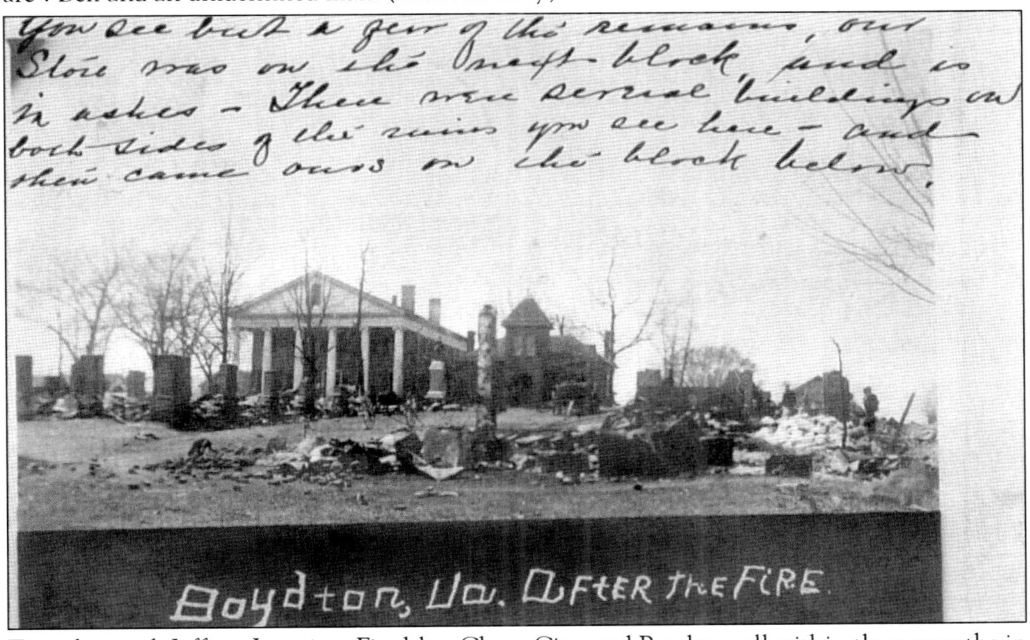

Tragedy struck Jeffress Junction, Finchley, Chase City, and Boydton, all within three months in 1909—fires. This postcard is signed M. O. Snelling, and "our store" was A. P. Snelling Drug Store at Washington and Jefferson Streets. Note the soldier standing guard on top of the monument amid the debris. (WCG.)

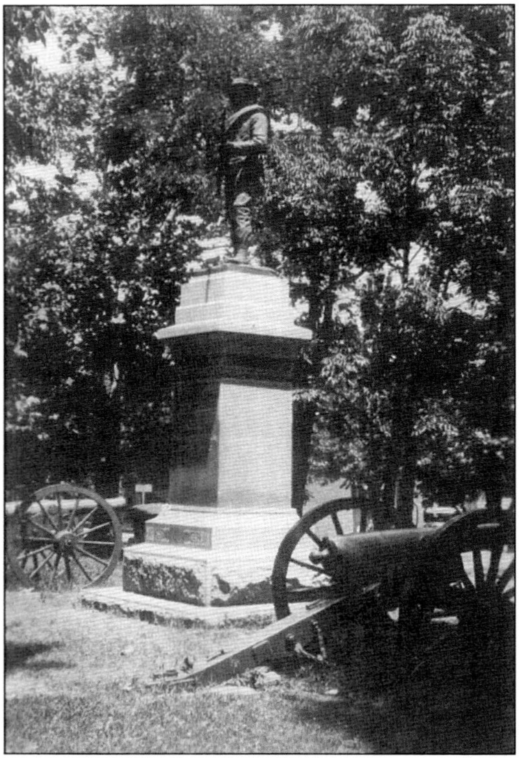

In August 1908, the L. A. Armistead Camp, Confederate Veterans, dedicated the statue of the Confederate soldier positioned on top of the monument. The soldier is 7 feet tall, weighs 1,600 pounds, and cost $1,000 to have made, delivered, and set in place. The soldier was positioned so he was facing the courthouse, indicating his loyalty to the county. (WCG.)

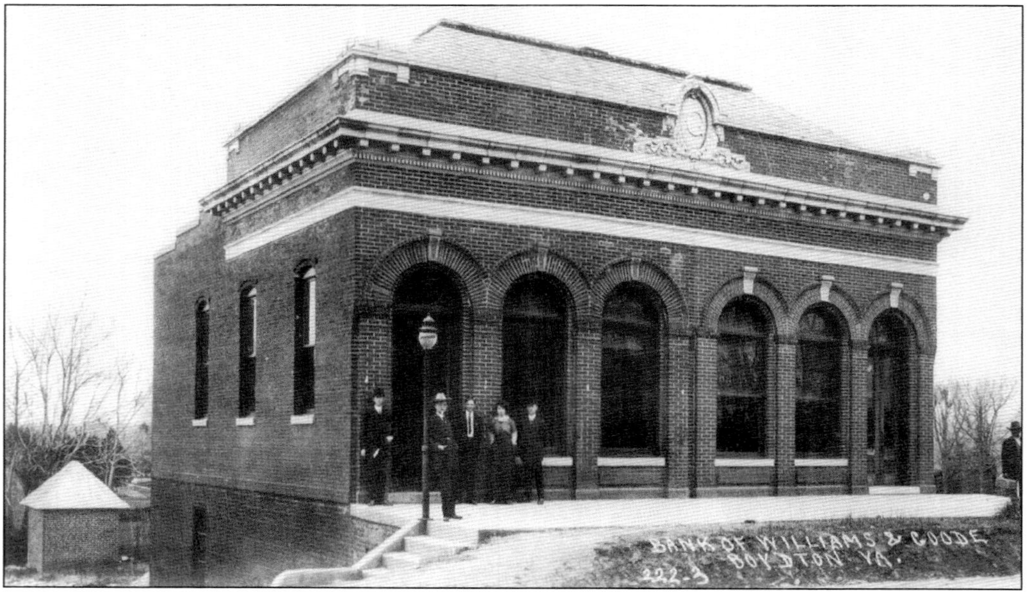

Completed in 1908, the Bank of Williams and Goode was built on the site of the former Exchange Hotel, which had burned in 1899. Since it was a brick structure, it was not harmed in the fire of 1909. Standing in the photograph are, from left to right, Carter N. Williams, Thomas F. Goode, and three unidentified bank employees. The building is clearly of very different architecture than any other building in town. (HBR.)

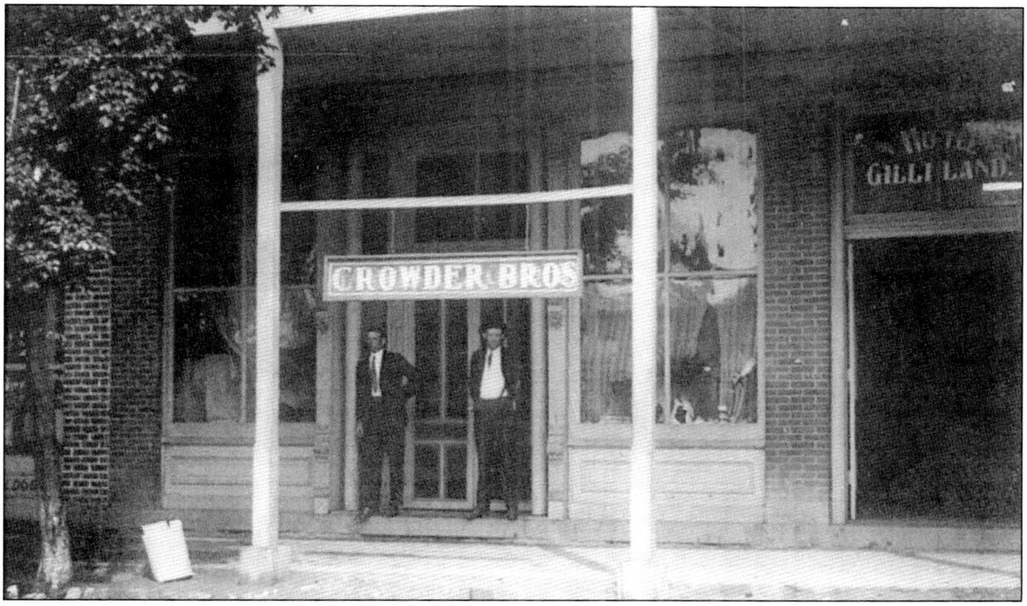

Bouldin Crowder married in 1905 while operating the Abbeyville general store and post office. His new bride didn't like the country, so he sold out, moved to Clarksville, and purchased half ownership of H. M. Harris dry goods store in the Gilliland Hotel. In 1917, a Mr. Wilkerson from the Fields community negotiated building a store for brothers Bouldin and J. Nelson Crowder next door to Davis Hardware directly across the street. In 1918, the brothers moved into their new building and began selling ladies' fashions. (BH.)

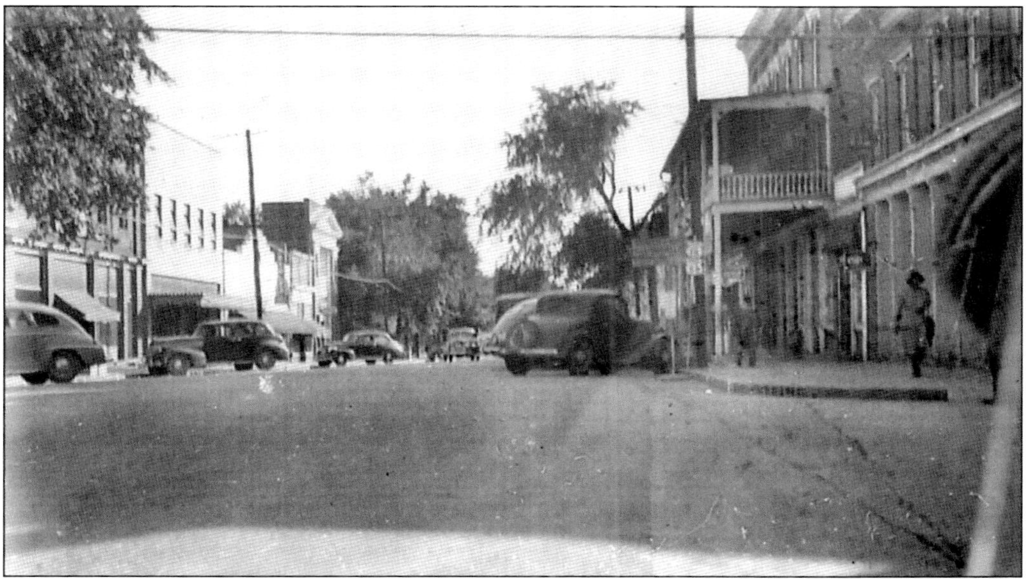

In 1919, Joe Howerton Sr. and Eugene Howerton moved to Clarksville from Halifax County, built a store next door to Crowder's, and opened a general mercantile business. In this 1935 photograph, the first store to the left is Crowder's, the store with the awning is Howerton's, next is Howerton meat market, and the building with a long awning over the sidewalk is the new Davis Hardware. The Gilliland Hotel is on the right. (Rebecca Cary.)

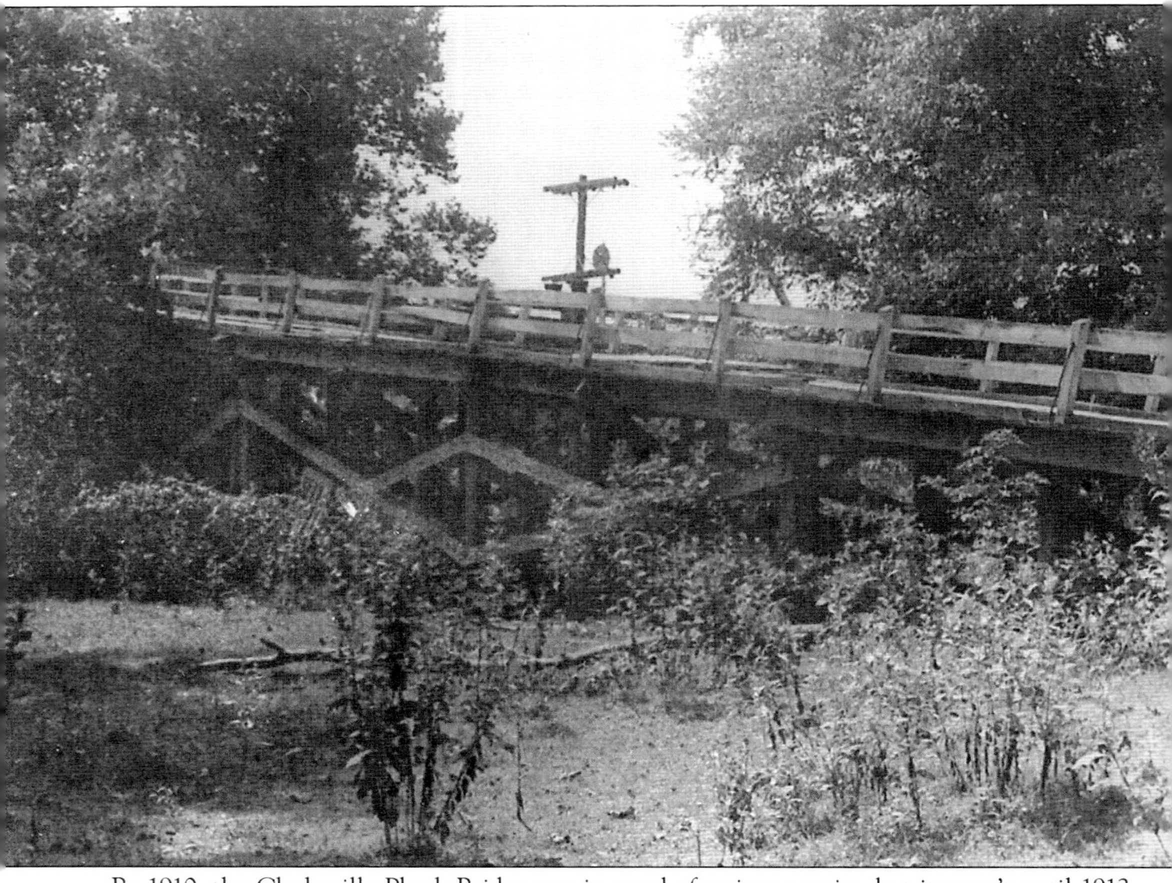

By 1910, the Clarksville Plank Bridge was in need of serious repairs, but it wasn't until 1912 that it was painted and 1914 that the floor boards were replaced. In 1916, F. J. Liipfort built an entrance ramp from his farm on Occoneechee to connect to the crossing bridge. Liipfort had remodeled the old Tolifaro home on the island and was operating a sawmill and hog farm. When the Smithsonian excavated in 1947, they found 34 village sites on the farm and on the south shore of the Dan River, 17 campsites, 41 flint workshops, and 2 Colonial-period sites. They uncovered 43 skeletons. (COE.)

The Wimbish family was large and located all over southern Mecklenburg and Granville Counties dating to the early 1800s. Lewis Wimbish was one of the cadets of Virginia Military Institute at New Market and later served as county treasurer. In this picture is Dr. William T. Wimbish, who set up his medical practice in Clarksville in 1910. (WCG.)

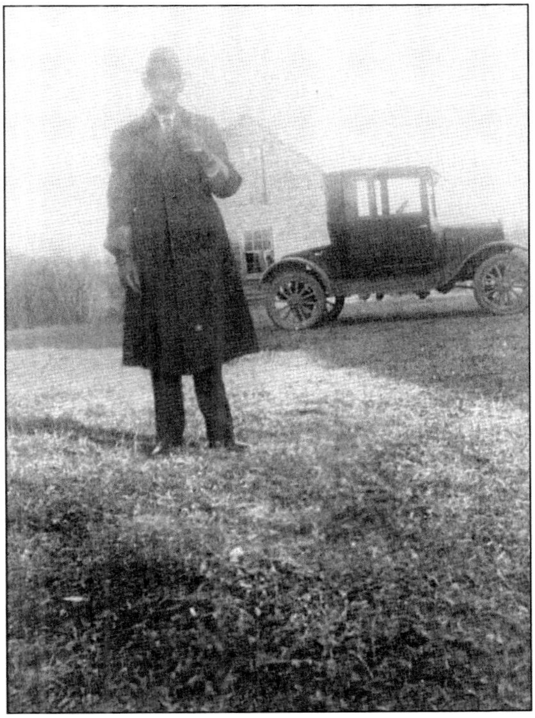

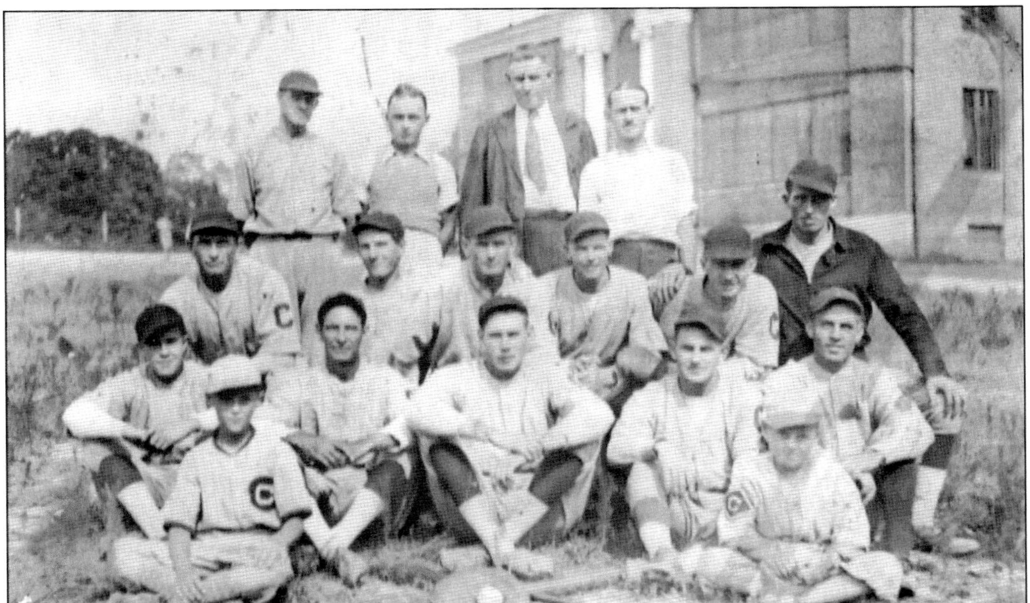

In the 1920s, Clarksville's B League baseball team posed in front of Clarksville High School. From left to right are (first row) Sam Davis, Will Collier, Joe Burnette, ? Elliott, James P. Taylor, Will Eubanks, and Walter Howerton; (second row) ? Walker, Eugene Eubanks, ? Walker, ? Wilburn, Ed Howerton, and Charles "Coon" Nunn; (back row) Dr. Lawrence Hoover (manager), Otto Sizemore, Ed Homer, and Luther Morgan. (Jeanne P. Morgan.)

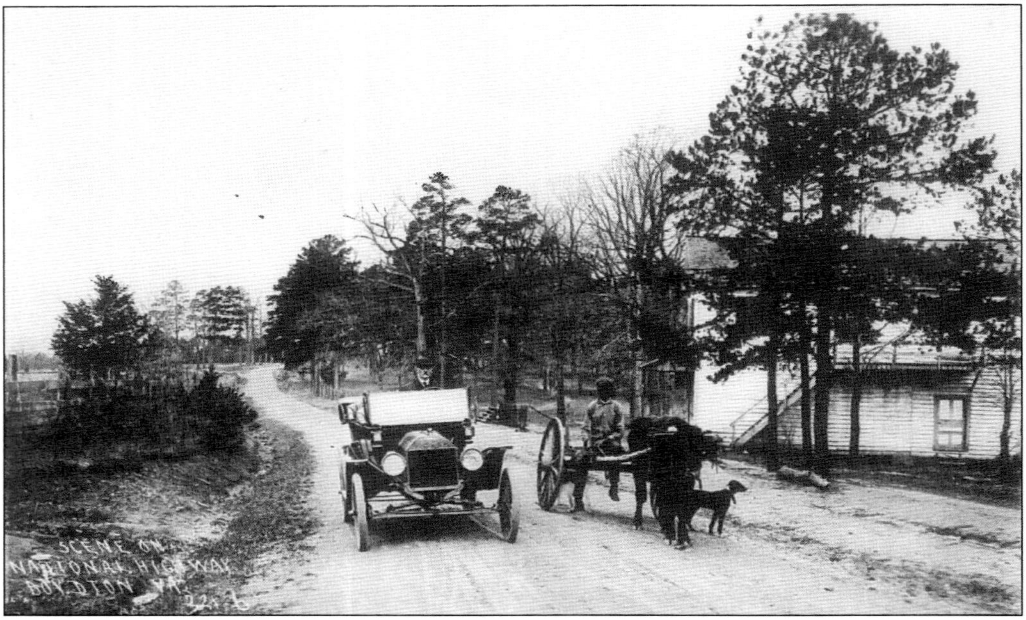

The Petersburg-to-Boydton Plank Road was the road of many names. Originally the Richmond to Catawba trading route, around 1800, it was Old Cox Road from North Carolina to Petersburg, then the Plank Toll Road, and after the Civil War, it was called Dixie Highway. (WCG.)

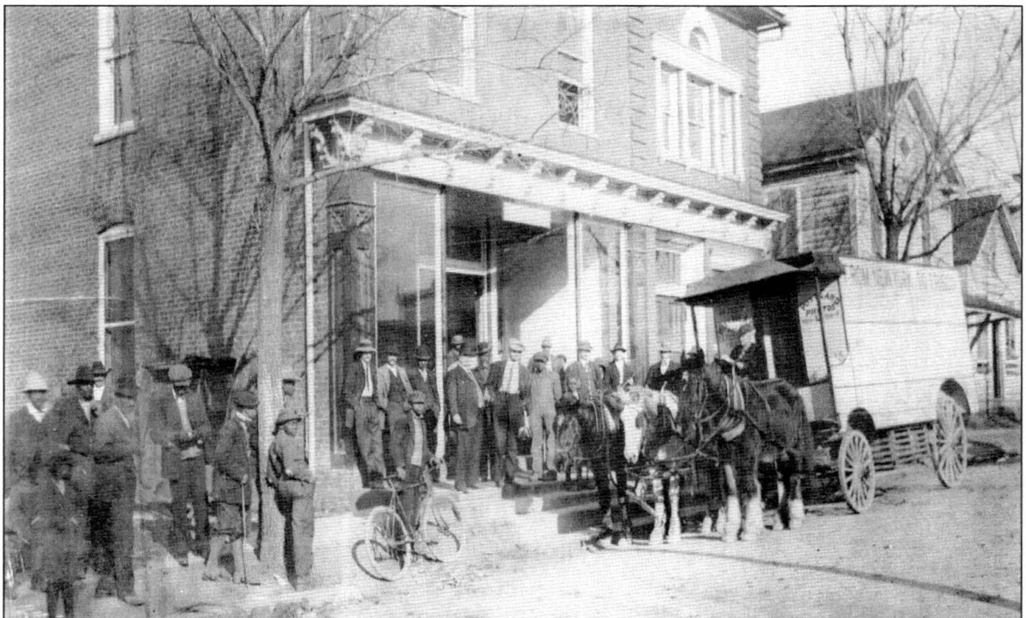

In 1905, a new town hall was completed in Boydton, with a second-floor auditorium/theater and a steeple atop the town hall section roof. The left side became the post office for many years. To the right is the Boydton Dispensary (a liquor store whose proceeds were used for new sidewalks), and to the left is a small tavern. This postcard is from 1913, when a postcard dealer/photographer came to town to earn traveling money. (HBR.)

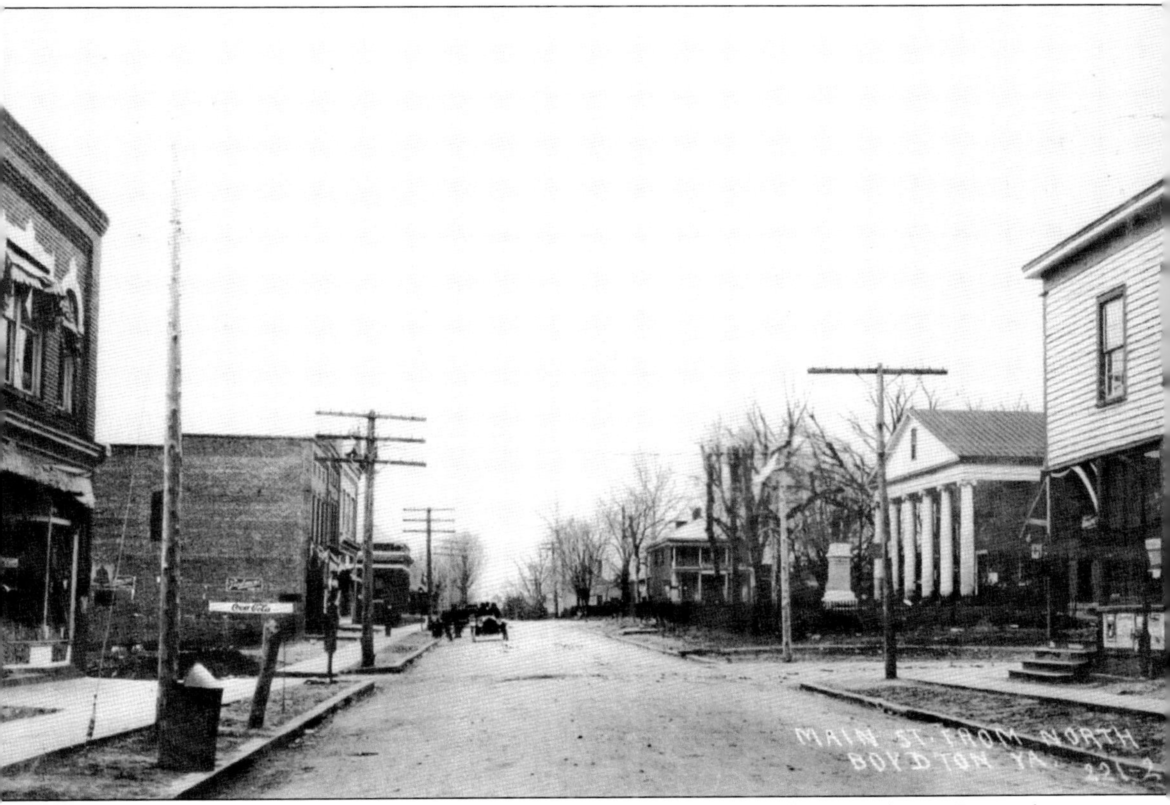

Looking down Washington Street, to the immediate right is Ora Waller's Hardware Store, the courthouse, Bruce and Sydnor Mercantile store, and the Washington Tavern in the distance. To the immediate left is the new Snelling's Drug Store at the corner of Madison Street. Across Madison is H. L. Turpin's grocery store, Mr. Pleasant's shoe and fabric store, and Abe Fine's Department Store. (HBR.)

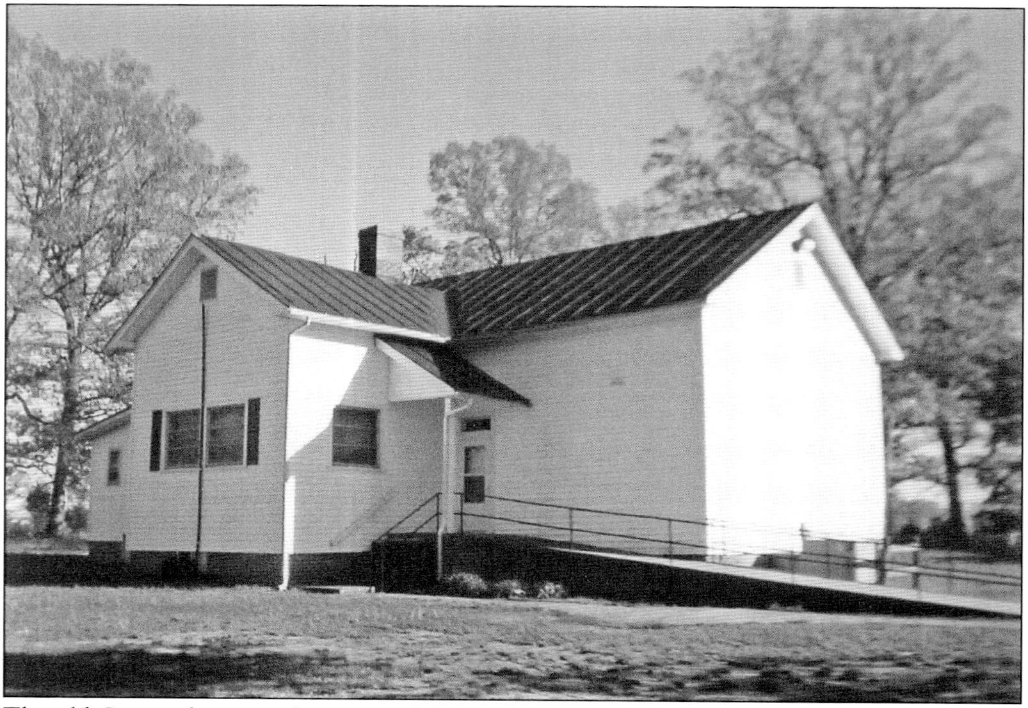

The old Concord meetinghouse, an African American church built after 1874, found a new purpose in 1899 as a public school for black children. It served as a community two-room school until the 1940s, when buses finally became available. The old meetinghouse still serves as an activities center for the African American Concord Baptist Church. (Lucille T. Hudson and W. P. Hudgins Sr.)

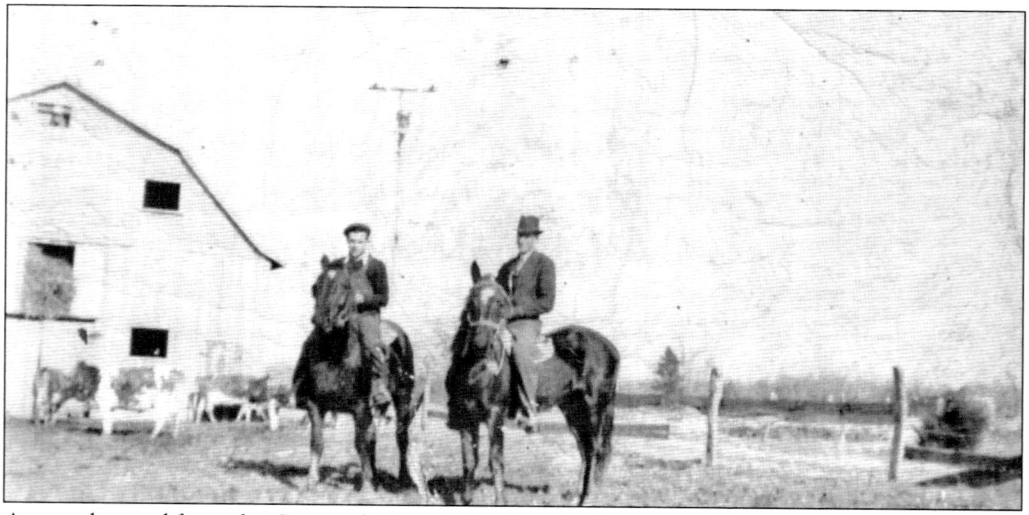

Across the road from the Concord Church developed a dairy owned by George W. and Etta Blue Kizer named the New Life Dairy, milking between 40 and 50 cows per day. In front of the barn are two of their sons, Walter (left) and John Kizer. Soon after this picture was taken, John went to college and became a minister, returned to Chase City, and taught returning veterans farming in the agriculture department of Chase City High School. (Thomas Carol Kizer.)

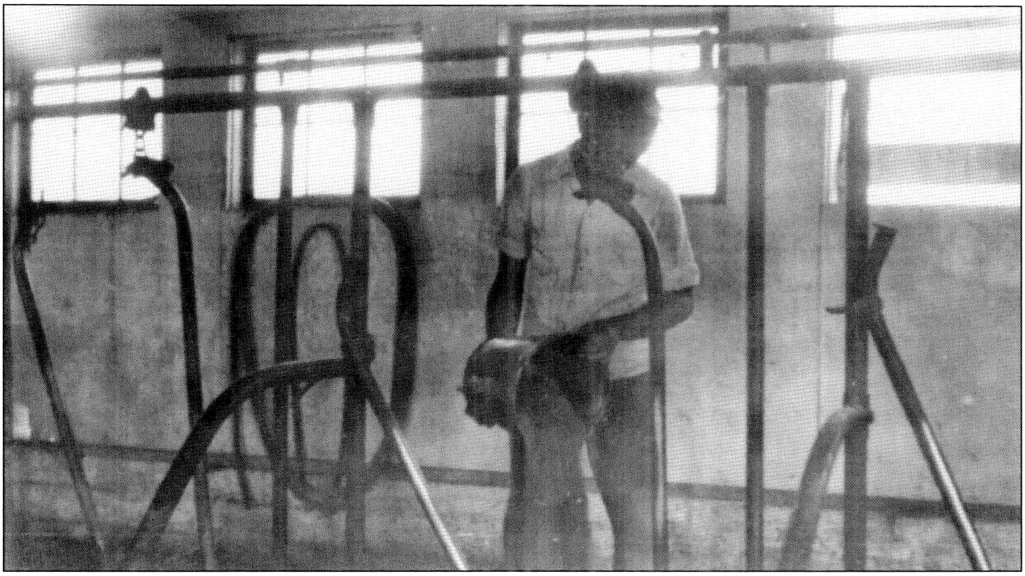

Inside the dairy were the milking stalls, and in this picture, another son, Thomas Carol Kizer, fills the feed trough. Thomas and his brothers Walter, William, and John were responsible for the milking. In the 1920s, a bottling operation was begun, and in 1928, a new delivery truck was purchased. Milk was delivered to most of the grocery stores in Chase City and the surrounding country stores, including Easters and Draperville. (Thomas Carol Kizer.)

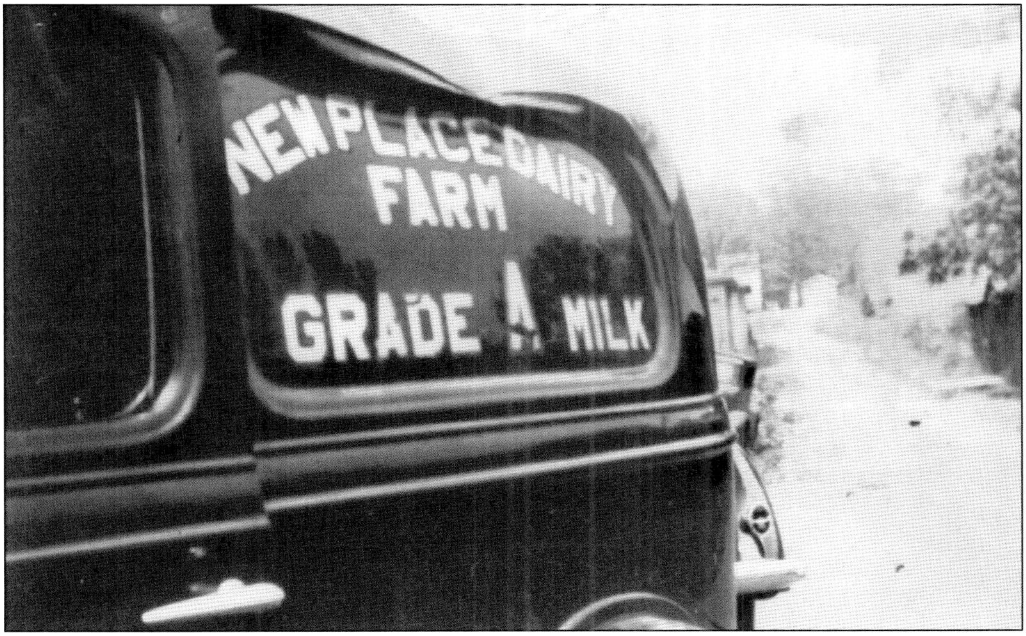

Surviving the Depression, the New Life Dairy was faced with a new obstacle—new federal regulatory control of the milk industry in 1936. With these new regulations, by 1939, all of the small dairies in the county were closed and out of business, ending another era in history. In this photograph, Walter was making a delivery when his truck ran off the road and overturned. (Thomas Carol Kizer.)

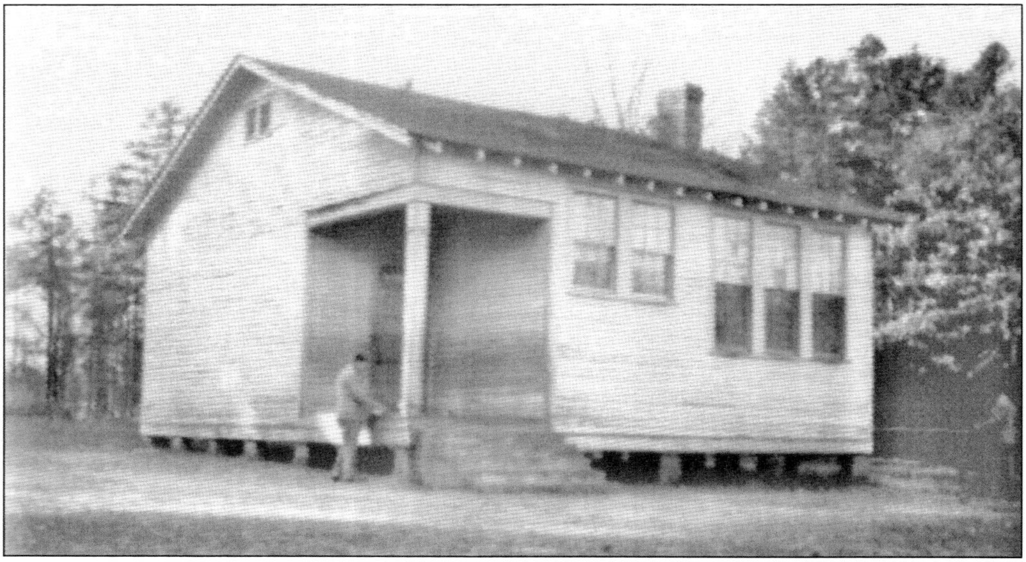

Located on the Chase City–to–Boydton Road, about halfway between the two towns, is the Crutchfield farm. In 1899, they donated land and a building for a community African American public school. The first teacher was William Smalley. One of its most distinguished graduates was Barbara Crutchfield George, who went on to Bennett College in Greensboro, North Carolina, then to the University of Iowa Law School. She first taught law at the University of Hawaii and then taught and established a distinguished career at California State University–Long Beach. (Lucille T. Hudson and W. P. Hudgins Sr.)

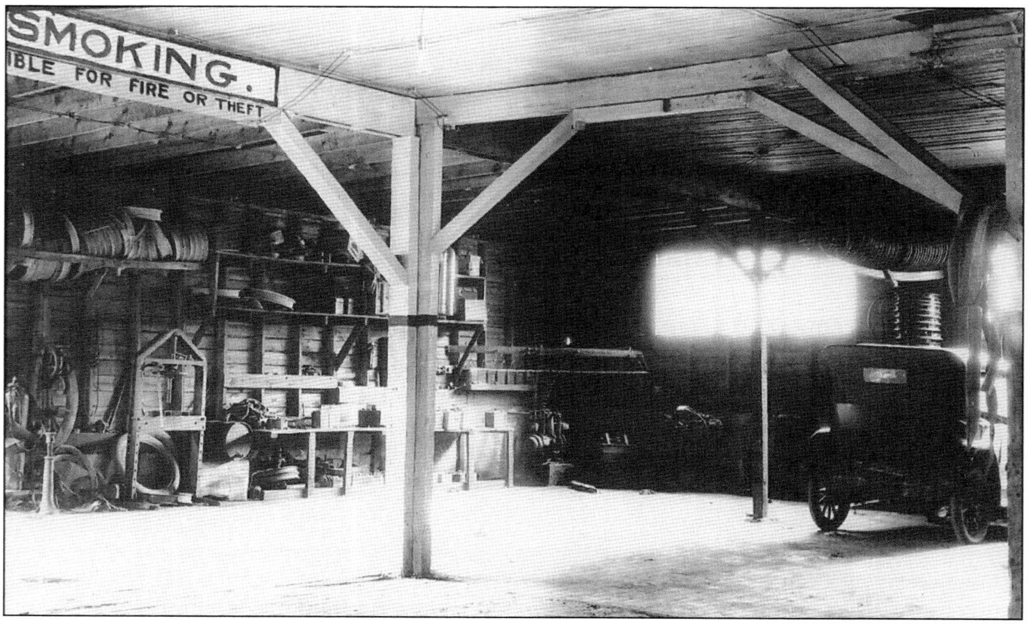

Carl Nicholson converted his blacksmith shop to a garage on June 1, 1914. In 1918, it was purchased by R. H. Park Sr., with an in-ground gas tank added in 1919. In January 1920, an addition was made to the building and he began operating the garage with a car for hire and auto livery service. (R. H. Park III.)

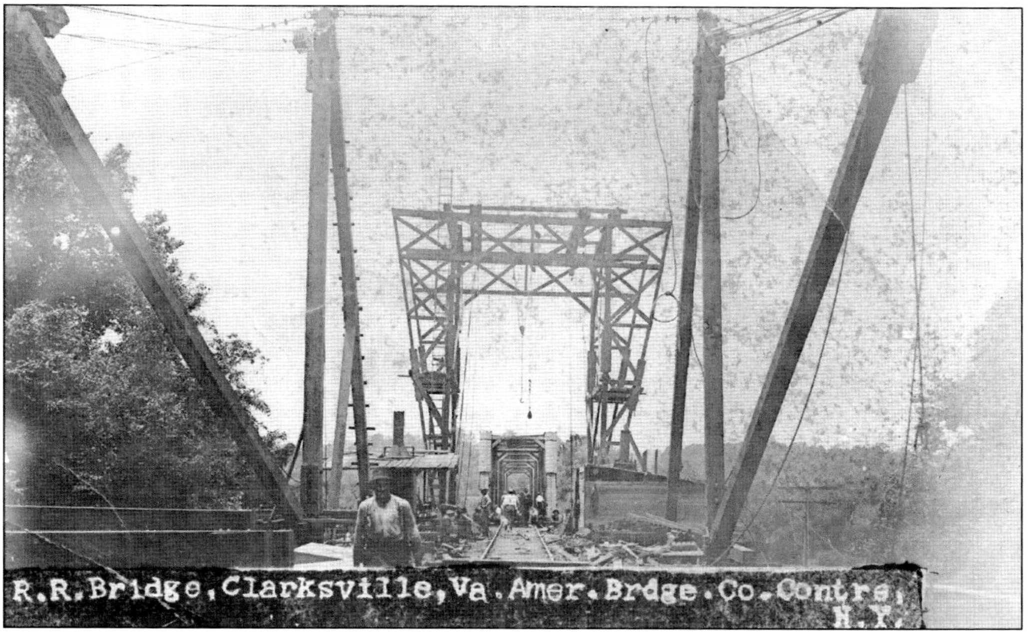

On August 1, 1912, the morning train from Richmond and the freight train from Danville collided on the trestle over Island Creek between Jeffress Junction and Clarksville in the low grounds near the river. It is said the sound could be heard 4 miles away in Finchley. Ten passengers were injured, and both engines and several cars were destroyed; no charges were brought in the accident, but for years after, there was a feud between the two station managers. This postcard is of the crew rebuilding the track in 1912. (Kathryne B. Routt.)

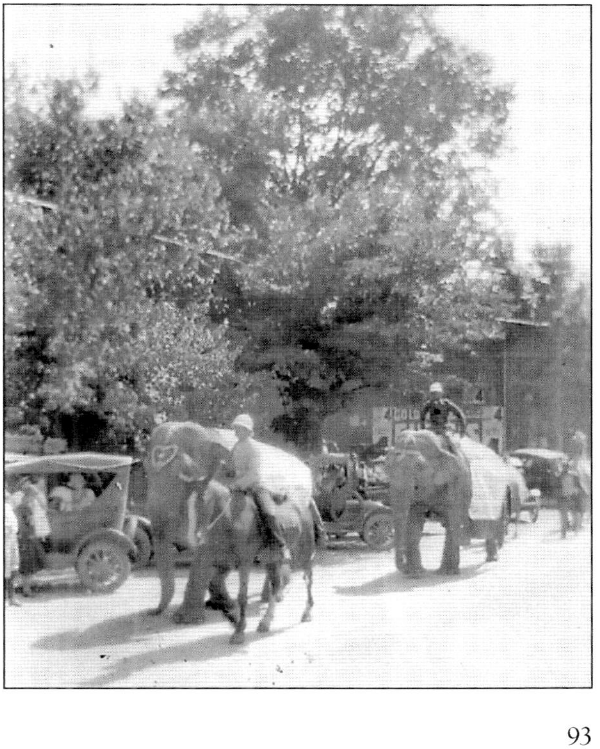

By 1920, a circus was common two to three times per year in Chase City, Boydton, and Clarksville. Even the schools would close for a day to attend the circus. Along with the circus were the vaudeville companies of entertainers that would fill the theaters for two or three shows daily. The circuses continued in the area until the 1950s. Of course, today most of what the traveling circuses represented is socially/politically incorrect. (Jeanne P. Morgan.)

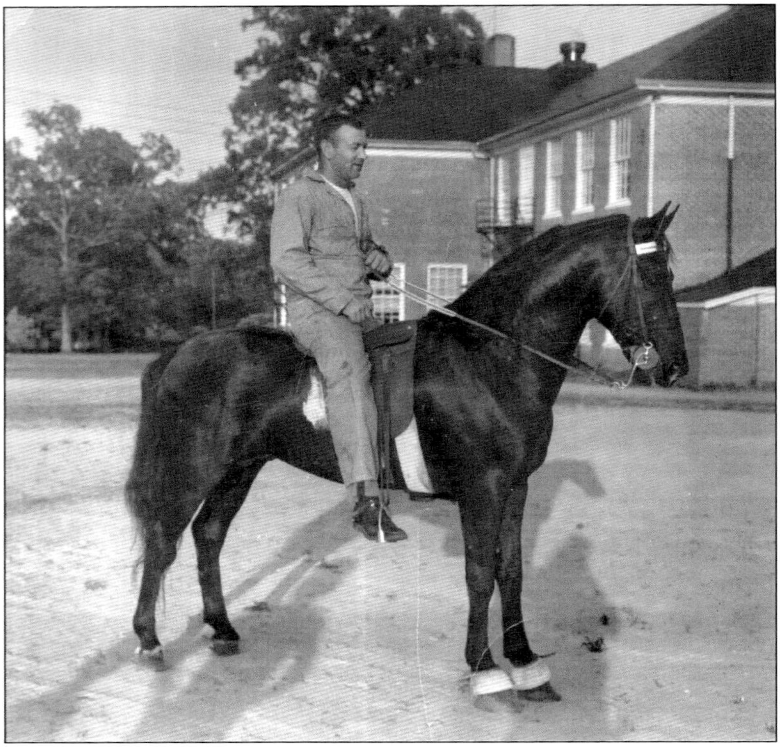

In this photograph is county deputy sheriff Haskins Cox displaying one of the first Tennessee Walking horses in the county, Glory's Co-Pilot, in front of the Boydton School in 1913. Cox spent many years training classic show and "trick" show horses and always attended the Boydton festivities. (Memory of Haskins Cox.)

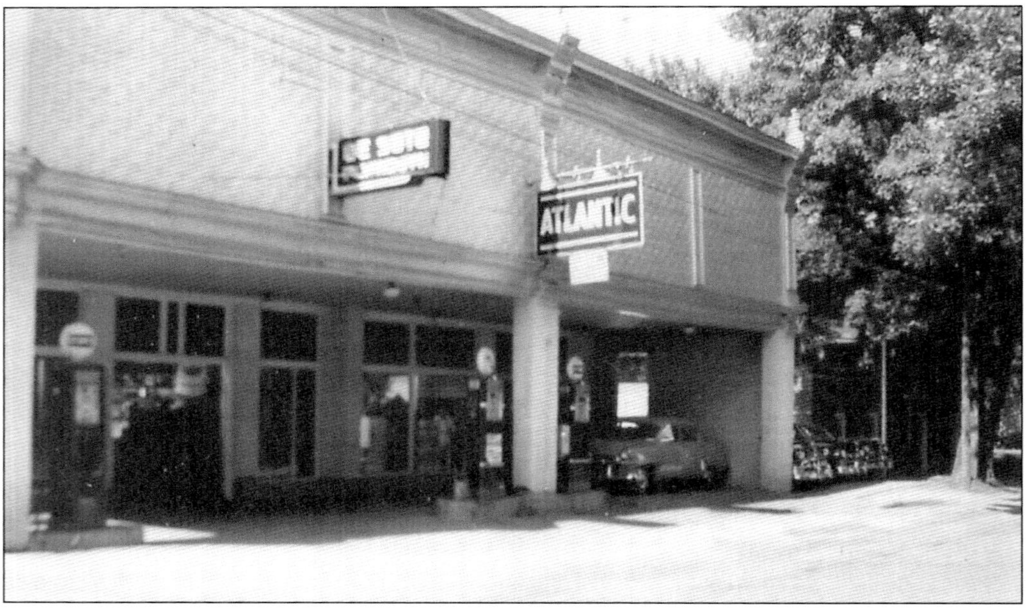

Marvin Beales, Frank C. Bedinger Sr., and Thomas W. Gregory Sr. began a Studebaker dealership in 1918, which included a full-service drive-up gas pump. The dealership was in front of the George E. Brown Wagon Manufacturing Company, which had been enlarged and remodeled in 1887. The motor company was enlarged in 1924, changed its name to Mecklenburg Motor Company, Inc., and began to sell Desoto and Plymouth products. (Henry H. Gregory Jr.)

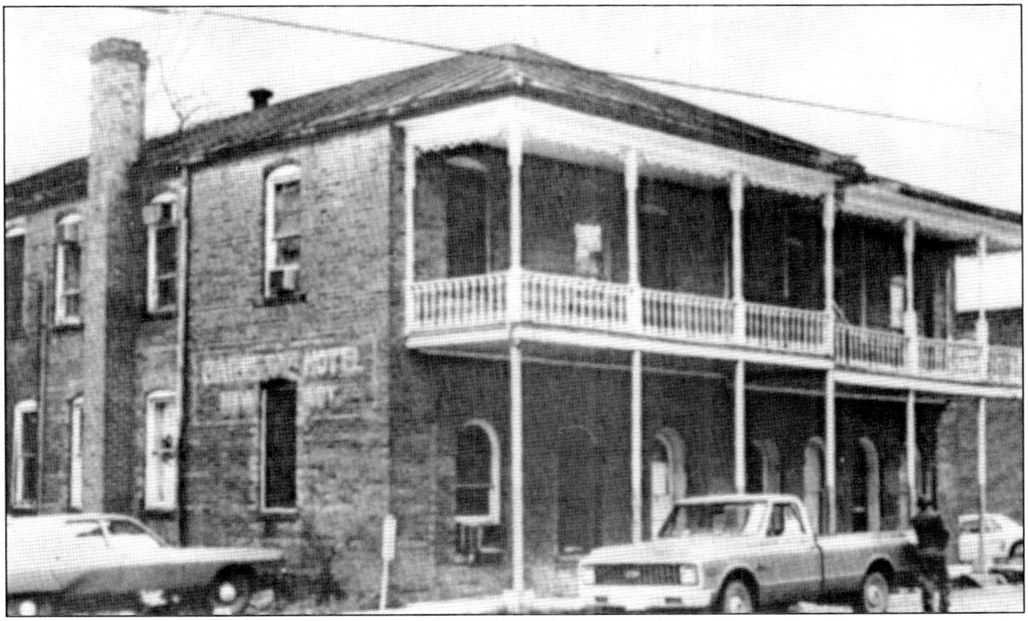

Sydney O. Barnett of Finchley purchased the Boydton Hotel in 1914 and sold it three months later, then purchased it again in 1917, the same year he was elected to town council. In 1918, he and his son opened a gas station, store, and garage, and he died in November 1918. His son, S. O. Barnett Jr., built the new Barnett Hotel directly across the street in 1922 and on July 20, 1922, sold the Boydton Hotel. (REC.)

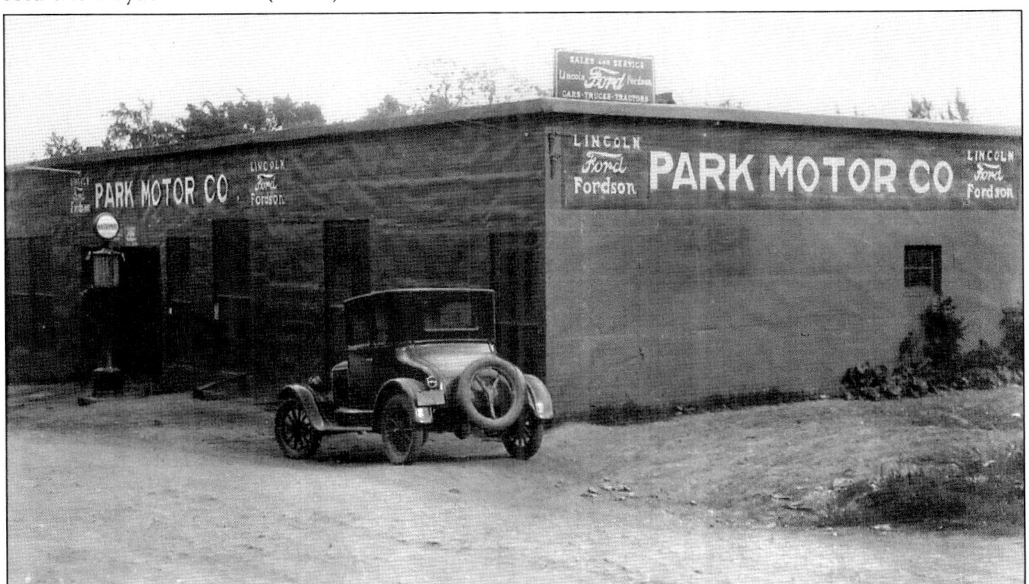

In 1924, Park Motor Company converted the old service center to a new car and tractor sales and service department for Ford Motor Company products. It remained in this location until a new building could be constructed. In 1928, it moved into the new building; it leased this building to Chase City Motor Company in 1935. Chase City Motors used the building for a filling station, service center, and used car lot, which closed with World War II in 1942. (R. H. Park III.)

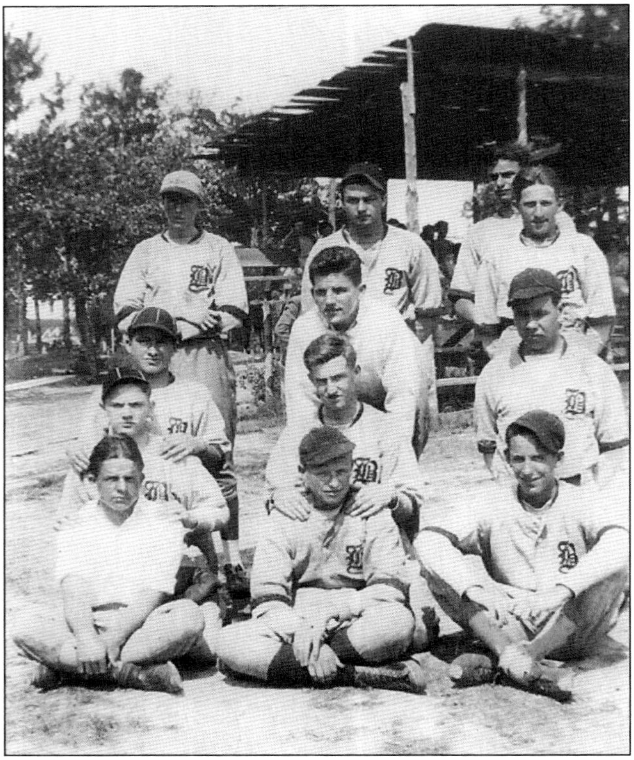

In the 1920s, "B" baseball became the all-American amateur sport, with leagues across the country. This 1935 photograph of the Boydton team players is, from left to right, (first row) Walter Wright Jr., Herbert Moss, and Dick Hendrick; (second row) Courtney Sheffield, Douglas Bishop, and Landon "Bumps" Crowder; (third row) Raymond Thompson and Chuck Snellings; (fourth row) Giles Propst, Thorpe Jones, John Propst, and Charles Gill. (Walter R. Beales III.)

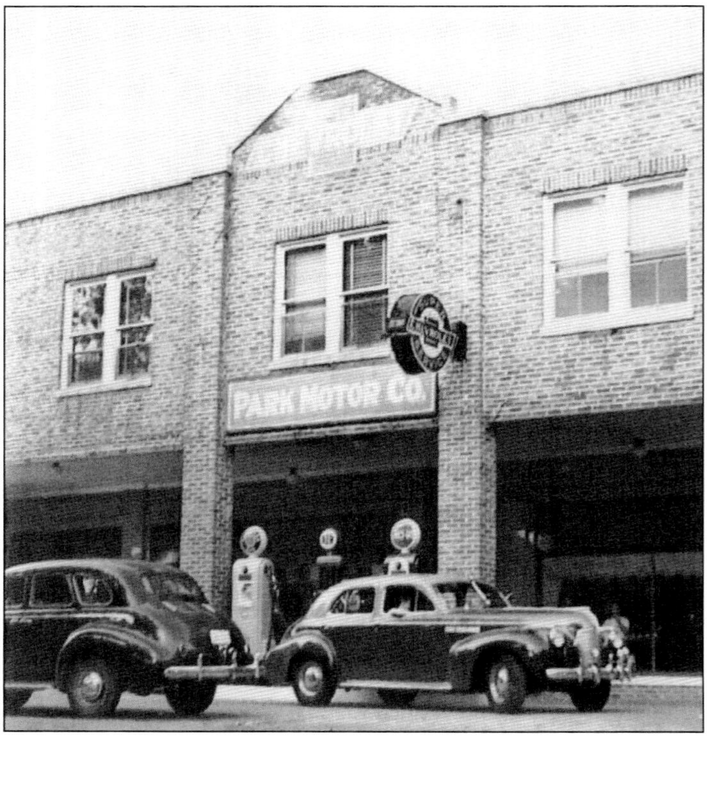

The new Park Motor Company located on Madison Street had a drive-through, covered, full-service filling station. After the Depression, R. H. Park Jr. became involved in the business, and they switched to Chevrolet automobiles and Allis Chalmers tractors, with parts and service for both. Later, in 1968, R. H. Park Jr. moved to the new U.S. Highway 58, sold Massey-Ferguson tractors, lawn mowers, and lawn tractors, and opened a garage. R. H. Park III joined the business; later the Highway 58 dealership was discontinued, but the garage continued. In 1996, the business was sold. (R. H. Park III.)

Walter R. Beales Sr.'s family brought him to Mecklenburg County from Loudoun County in the 1880s by train. In 1904, he was elected county sheriff and is the longest serving sheriff in the county, truly respected and held in high regard by county citizens. Wherever Sheriff Beales went to serve warrants, make arrests, or chase suspects, he would deputize a local law officer or upstanding citizen to assist him. (Walter R. Beales III.)

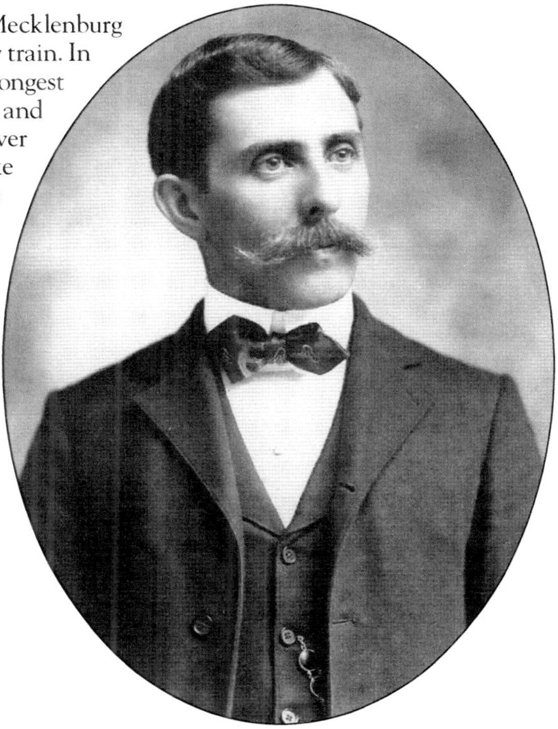

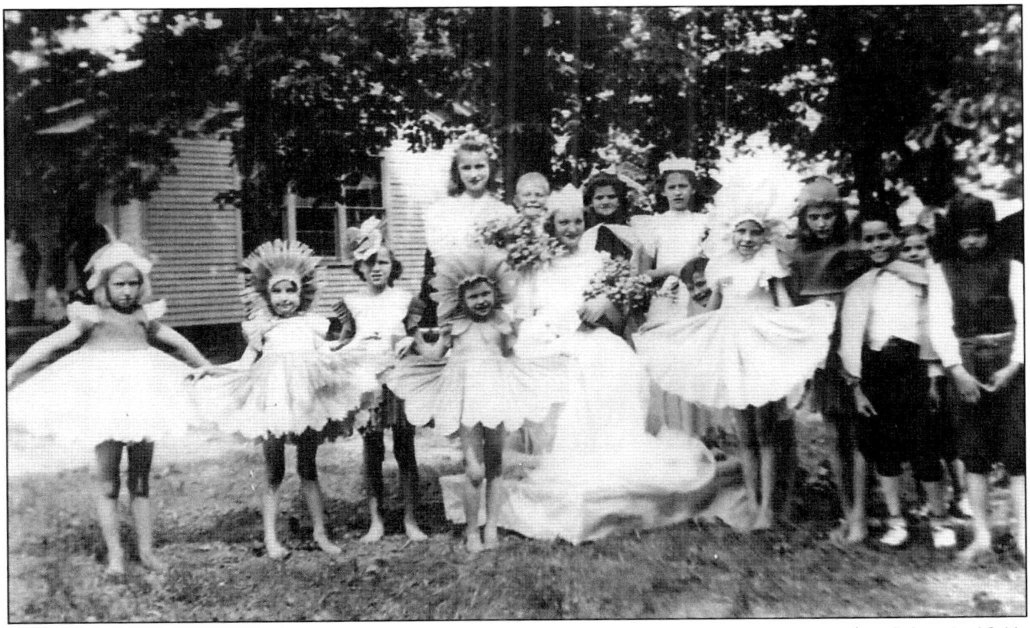

Around 1900, Liberty School, a public two-room schoolhouse, was begun. In this May 1, 1941, photograph, the students are celebrating "Child Health Day—May Day" with health queen Mary Emma Puryear (seated), princess Barbara Carter (behind Puryear to the right), and "May Day" Kathleen Carter (back left). Other students were "Brown Bear"—J. B. Claiborne, "bumblebee"—Robert ?, and "1st of May"—Virginia Elliott (to the right of the queen). (Barbara Carter Royal.)

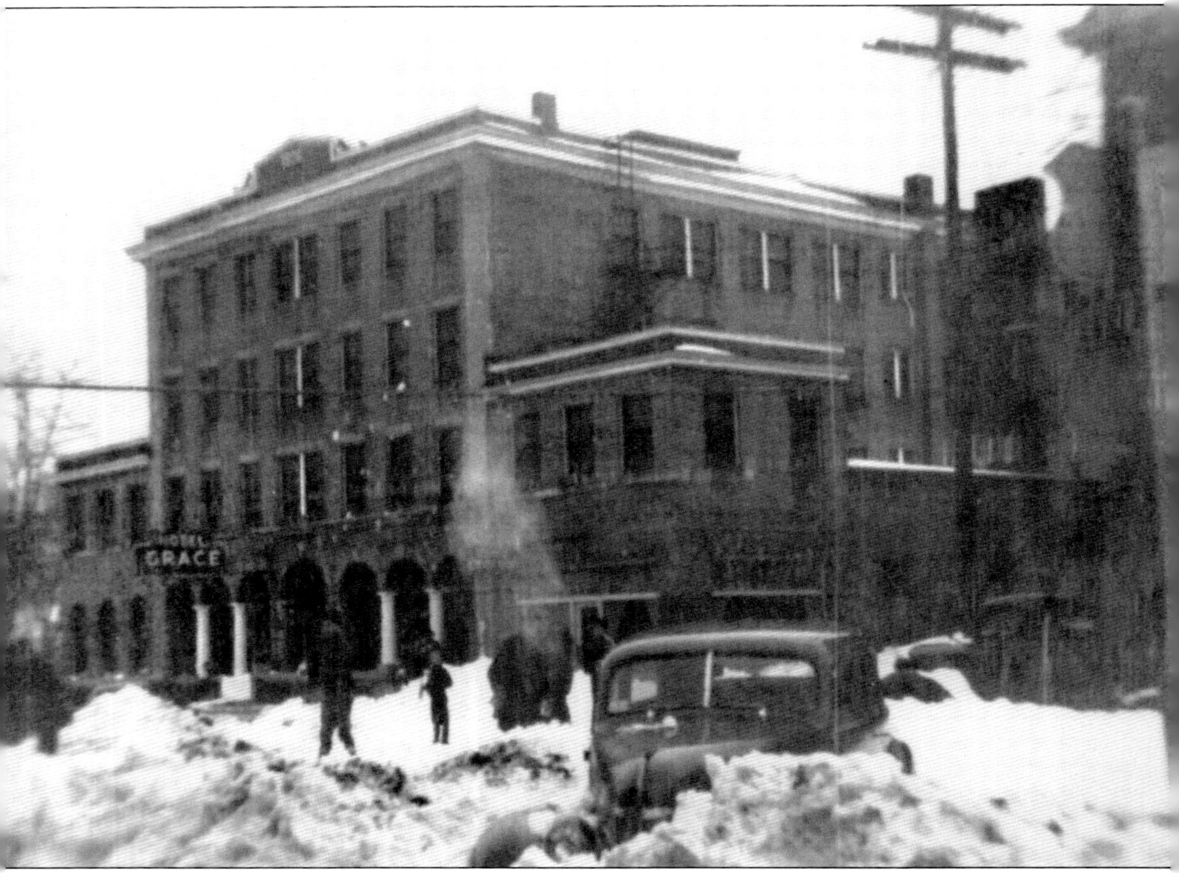

The Grace Hotel caught fire in the late fall of 1925. Remodeled, updated, and expanded to a new, bigger, and better facility, it scheduled its grand reopening with a New Year's Eve ball in 1926. This photograph was taken during the big snowstorm of 1940, the year of the great flood. (CRM.)

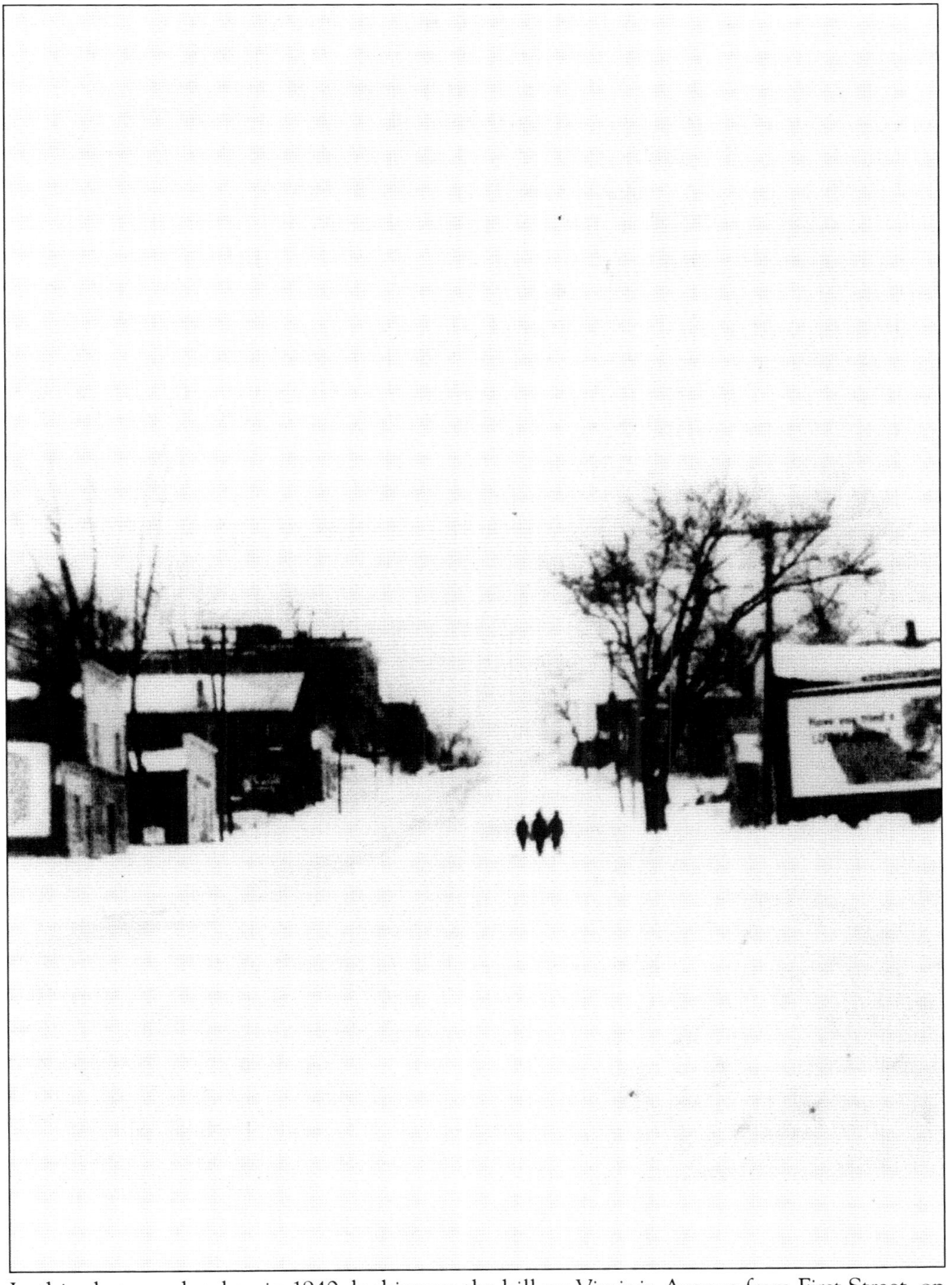

In this photograph taken in 1940, looking up the hill on Virginia Avenue from First Street, on the right side is Aaron Carter's service station. On the left are the Place, a café owned by Charlie Harris; Edward Ross's blacksmith shop; the J. P. Taylor warehouse; Reid's Barbershop; and Dew Drop Inn and dance hall, owned by Marion Lewis. (CRM.)

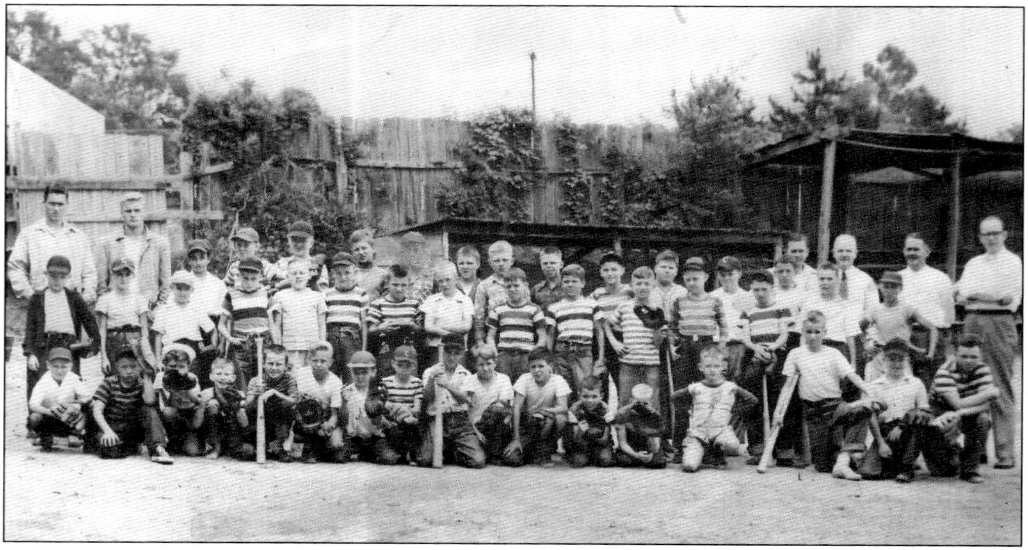

To meet the needs of B League baseball, the town donated land in 1927 to build a community park along Blue Creek. The embankment of the creek served as a grandstand, and the park became popular not only for amateur baseball but for the high school games and rallies, Little League, and for the town in general. This photograph taken of a Little League team in 1951 shows the last year it was used. Forty of the 48 persons shown are identified, but space does not permit the listing of their names. (Jack Hite.)

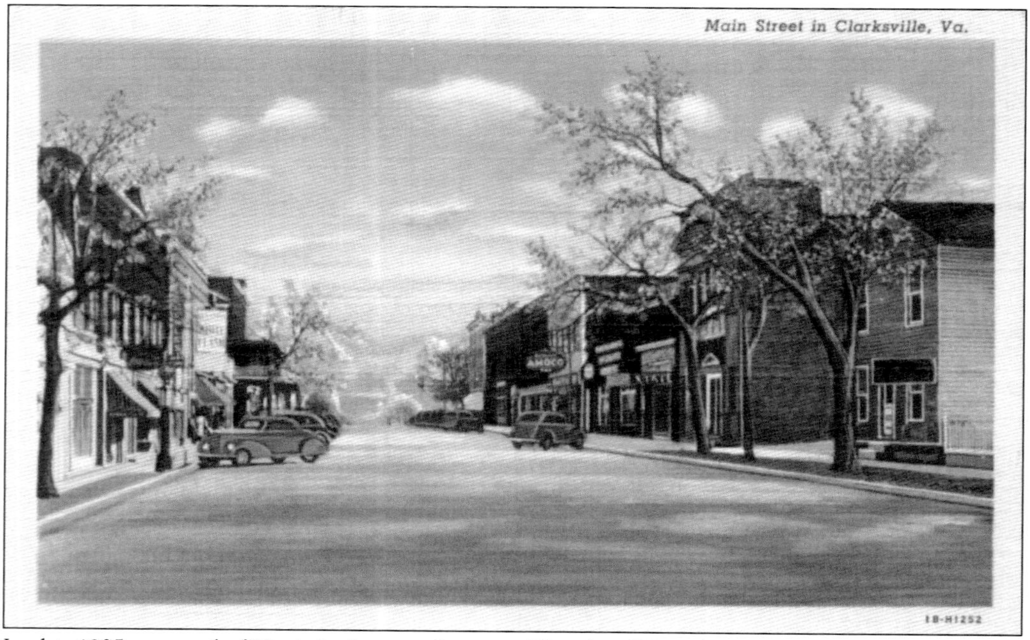

In this 1935 postcard of Virginia Avenue, between Third and Fourth Streets, on the right, nearest, is a grocery store, "the horseshoe lot," Citizens Bank and Trust, the State theater, Carrington's garage and Amoco station, and Davis Hardware (the white-fronted building). On the left, the small white frame building was a furniture store; also shown are the Rennie Department Store, Planters Bank building, and the Gilliland Hotel. (CRM.)

Pictured in 1940, the State theater is now Clements Drug Store with a café inside; note the penny weighing scale on the sidewalk. Carrington's garage is being renovated for the new Peeble's Department Store. (Jeanne P. Morgan.)

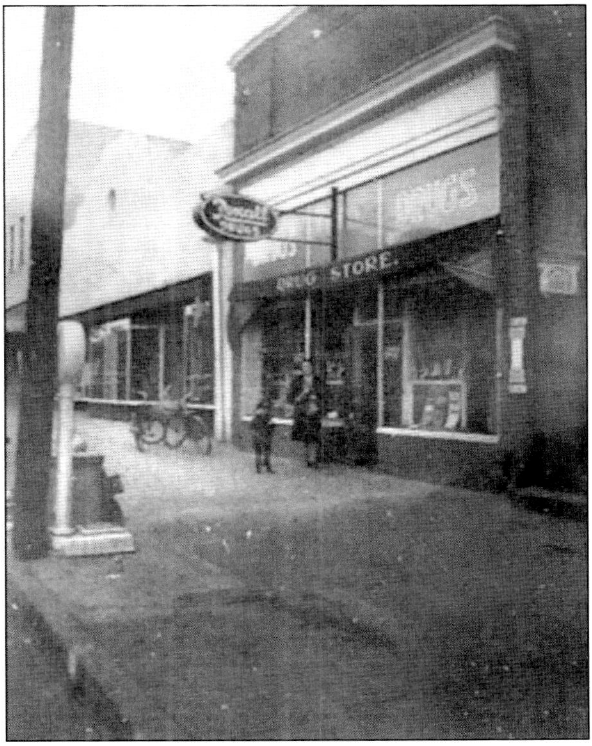

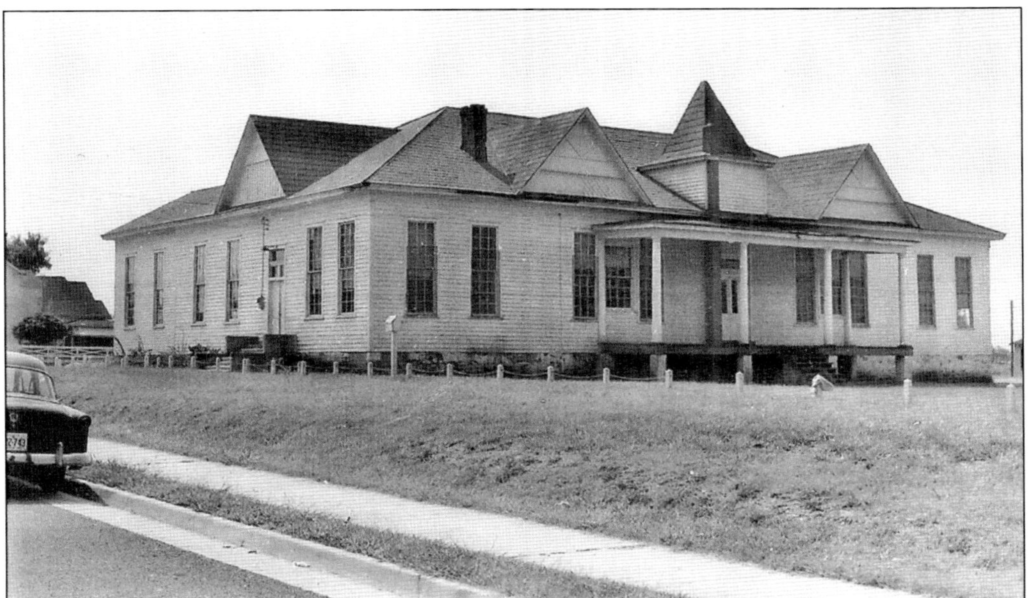

Being turned down by the county school board for a new high school, surrounding schools, farmers, and African American churches and businesses conducted fund-raisers and began to build a new high school on Caroline Street, near Blue Creek and the old community park. The main building opened for classes in the fall of 1935, with Robert D. Harris as the first principal. An auditorium and a science classroom were added. (COE.)

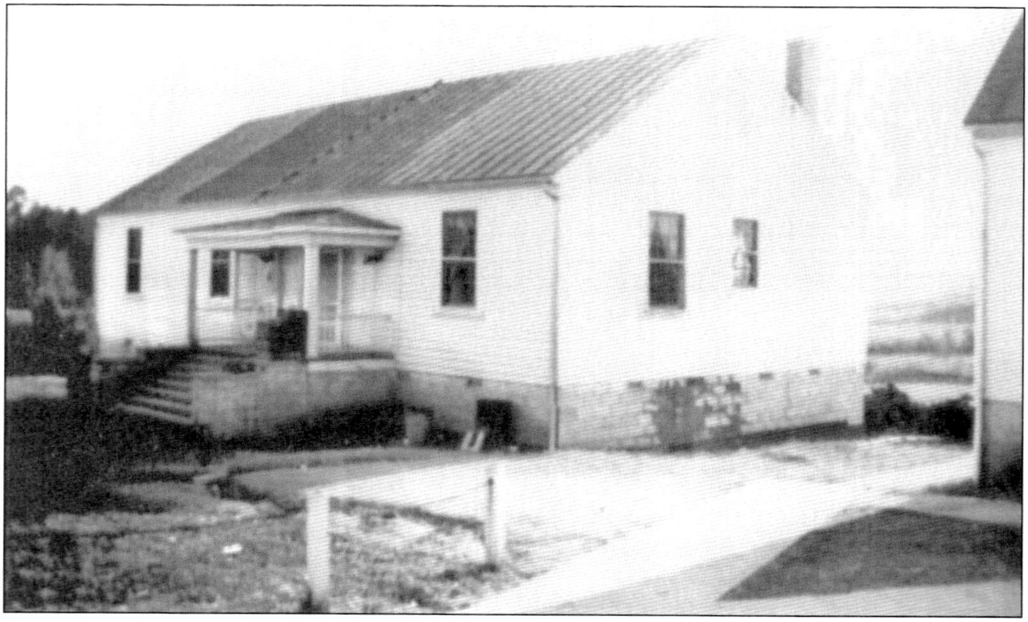

Construction and fund-raisers continued, and in 1938, home economics and cafeteria buildings were completed. In 1939, a building for vocational agriculture was added, and the first graduating class had 20 students graduating on June 2, 1939. In 1950, the school was taken over by the Corps of Engineers and was closed and sold. This is a picture of the economics building. (Lucille T. Hudson and W. P. Hudgins Sr.)

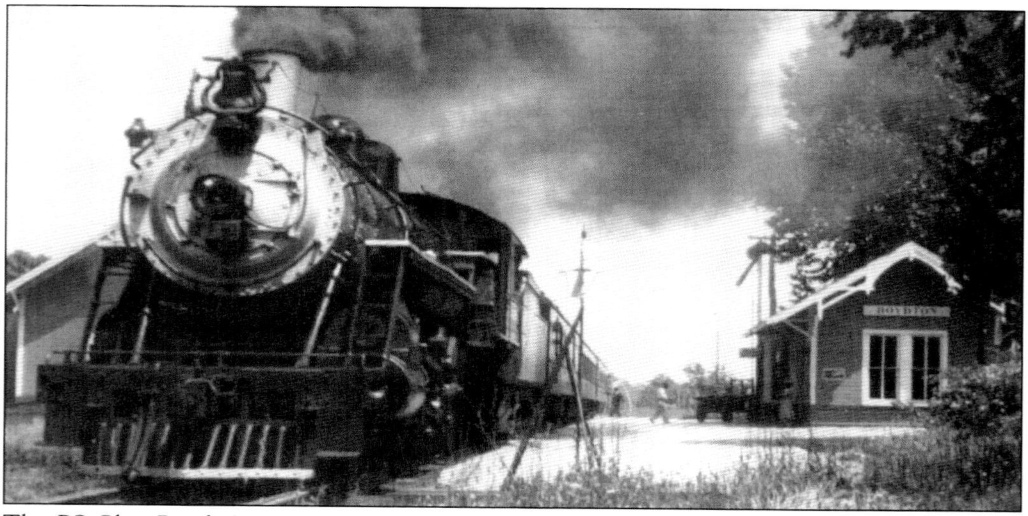

This PS-Class Pacific No. 1227, Train 1, is leaving Boydton en route to Danville in May 1937. The last passenger trains came through in 1969 and the last freight in 1974. (HBR.)

Four

The Dam

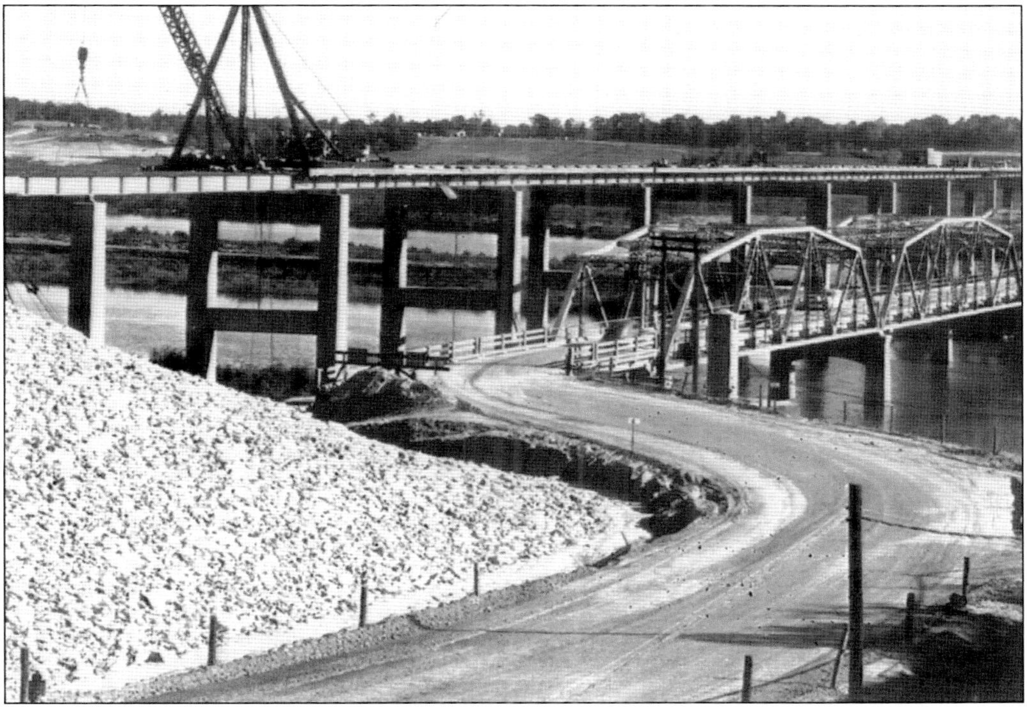

In 1951, the Corps of Engineers was constructing a new elevated bridge into Clarksville that would enter town at Second Street. All along U.S. Highway 58, the road had to be elevated, in places as much as 43 feet, to accommodate the coming of the new Buggs Island Lake with over 800 miles of shoreline. Clarksville was and is the only town on the lake. From this photograph, one can see the new 1927 steel bridge into town, built by the Virginia Department of Highways. (Betty Jack Ligon.)

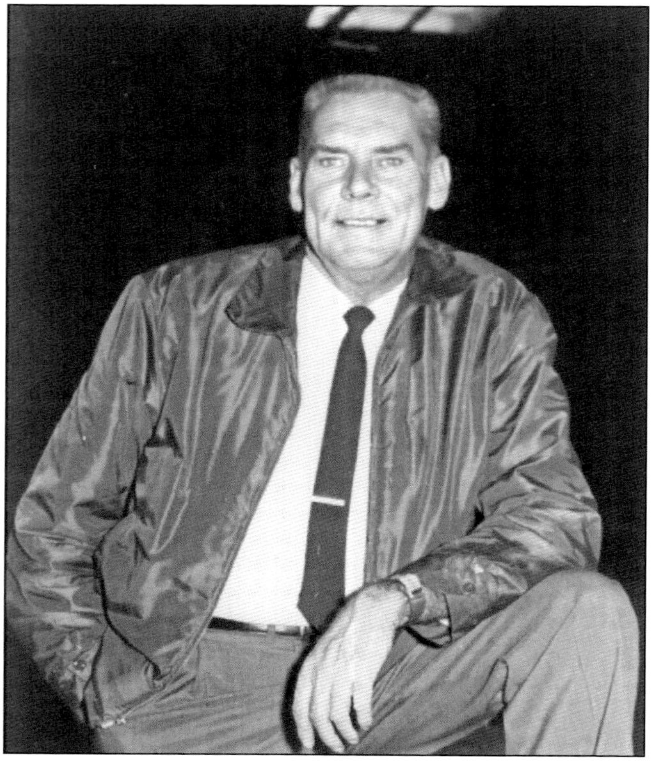

Of 50 world-titled tobacco auctioneers, 12 are from Clarksville/Buffalo Springs. The most famous was Joe Burnett ("Smokey Joe" of television and radio's *Sold American*) from Buffalo Springs. He was sought after as an auctioneer in Florida, Kentucky, North and South Carolina, and Virginia. In 1948, he decided to only sell in Clarksville. (CRM.)

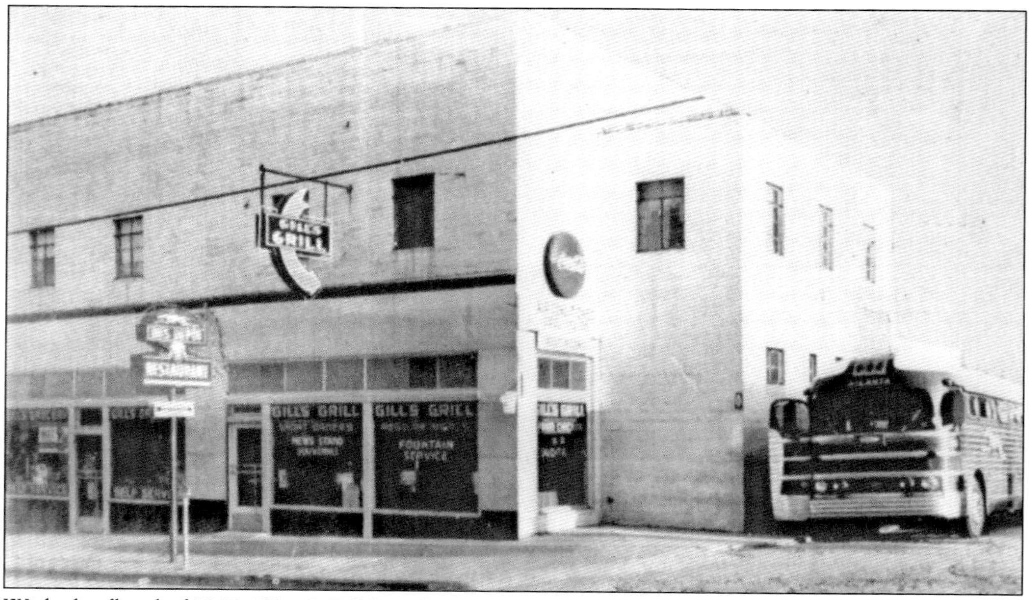

With the flood of 1940, "Doc" Gill hired contractor Charlie Buchanan to build a new Greyhound bus station on Virginia Avenue and petitioned to move it from North Clarksville. Once completed, it housed the bus station, a café and soda fountain, and Sally Morgan's Grocery store. It became a very popular establishment during World War II, as the soldiers would go and come on furlough by bus. (BH.)

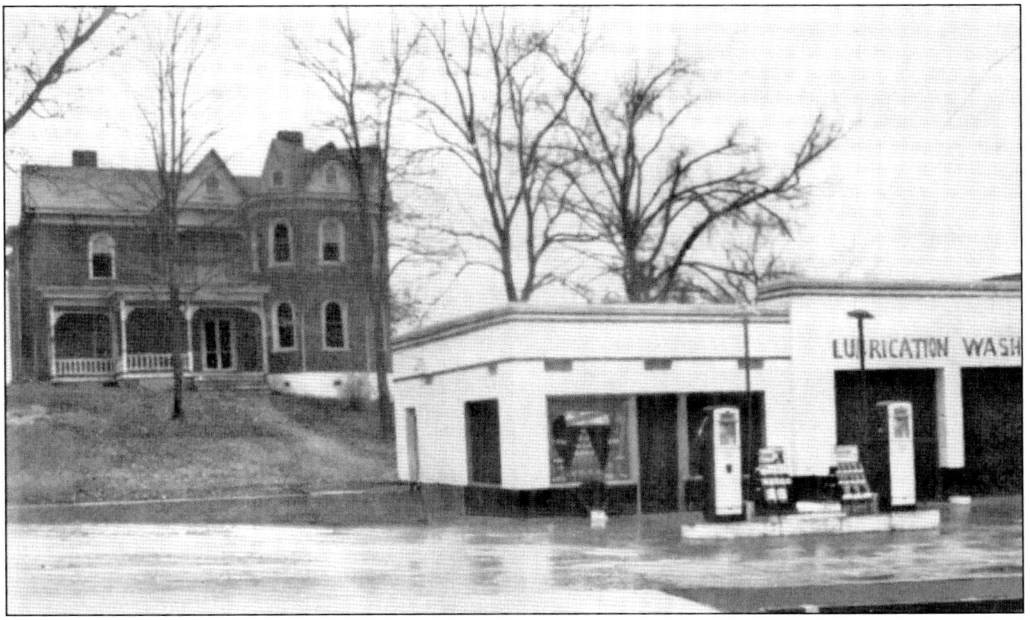

Across the street, Charlie Buchanan had purchased the Magee House, previously owned by A. Preston Magee, who had begun Magee Lithia Water Bottling Company on First Street in 1911. Buchanan was contracted to build the new Preston and Stuart Magee ESSO Service Center and snack shop in 1942. Throughout his career, Charlie Buchanan built 25 businesses and over 50 homes in Clarksville and the surrounding community. (Dylan Willis.)

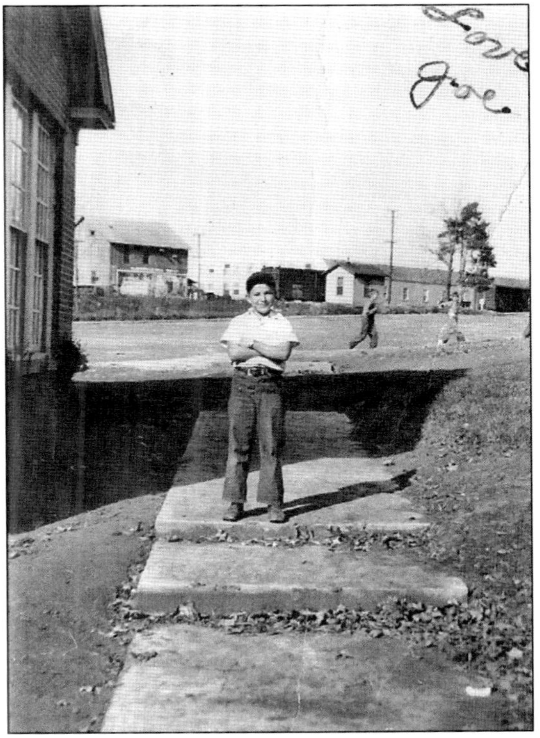

From the front lawn of the Clarksville High School, the sports field was between the school and the railroad tracks. In the distance to the right is the Southern Railway station, which was sold, dismantled, and moved to Roxboro, North Carolina, where it is still being used as a restaurant. To the left is Clarksville Supply Company, built in 1912. Standing on the walk is Joe Weary. (Jack Hite.)

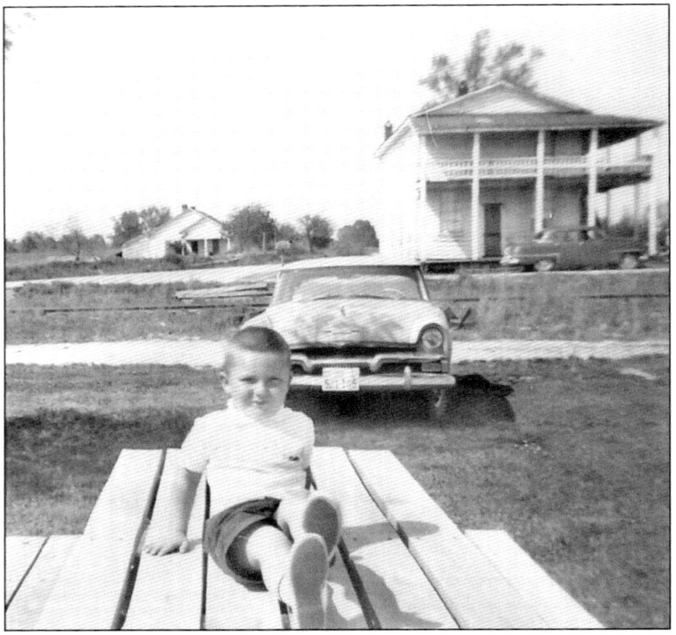

Harvey T. and Elizabeth Wootton moved from the Field's community to open a store in Finchley in 1932. By 1949, Moore's store, located across the road, was owned by Jake Jackson, and Harvey Wootton suffered a stroke, closing his store. That same year, in December, Ben Fuller shot and killed Joe Thompson in front of Jackson's store. Fuller was convicted of murder and became the only resident of Mecklenburg to receive the death sentence. On the picnic table is Wallace Carter. (Barbara Carter Royal.)

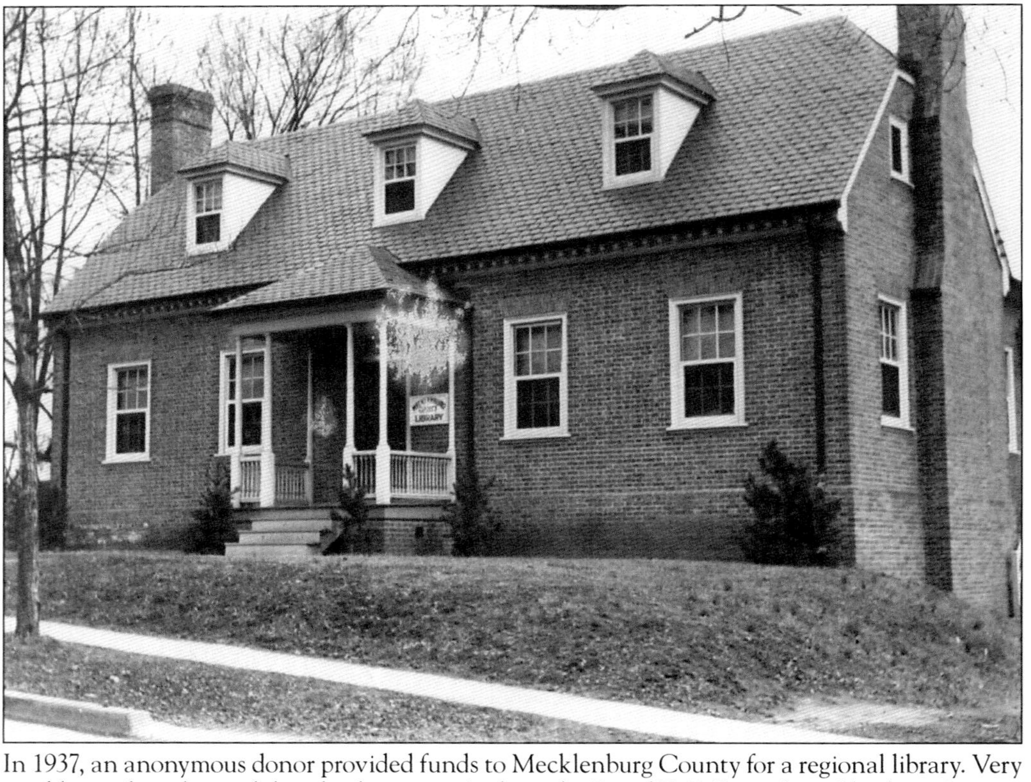

In 1937, an anonymous donor provided funds to Mecklenburg County for a regional library. Very quickly, residents learned that the donor was Ambassador David K. E. Bruce from Charlotte County, who had done likewise there and also in Halifax and Lunenburg Counties. It was his belief that learning through reading might help prevent another depression. (Southside Regional Library.)

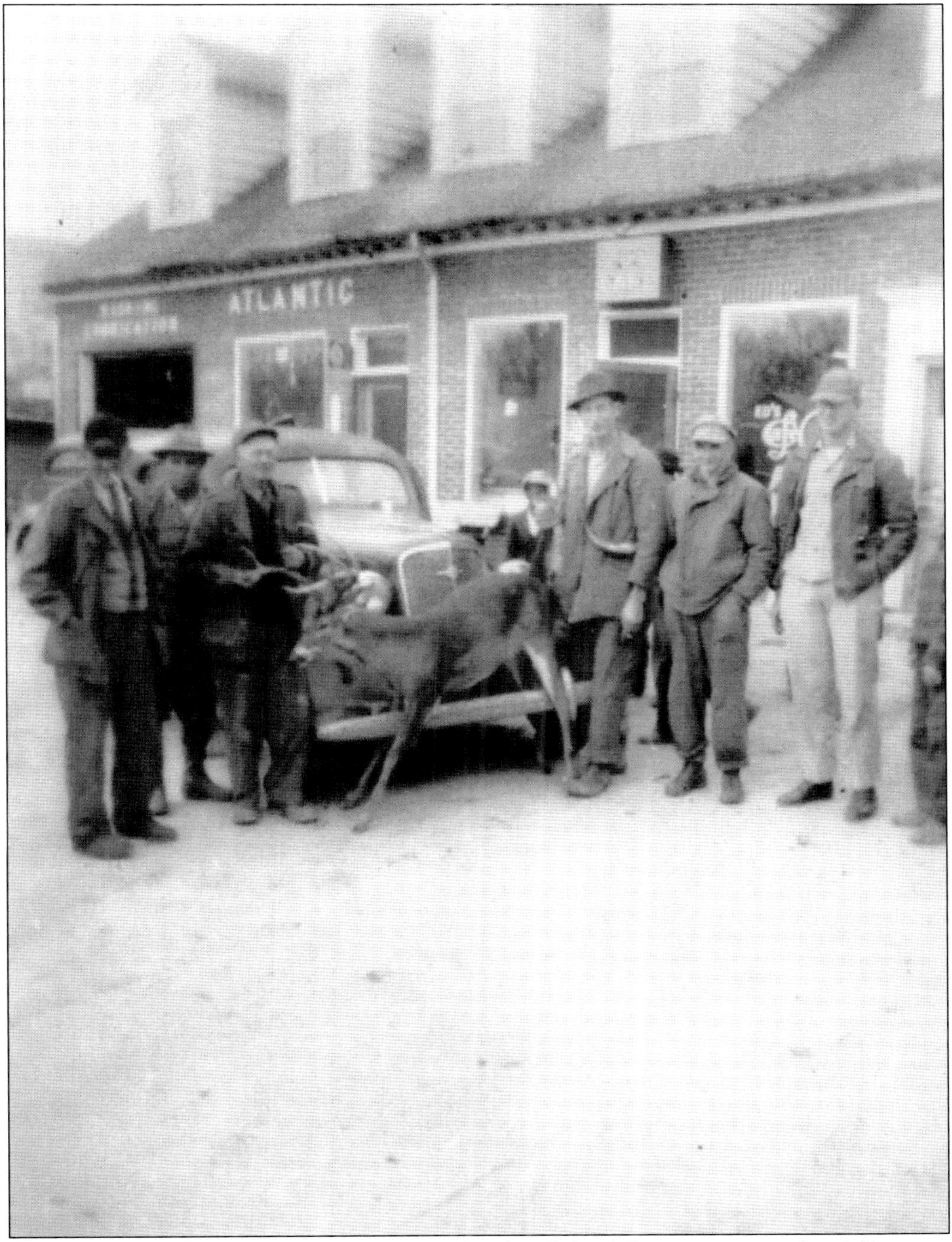

In 1948, the new Atlantic building was completed and the Atlantic station with a full-service garage was opened. Next door was Ed's Café. This building was owned by Thomas Gregory Jr., who had been deferred from World War II because of his trucking business but served in the Virginia Home Guard of Boydton and rose to the rank of corporal. (Henry H. Gregory Jr.)

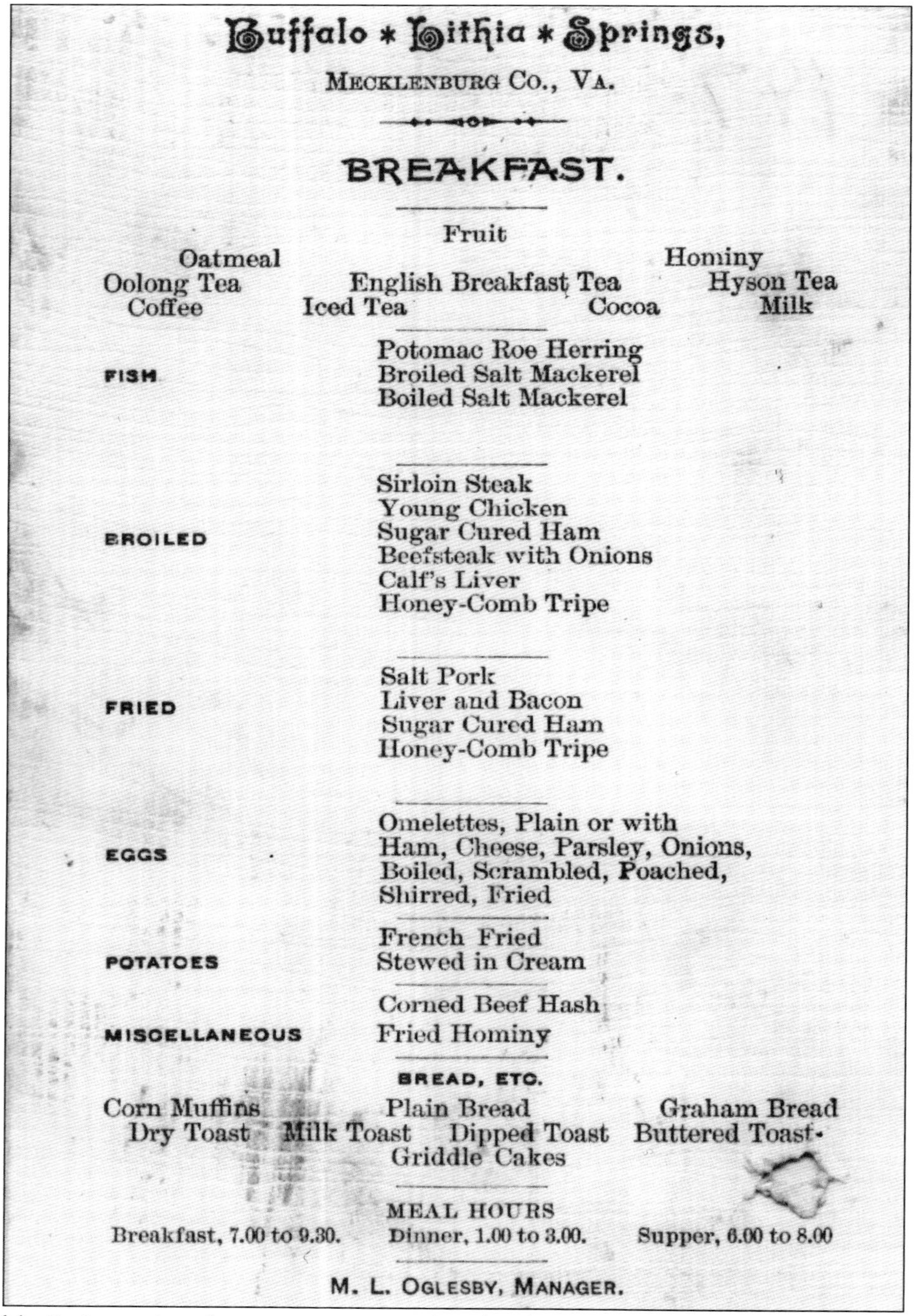

Buffalo * Lithia * Springs,

MECKLENBURG CO., VA.

BREAKFAST.

Fruit

Oatmeal Hominy

Oolong Tea English Breakfast Tea Hyson Tea

Coffee Iced Tea Cocoa Milk

FISH
Potomac Roe Herring
Broiled Salt Mackerel
Boiled Salt Mackerel

BROILED
Sirloin Steak
Young Chicken
Sugar Cured Ham
Beefsteak with Onions
Calf's Liver
Honey-Comb Tripe

FRIED
Salt Pork
Liver and Bacon
Sugar Cured Ham
Honey-Comb Tripe

EGGS
Omelettes, Plain or with
Ham, Cheese, Parsley, Onions,
Boiled, Scrambled, Poached,
Shirred, Fried

POTATOES
French Fried
Stewed in Cream

MISCELLANEOUS
Corned Beef Hash
Fried Hominy

BREAD, ETC.

Corn Muffins Plain Bread Graham Bread

Dry Toast Milk Toast Dipped Toast Buttered Toast

Griddle Cakes

MEAL HOURS

Breakfast, 7.00 to 9.30. Dinner, 1.00 to 3.00. Supper, 6.00 to 8.00

M. L. OGLESBY, MANAGER.

Buffalo Springs mineral water was registered under the Pure Food and Drug Act of 1906 by the new owners. In 1929, Dr. W. E. Finch filed suit against the springs for back debts and taxes, and the complex was sold at auction to a Wall Street investment firm. This 1930 menu from Buffalo Springs shows the variety offered. Their slogan was "not or, but and" when one placed an order. (CRM.)

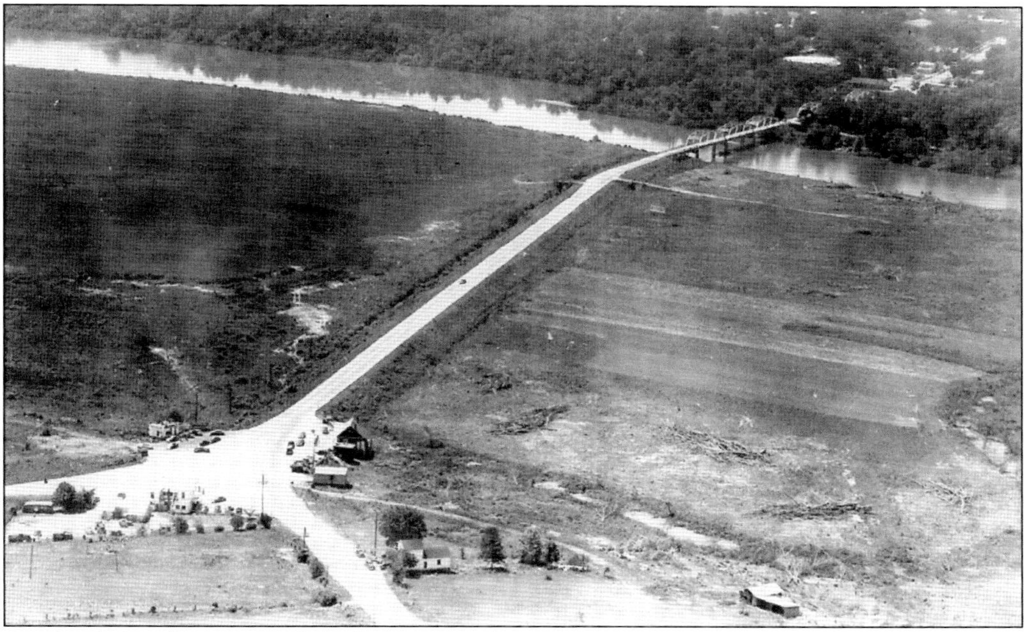

North Clarksville was established in 1926, and in 1927, with the new steel bridge, it grew rapidly. In this photograph is the old "Y" intersection of Highways 15 and 58 for crossing the bridge. On the left is Dick Long's Hotel/bus station/restaurant and parking lot. To the right is Keiffer Yancy's curb-service barbecue restaurant, a small store that sold fresh hams, and "Mama Johnson's" tavern. This area is now part of the lake. (COE.)

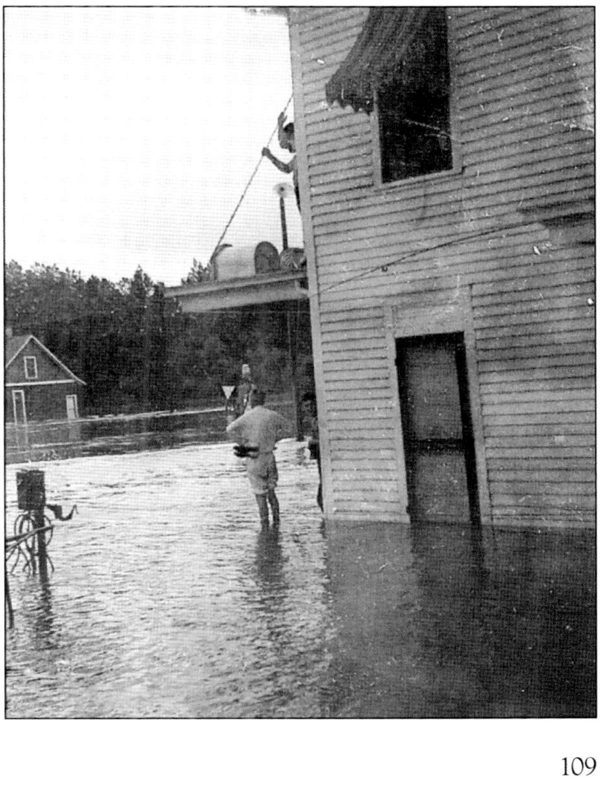

The flood of 1940 is clearly demonstrated in this photograph, taken in the parking lot at Long's. Not only were the low grounds underwater, but the higher ground of North Clarksville was under a foot of water even before the rivers crested. Compare the two photographs and imagine the bridge underwater. Long's boasted "good food, reasonable prices and good accommodations." (Lucille Tisdale Campbell.)

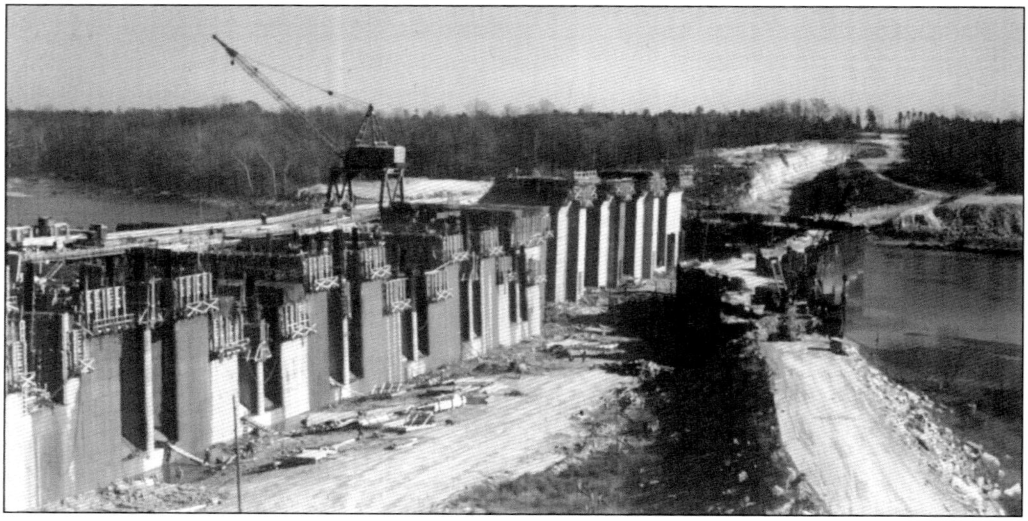

In 1946, construction began on the John H. Kerr Dam to impound the waters of the Roanoke River and create the Buggs' Island Lake. This picture is of the beginning stages of building the cofferdam. (Mecklenburg Electric Cooperative.)

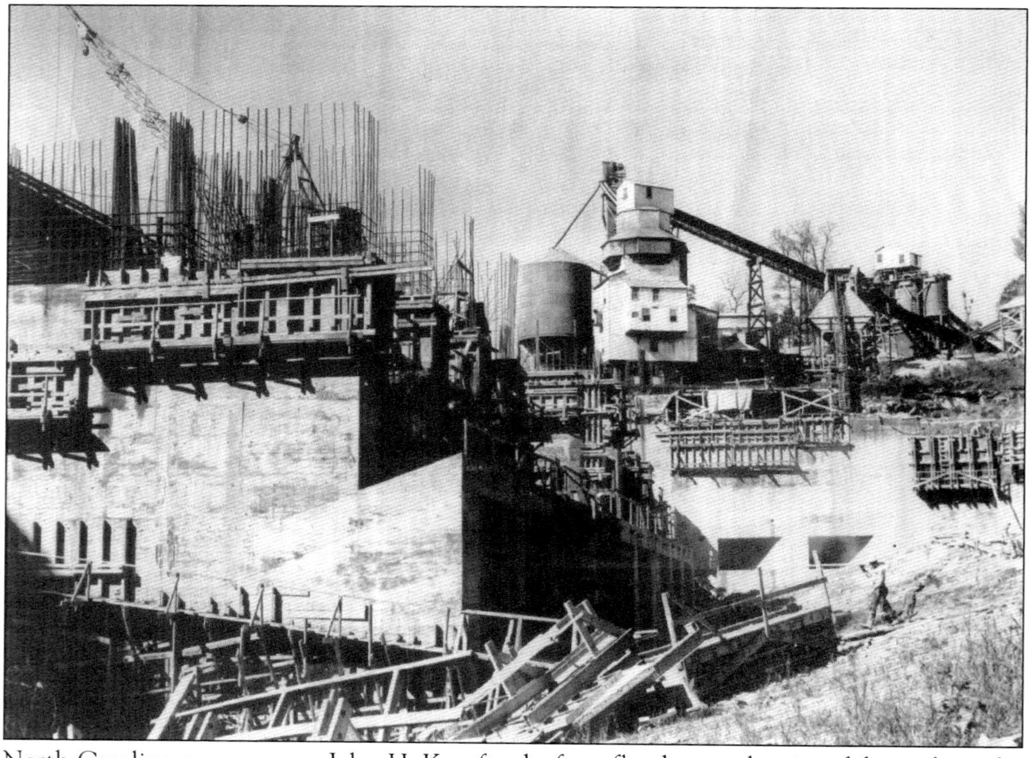

North Carolina congressman John H. Kerr fought for a flood control series of dams along the Roanoke starting in 1925, but with the Depression and the war, it was 1945 before it received approval. The total cost of the project was over $92 million. This photograph shows part of Kerr Village with the cement plant in place in late 1947. The forms have been removed from the foundation, and the steel is in place to begin the walls. (Mecklenburg Electric Cooperative.)

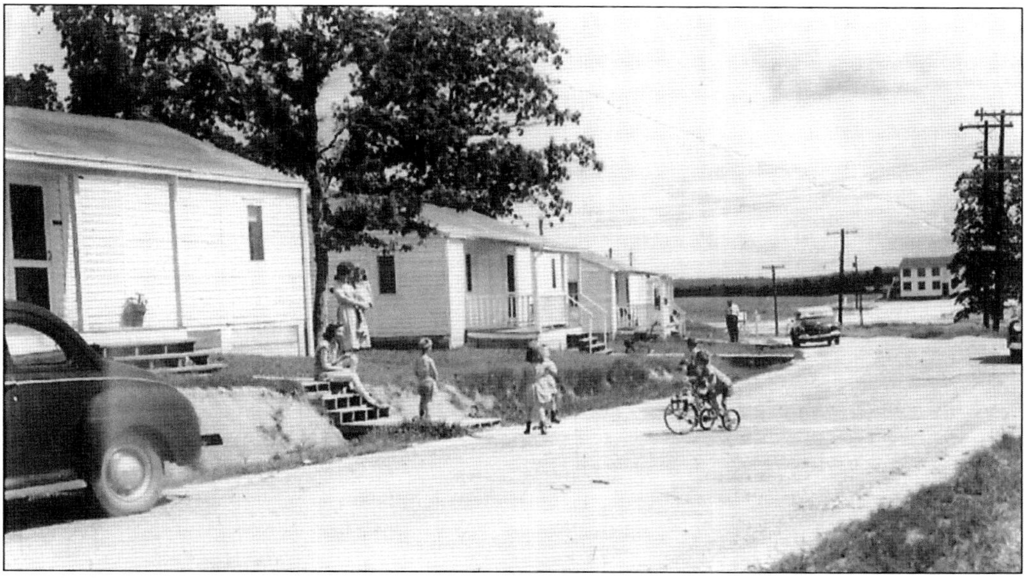

For all the workers arriving at the site, a community was built in 1946—Castle Heights. Over 1,000 workers, many from out of state and expecting a three-to-five-year job, moved to the area with their families. Each family was given a 12-page booklet of instructions and regulations for living in the "Heights." In this photograph is a small portion of the community with the street that would become the new Route 4 across the dam into North Carolina. When the dam was completed, the buildings were sold and moved. (COE.)

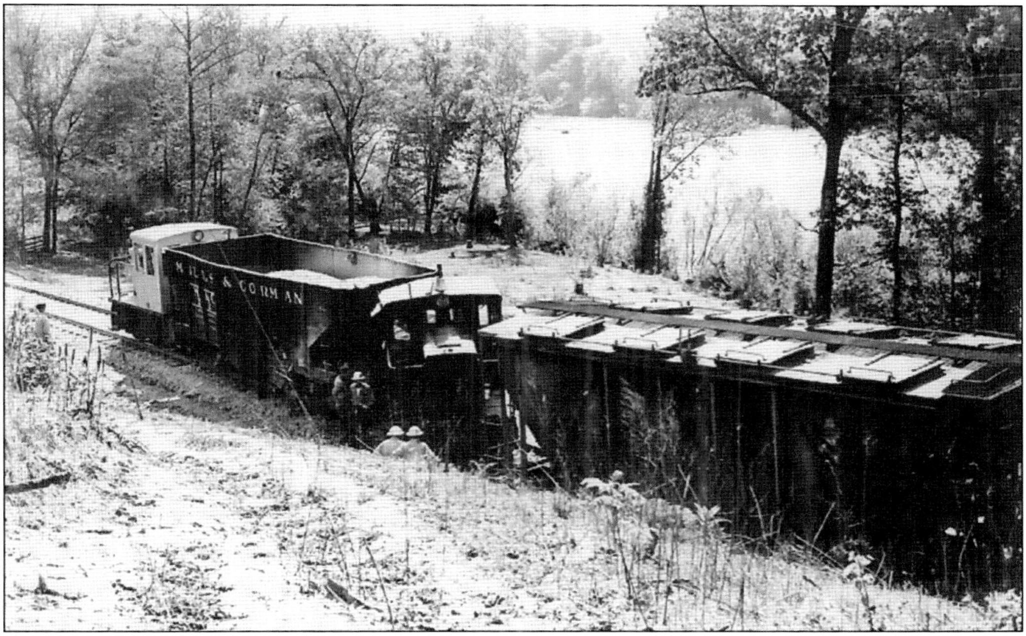

This May 6, 1950, photograph shows the collision of two dinkies that were designed to work in close quarters for moving the railcars to and from the work site to the quarry, cement mixer, and lumber and gravel yards. Over 7 miles of railroad tracks had to be laid to support the Kerr Dam project. Upon completion, the lake impacted five counties in North Carolina and Virginia. (COE.)

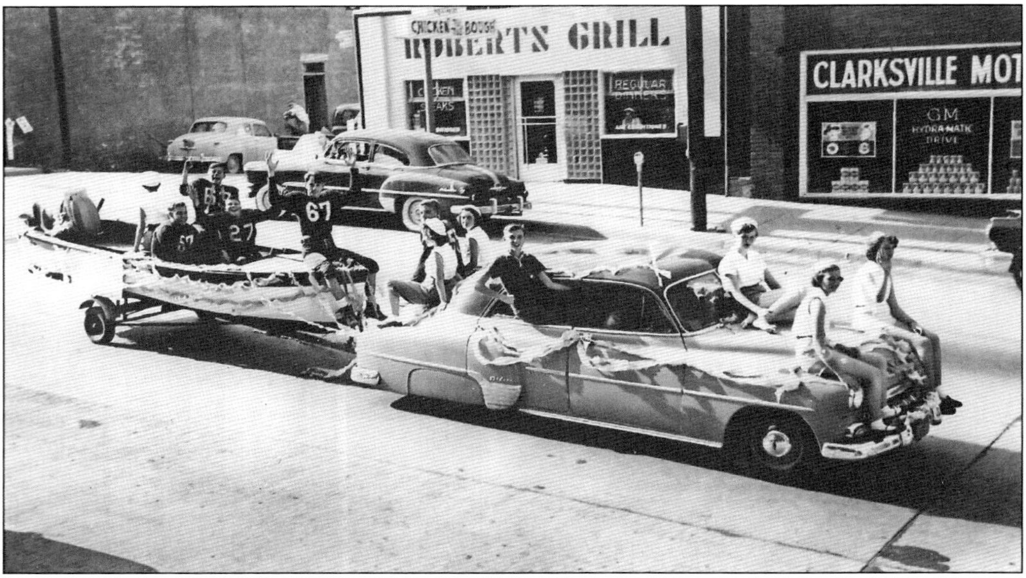

Especially after World War II, Clarksville demonstrated a great team spirit, supporting all sporting events in grand fashion. This 1952 spirited group of Clarksville High School football players and cheerleaders includes, from left to right, Bob Wilkerson, Marshall Shearin, No. 27 Gordan Yancy, No. 67 Sal Thomasson, B. Clinton Hayes, Martha Yancy, unidentified, Jack Hite (hanging out of the car), Zelma Riggins, Barbara Hash, and Joyce Clark. (Jack Hite.)

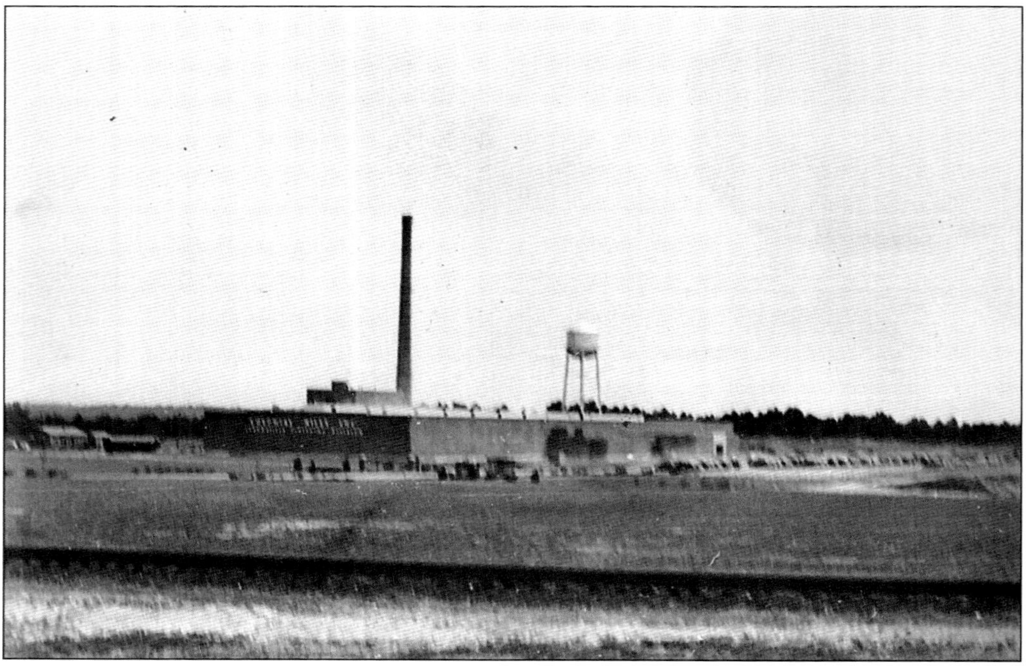

Begun in 1946, the new Colonial Farm Textile Corporation's Rayon Finishing Mill opened in the spring of 1947. The Robbins family, who owned the mill, made many significant contributions to Clarksville and changed the name to Robbins Mill in 1948. (COE.)

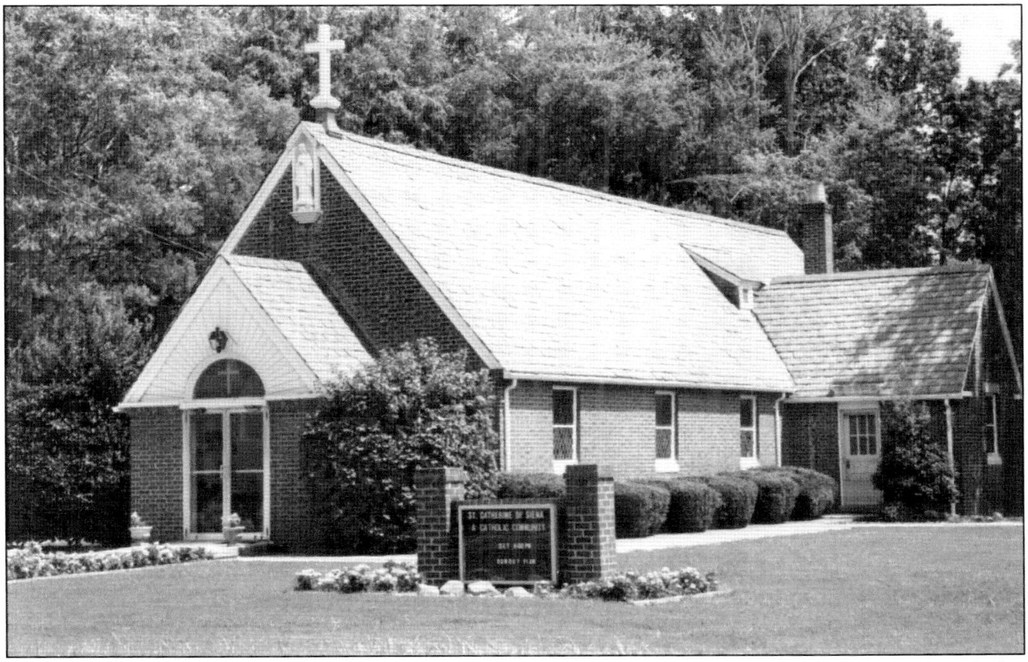

Catholics had been meeting at the home of a layman since the 1930s, and finally a new Catholic church was granted in 1947—the first in western Mecklenburg. St. Catherine of Siena was dedicated on September 23, 1947, by R. Rev. Msgr. Leo J. Ryat, vicar general of the Catholic Diocese of Richmond. (Rebecca Cary.)

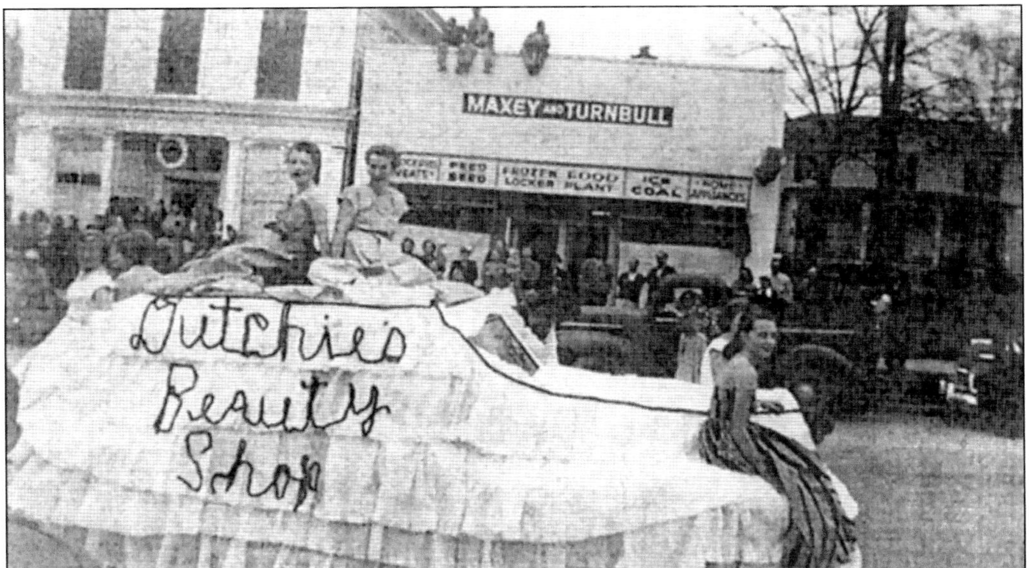

This parade photograph from 1947 shows the former Charlie Tisdale Jewelry store, now Maxey and Turnbull's Grocery and freezer locker plant, next door to the J. S. Johnson Variety Store. Dutchie's Beauty Shop is still over the drugstore, and this appears to be a May Day parade. Note the crowd on the store roof watching the parade. (BH.)

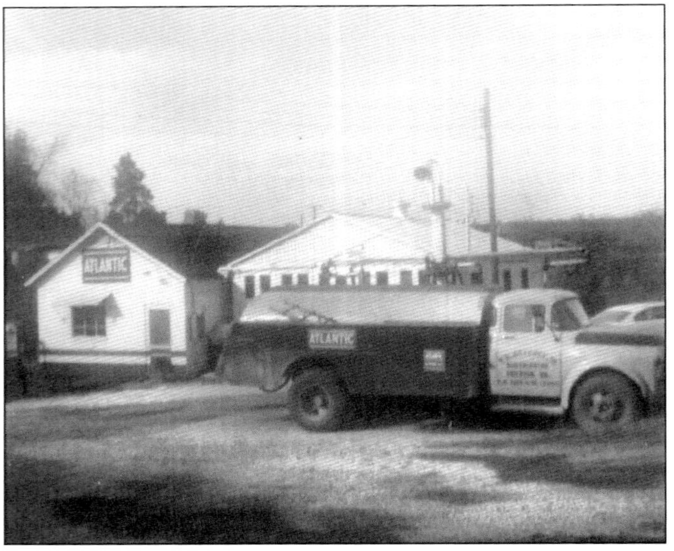

In 1937, Thomas W. Gregory Jr. began a trucking company for general hauling. With the 1939 regulations, it became government controlled, but with World War II, business boomed. He purchased a second truck and hired a driver, Skinner Wells. By 1947, the government restrictions were such that an independent trucker could not compete. He sold out and began this petroleum dealership. He was elected to the Virginia House of Delegates in 1949 and eventually sold his business in 1986. (Henry H. Gregory Jr.)

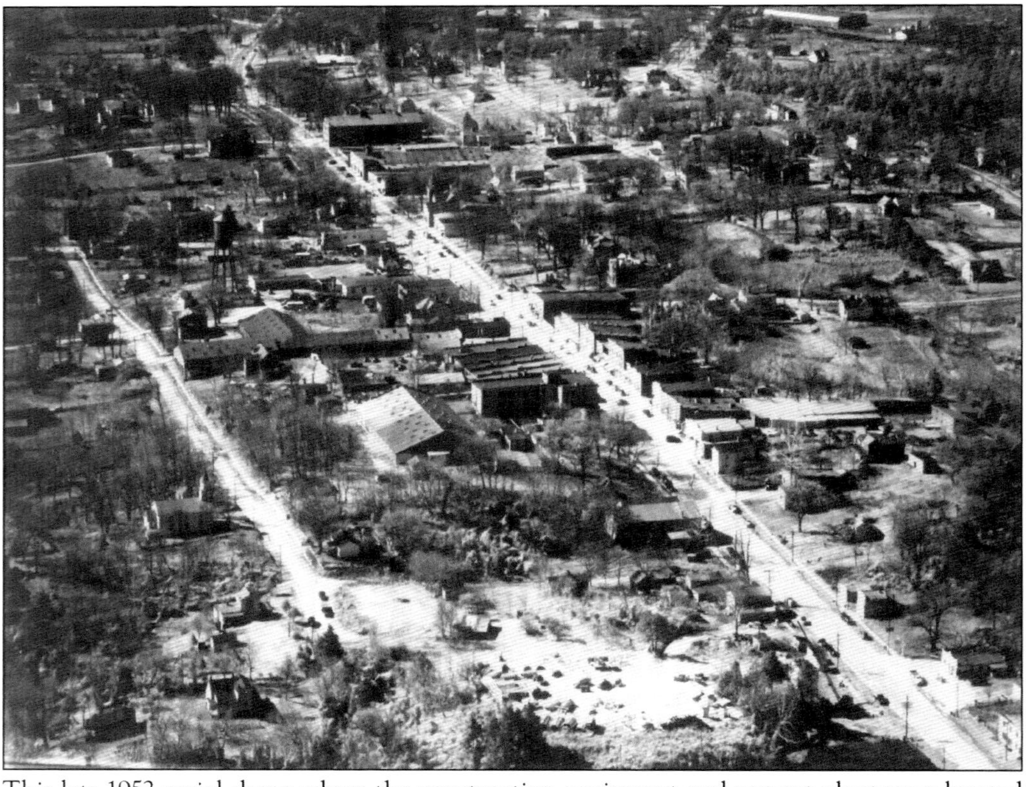

This late-1952 aerial shows where the construction equipment and cement plant were located (bottom center) for building the new Clarksville bridge. First Street is now underwater. This picture starts with Second Street looking south. To the left on Market Street are two homes and Mount Zion Baptist Church. The bottom right edge of the picture is the old city hall and jail. Virginia Avenue runs through the center, and the distant end of Virginia Avenue is the old Moss tobacco factory/warehouse, next door to the Planter's Warehouse 1 and 2. (COE.)

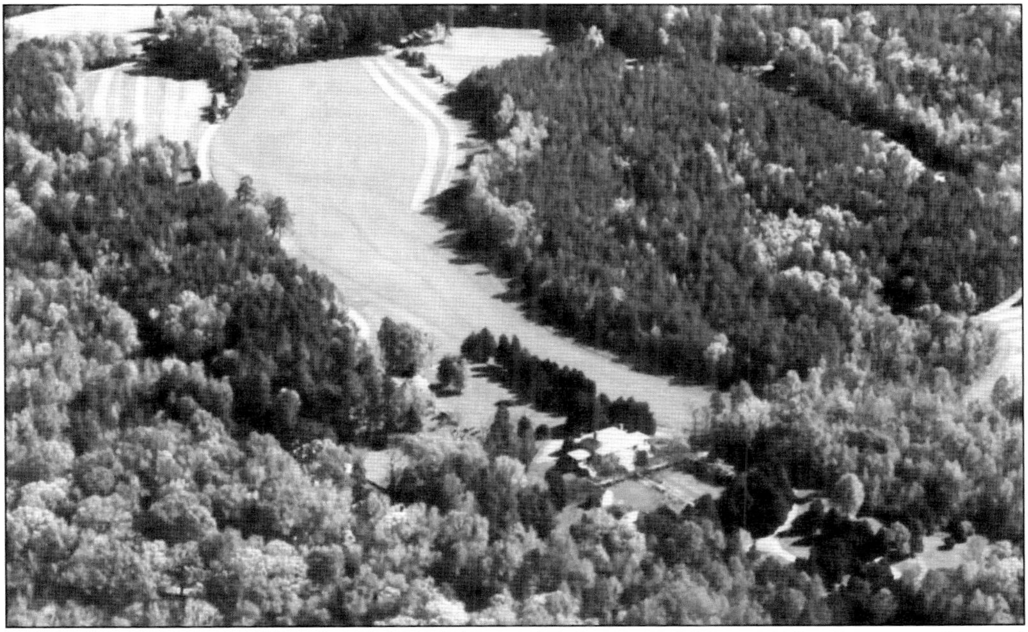

In 1948, the Karl Robbins family purchased the Kinderton estate. The manor house was modernized and bedrooms added to the basement so that when guests would come to visit or consult at the mill they could stay close by. A nine-hole course, clubhouse, store, club pro shop, and dining hall for members are open year-round. Currently, the club sponsors four significant tournaments annually. (Joe Noah.)

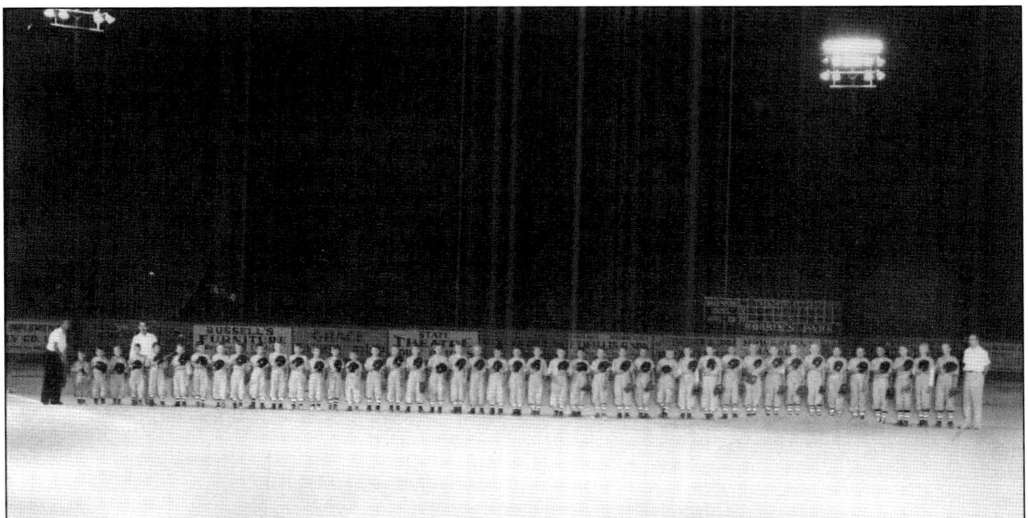

With the Corps of Engineers closing the community park in 1951, the Robbins family purchased a parcel of land and built the new Robbins Field, complete with lighting for evening games. They also sponsored a B League baseball team: Clarksville Robbins. Here the Little League team is lined up for a portrait across the lighted field before a game. This is the same team pictured a year earlier on the community park field on page 100. The Little League is still a significant part of Clarksville's sports. (Jack Hite.)

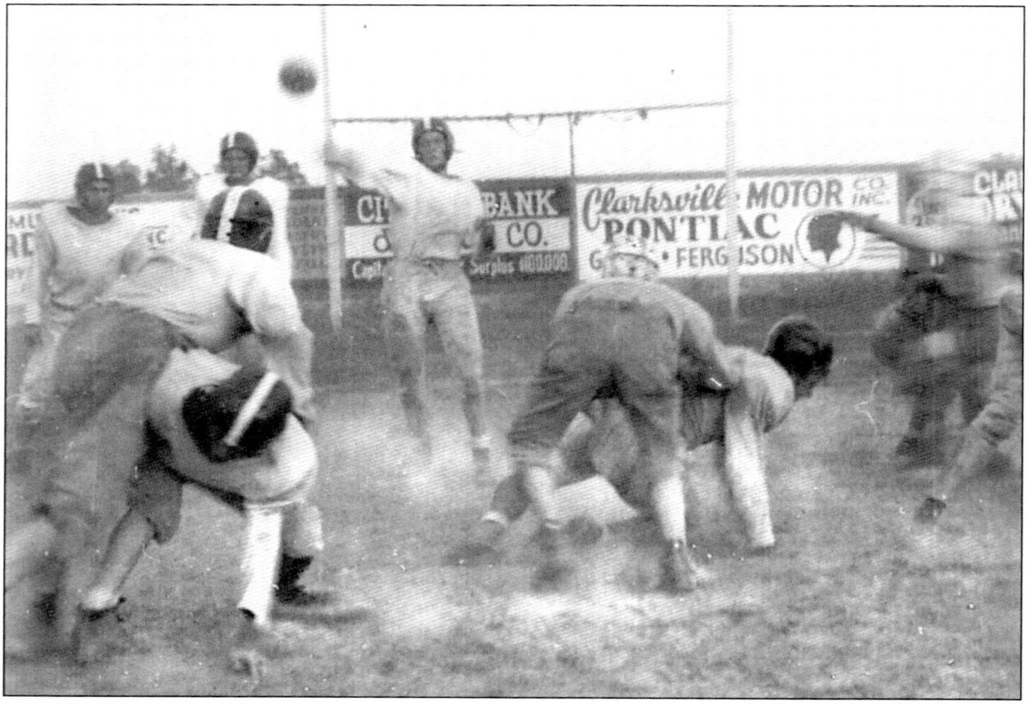

In 1952, the new Robbins Field was also host to the high school team sports and recreation. Football, baseball, track, and other sports for the school and community were practiced and played on this field. The B League team practiced and played here. In this photograph, the Clarksville High School football team is scrimmaging in preparation for their game against their archrivals South Hill. In 1955, the schools were consolidated and there became only two high schools in the county. (Jack Hite.)

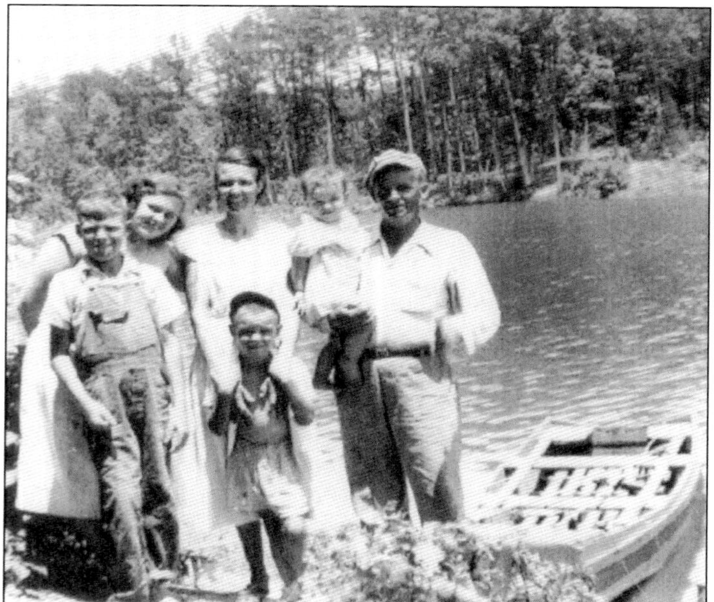

With 20 new boat ramp access areas and 15 state park areas in western Mecklenburg County, many families spent entire weekends on the lake fishing and camping. In this 1954 picture, the McKinney family has the boat in the water and is readying for the weekend. Pictured from left to right are (first row) David; (second row) Howard, Rachael, Pearl, Arlene, and Arthur Faye. (BMC.)

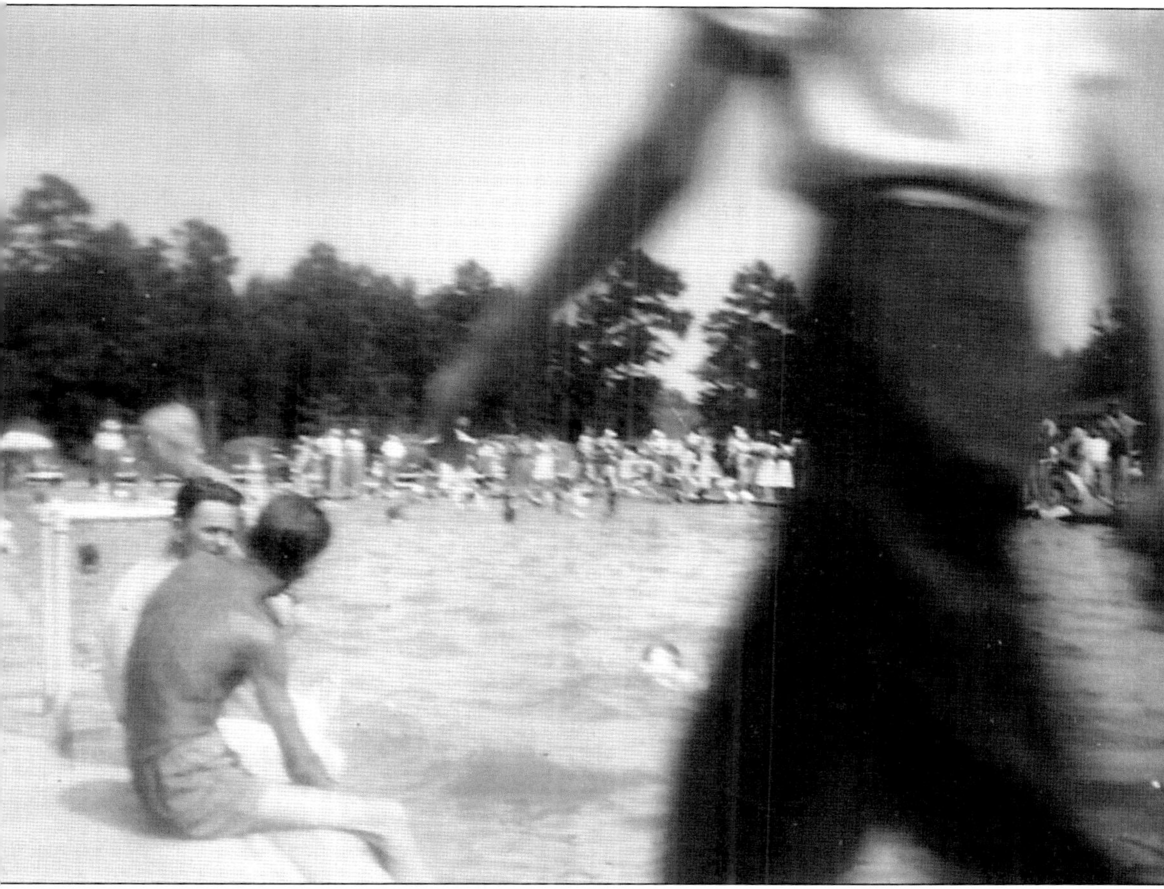

Later a general store was added and expanded to include a large swimming pool with two bathhouses, a "juke shack," and a concession stand with outdoor grill. This became such a popular local spot that in the late 1950s, Bluestone High School would schedule a seniors' "sneak day" each year before graduation and this became the destination for most of the class. (Garnett E. Clark.)

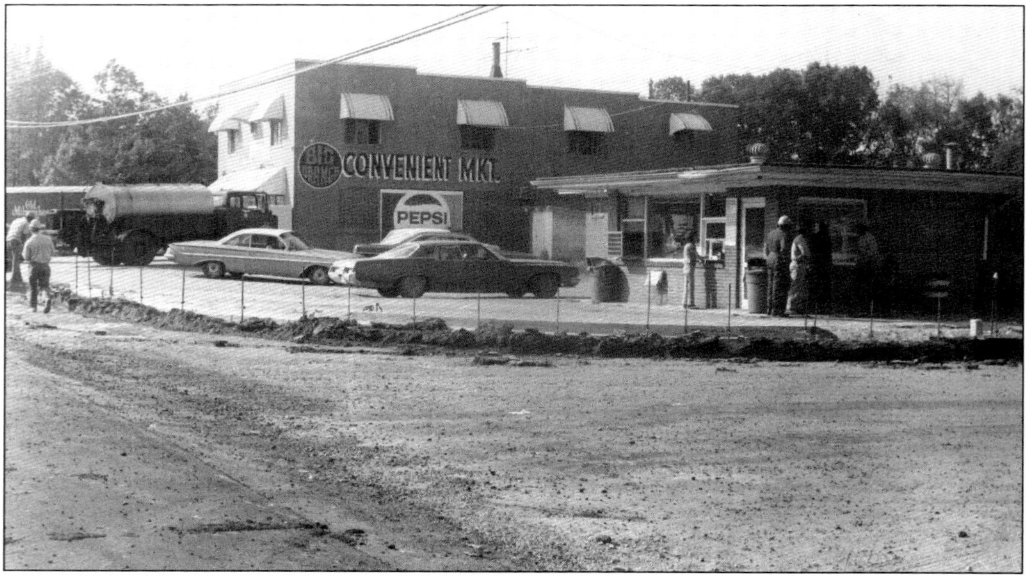

Around 1949, Frances P. "Flick" Rawls opened the Penguin drive-up restaurant. There was seating inside, but one had to be careful, as Flick always had words of advice for his young customers. Next door, the Big Orange Crush soda fountain and convenience store of Frank Easley opened in 1952; it was later purchased by Sammie Bass. (Jessie Thompson.)

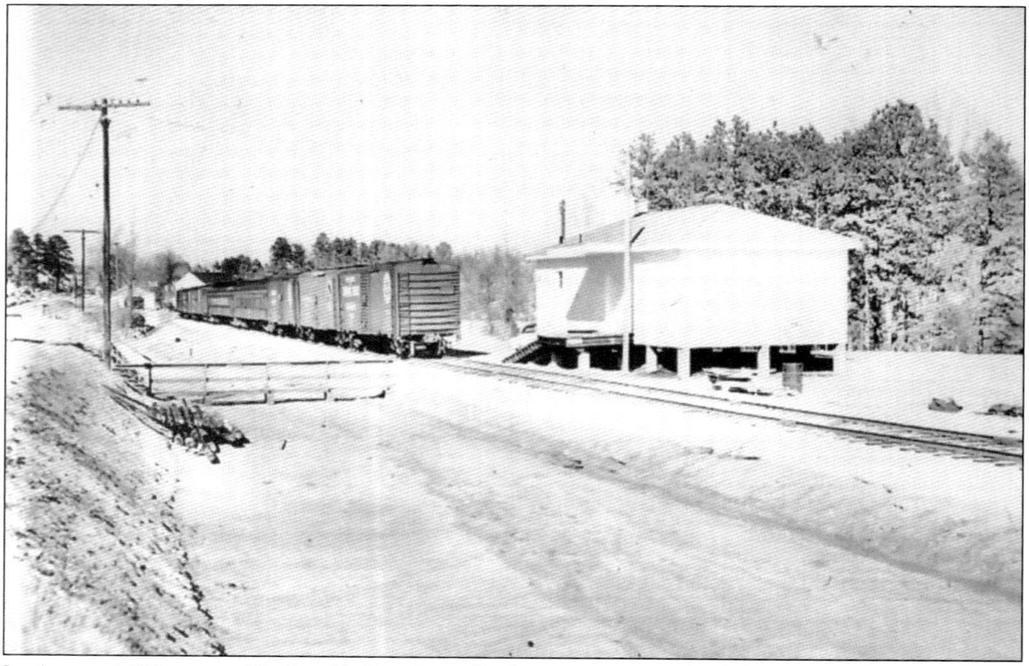

In August 1953, a new Clarksville Southern Railway station was built by the Corps of Engineers. The old station sold and moved; the new station was located across Highway 58 behind the new Garland's Community Center and was very small. Passenger service was slow, with one train per day, and freight was equally slow. The station was recently torn down and removed. All that remains of the train era is a muddy road atop the hill next to the track in the woods. (COE.)

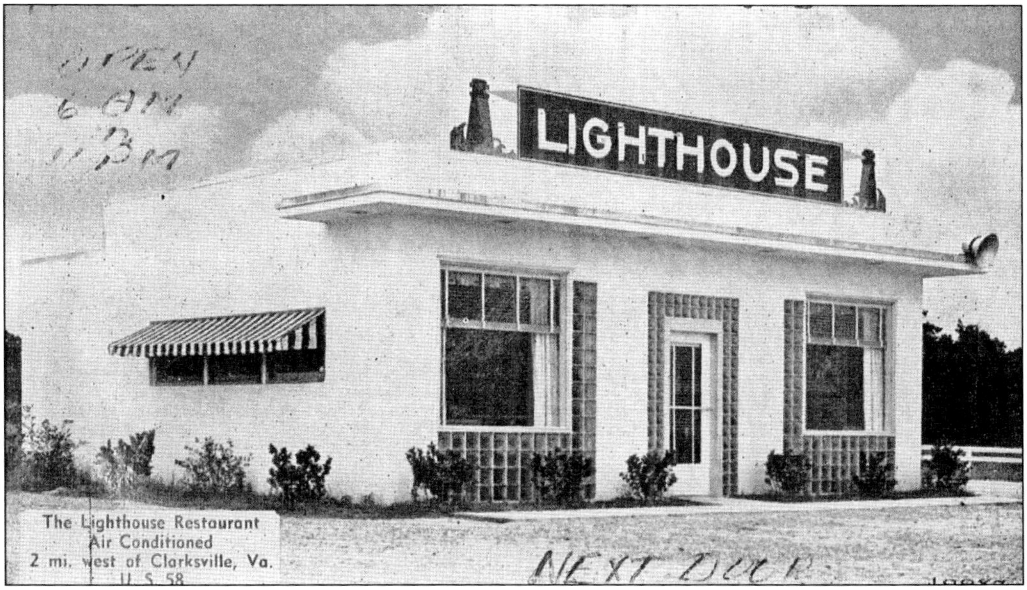

One mile farther west on Highway 58 was the Lighthouse Motel, restaurant, and swimming pool built by Dick Smith, opening in 1951. In the day, it was quite modern, with a television in every room. It became the place to go after dances and ball games, or just on late-night outings, for sodas, snacks, meals, or just socializing. Smith lived directly across Highway 58. One evening in 1959, not paying attention, he was walking across to the restaurant and was struck by a car and killed. (WCG.)

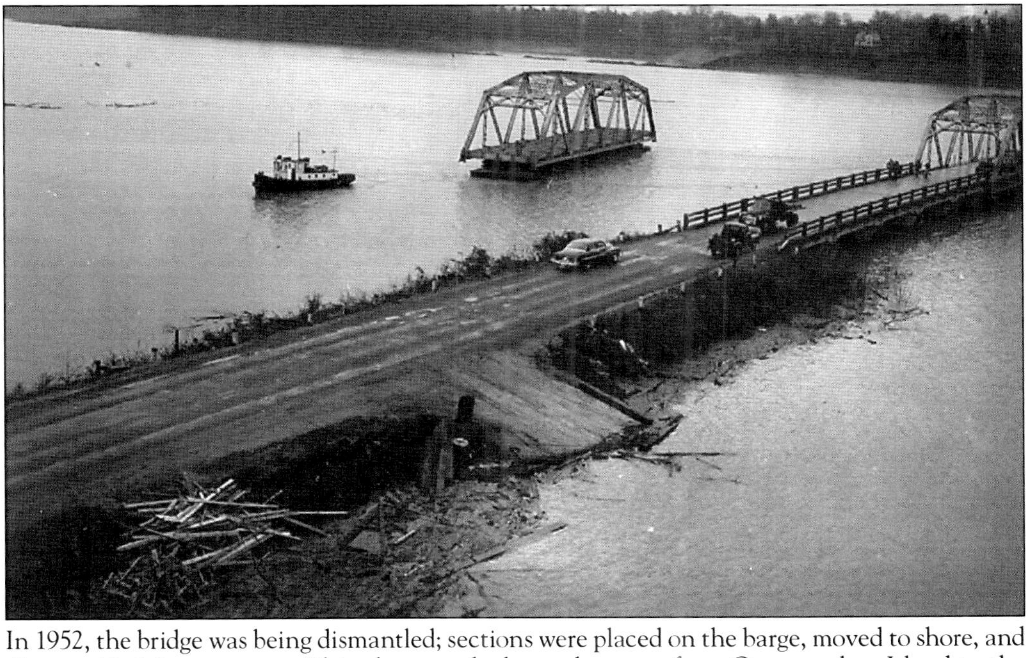

In 1952, the bridge was being dismantled; sections were placed on the barge, moved to shore, and disassembled for transport. This photograph shows the ramp from Occoneechee Island to the Clarksville bridge both nearly underwater. Tugboat *Dan* was built in 1937 in Duluth, Minnesota, and is 50 feet in length. (COE.)

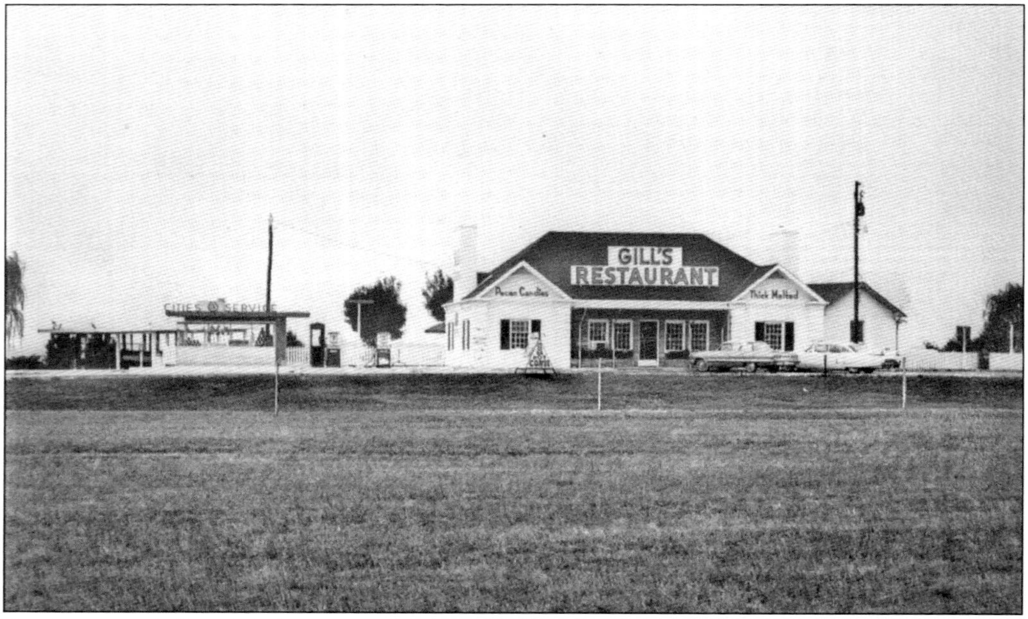

The lake was full and dedicated in the fall of 1952. The right-hand corner of property between the newly located Highways 15 and 58 intersection abutting the lake was purchased by Doc Gill for his new restaurant. The store boasted pecan candies and Virginia hams, with the restaurant advertising "thick malted's." (Richard Burnett.)

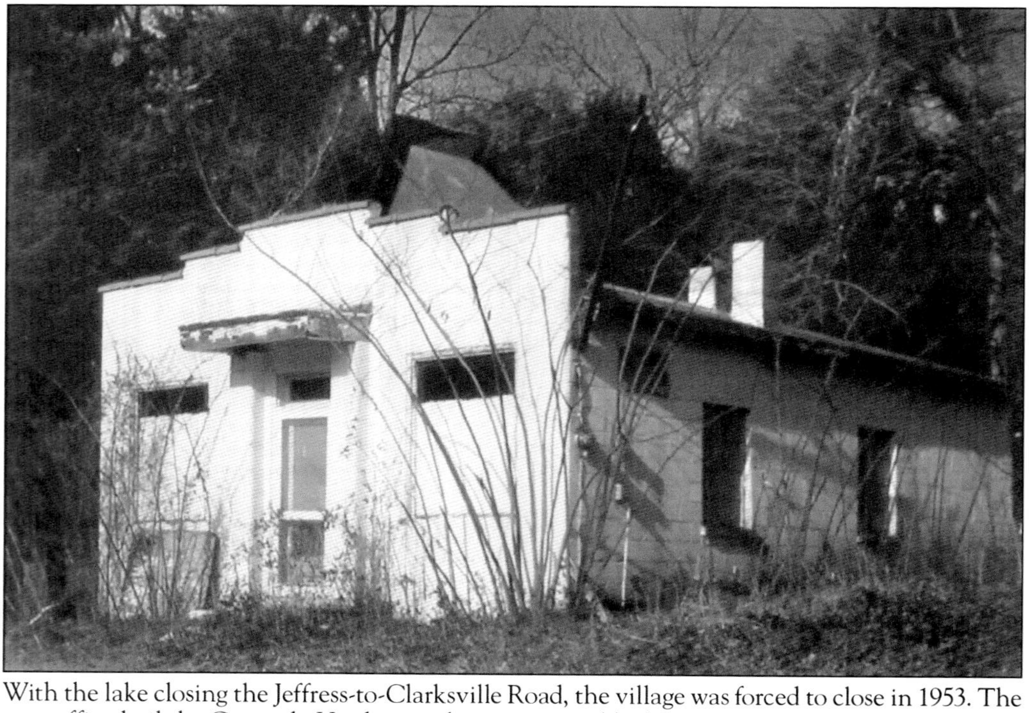

With the lake closing the Jeffress-to-Clarksville Road, the village was forced to close in 1953. The post office built by Gertrude Hardy, now being operated by her younger brother, James Dabney Hardy, burned again in 1945. The post office closed in 1953 and relocated to Skipwith. (BMC.)

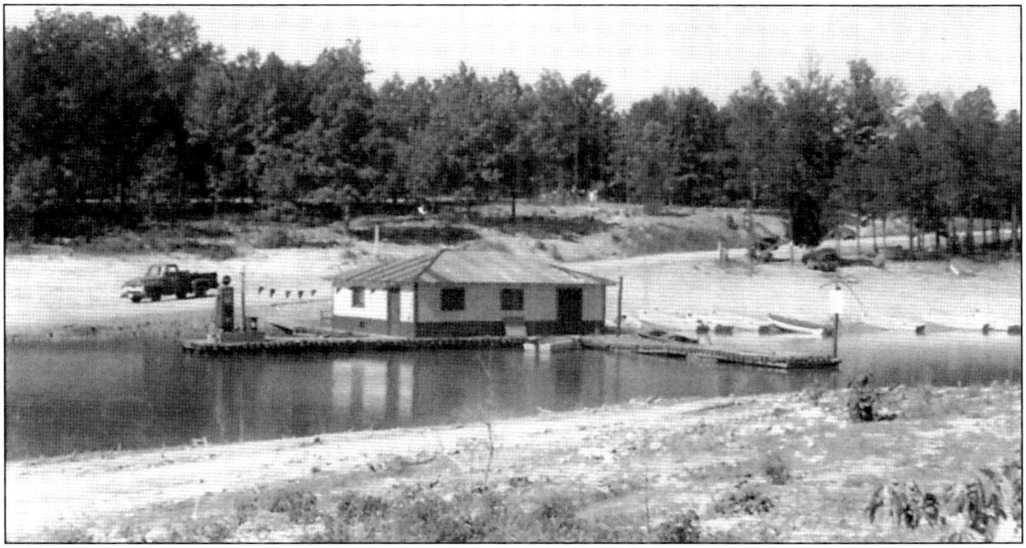

In 1952, those traveling south on Beauty Street would be underwater when arriving in Soudan. Pictured here is the Soudan Marina on Grassy Creek with the old U.S. 15 in the background. Soudan did have four stores, a post office, train depot, gristmill, sawmill, and a two-room school, but no church. (COE.)

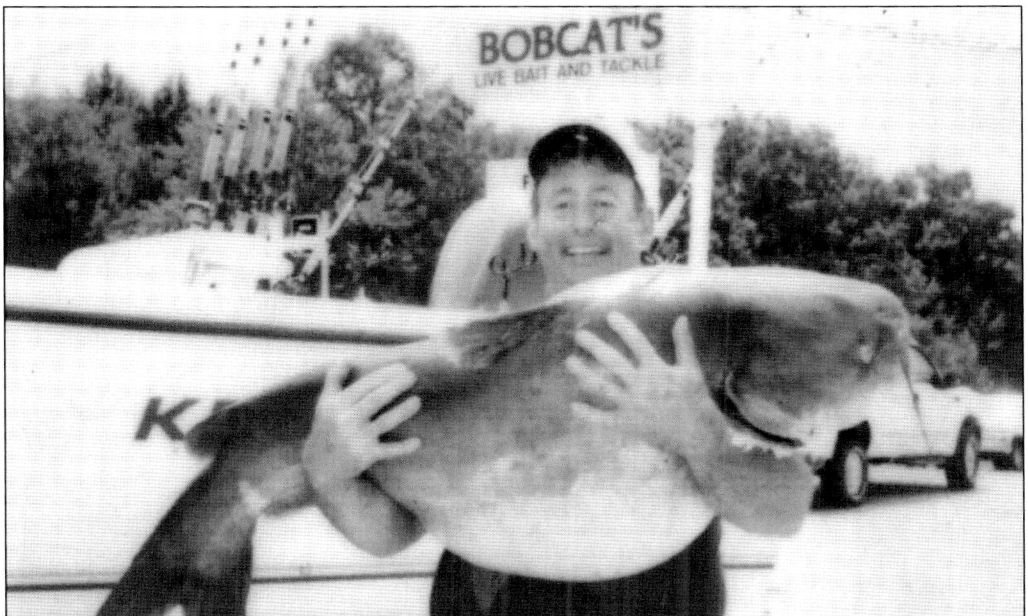

When the lake was completed and Highway 15 relocated, Grassy Creek bridge and state boat launch and two country store/gas stations opened. One of the most popular today is Bobcat's bait and tackle shop. Bobcat's sponsors and hosts a crappie tournament 10 months out of the year. Being an official station with certified scales, Bobcat's weighs in many trophy fish from the lake, such as this state-record blue catfish caught by William Zost in 2004 and in 2008 the state-record freshwater drum caught by Mike Fuller. (Bobby "Bobcat" Whitlow.)

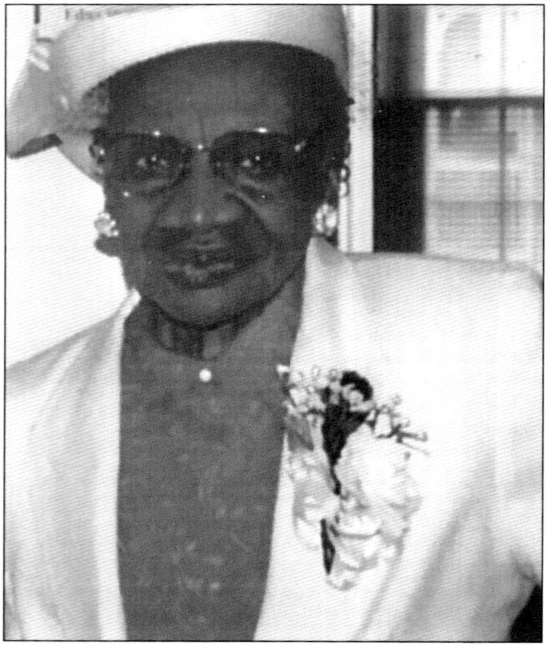

Annie Jones Garnett of Buffalo Junction moved to Clarksville after 19 years in Maryland and in 1951 became the first African American southside newspaper writer. Her column, "Clarksville Colored News" for the *Clarksville Times*, ran for almost 20 years. Her column became important to the African American community, as many lived along Blue Creek and were displaced by the lake. Through her column, she was able to keep the community in touch with the goings on of the area. (A. Garnett Miller.)

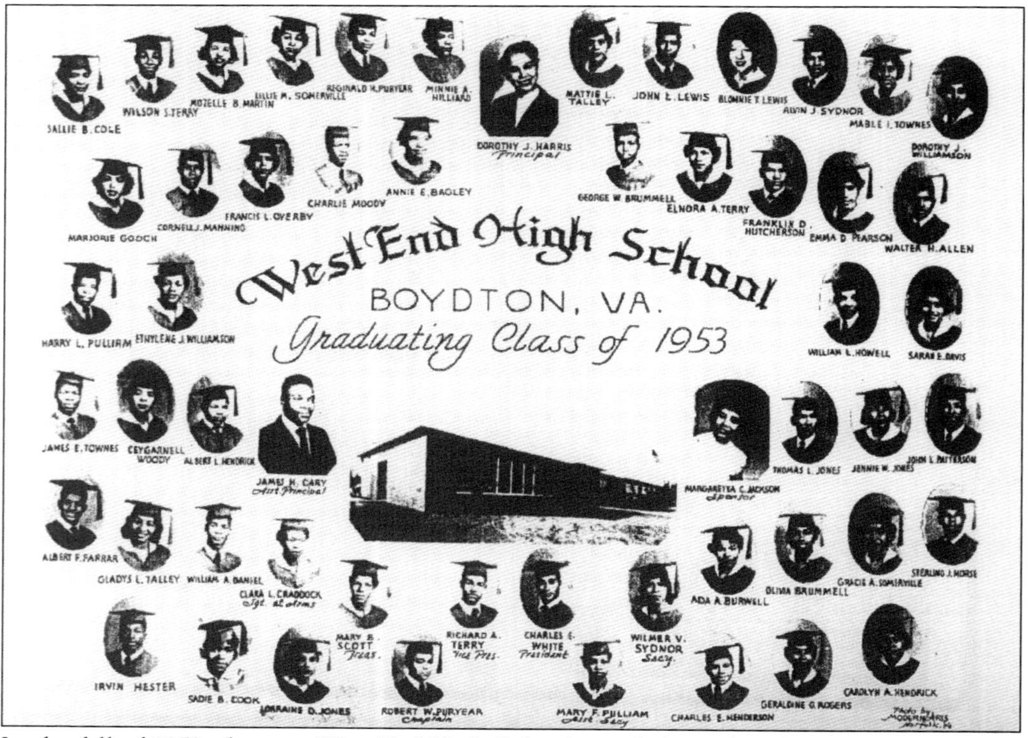

In the fall of 1952, the new West End High School was dedicated and opened in Skipwith, Virginia. The first graduating class held commencement in June 1953. The school served the black community of western Mecklenburg County until 1969. This is the class photograph of 1953 graduates with the new high school featured in the middle. (A. Garnett Miller.)

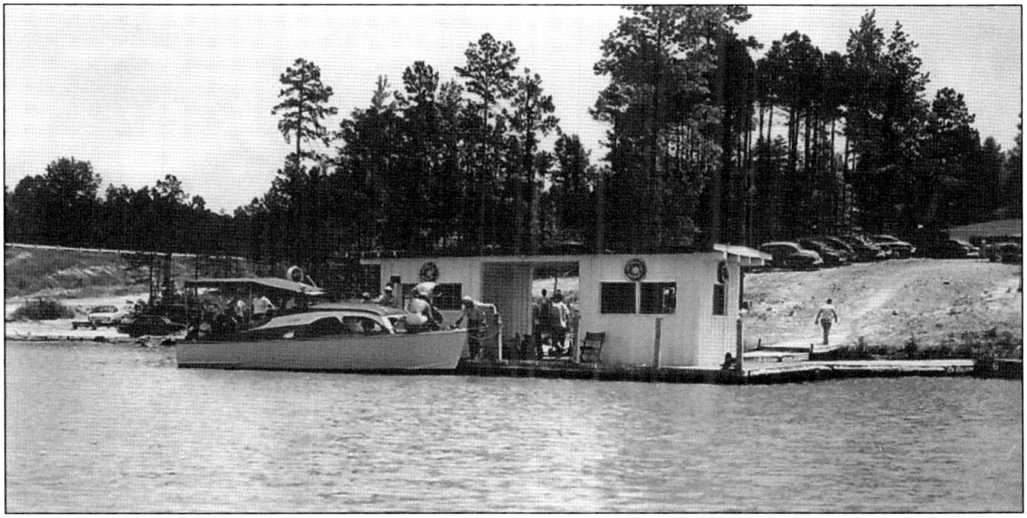

The new Occoneechee State Park on Buggs Island Lake opened in 1953. The park has a 15-mile multipurpose trail for hiking, biking, and horseback riding, a visitor museum, and a simulated village example of how the former Occoneechee Indians lived. The marina in this picture was the host site of the first Water Carnival in June 1953 and hosted many other activities until 1974, when it closed. (COE.)

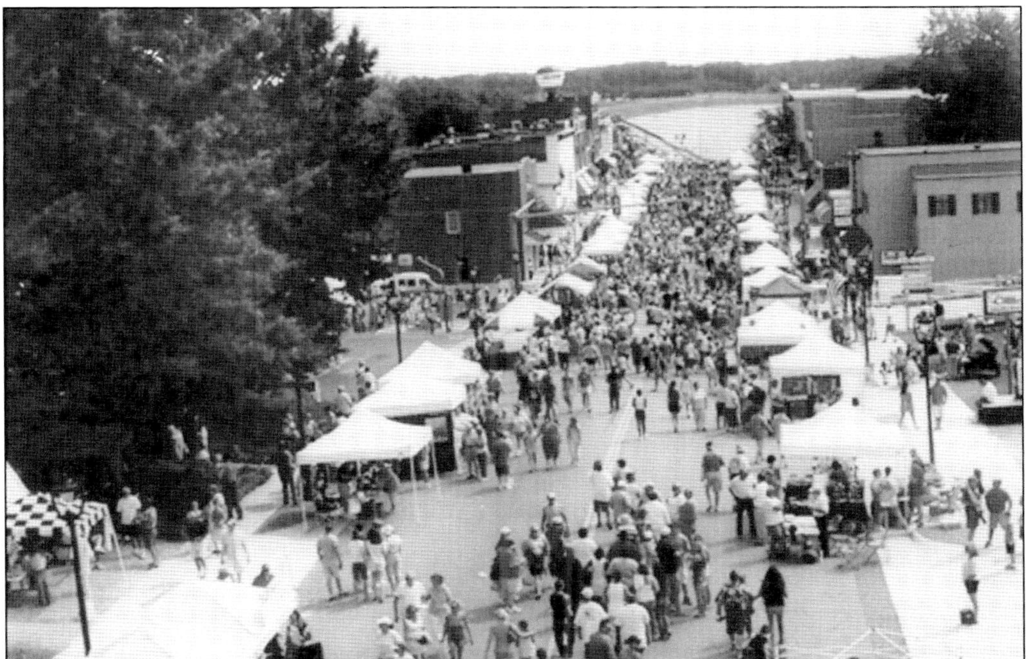

From June 13 to 15, 1953, the Clarksville community was host to the first Water Carnival. The Water Carnival Queen was Lu Long Ogburn, the 1951 Miss North Carolina and the 1952 first runner-up in the Miss America Pageant. In 1976, the Water Carnival began anew on Virginia Avenue in Clarksville and today is called Lakefest, with as many as 50,000 guests coming for the third weekend in July. (Joe Noah, Lakeside Flight.)

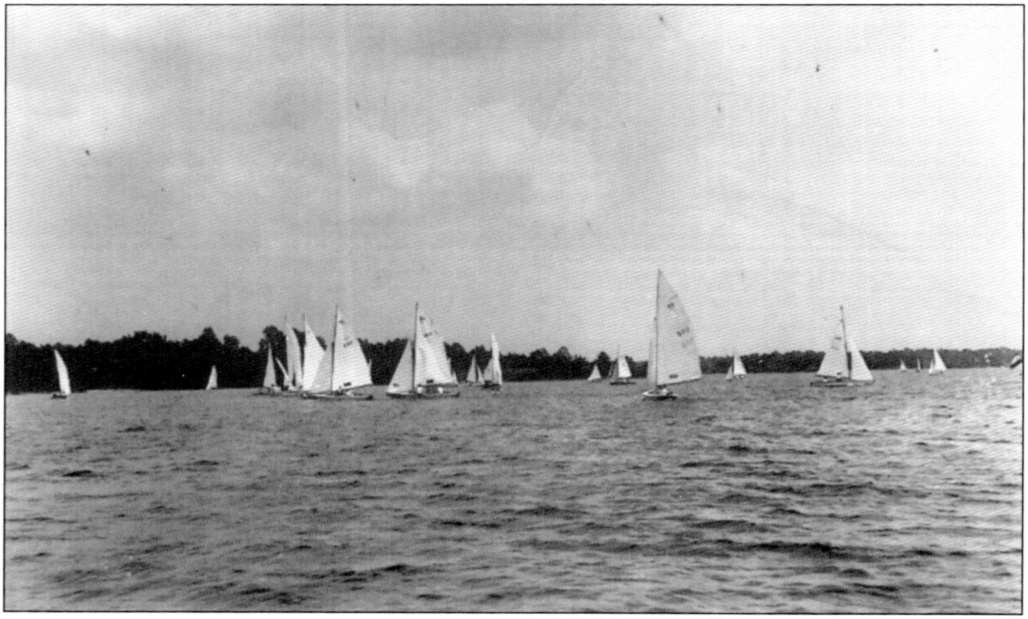

Virginia's dual-state sailboat racing takes place in Clarksville eight times per year. Beginning in the 1950s as an occasional variety of sailing events, over the years, it has become much more organized. This picture from 1958 shows sailing was very popular early on with the new lake, but today there are events for the serious racers, families, children's day, and just for fun. (COE.)

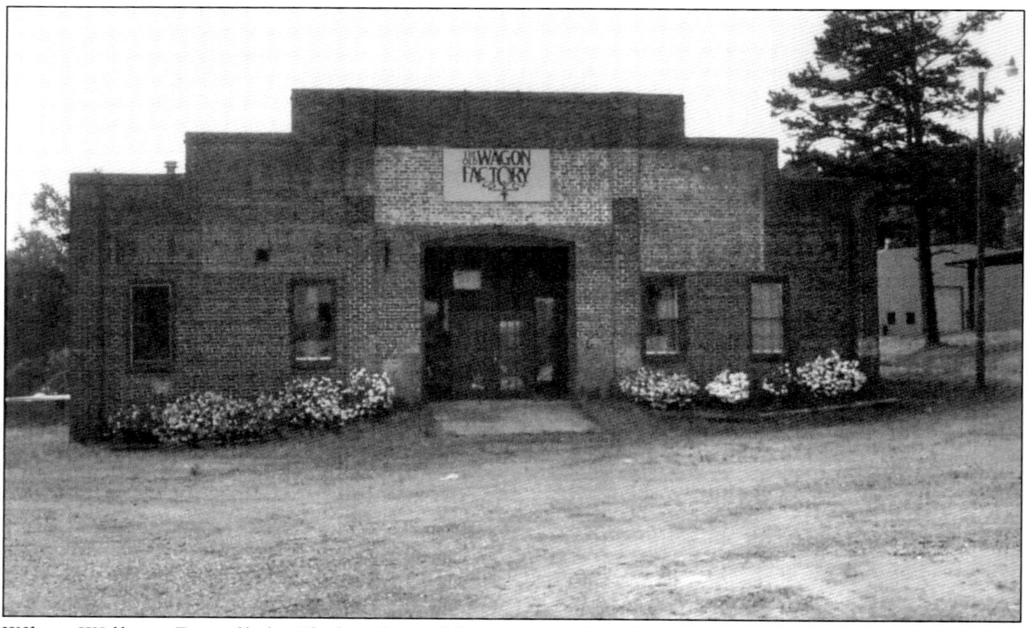

When William Russell decided to leave Virginia Tech and return to Clarksville in 1888, as a wedding gift, Charles Russell made him a partner in the company. The new Russell and Son began a full-scale production of wagons that spanned over 70 years. It was the last wagon factory in full operation in Virginia. (BH.)

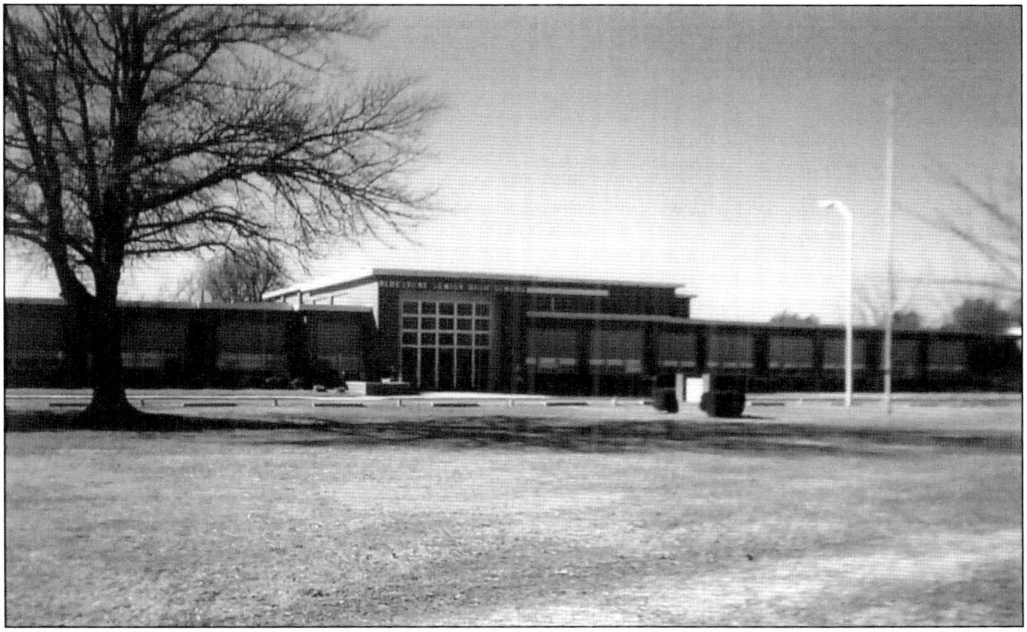

The new consolidated Bluestone High School opened for the fall 1955 school year in Skipwith. By combining the talents of the western part of the county, the school Drama Club received a superior rating for one-act plays every year from 1955 to 1962 from the University of Virginia. The school continues to thrive, break records, and serve the western county students. (John Caknipe.)

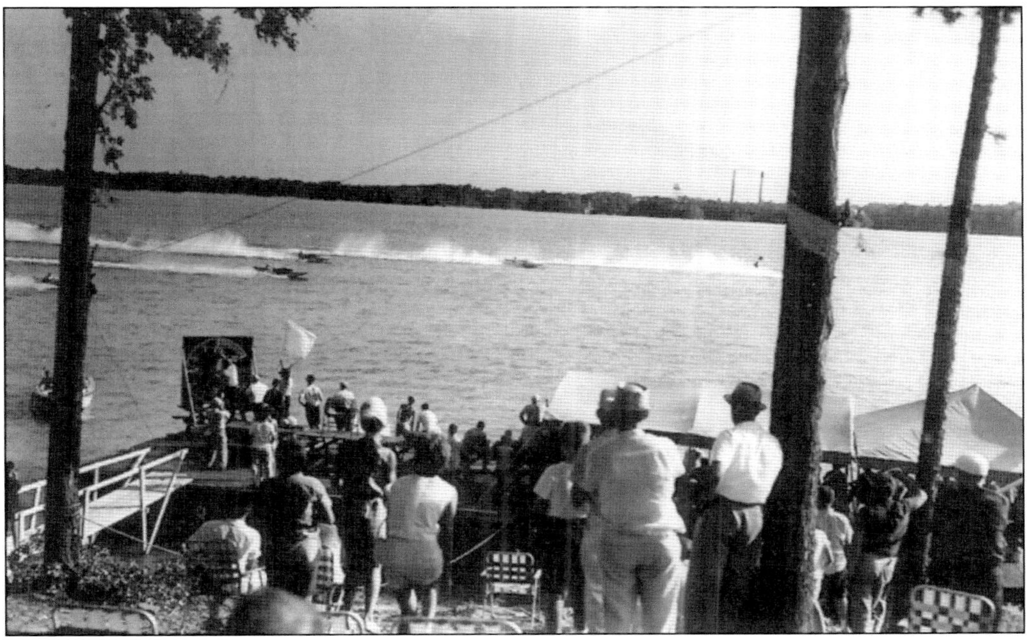

With a concerted effort by the Clarksville Veterans of Foreign Wars, hydroplane races came to Buggs Island Lake in Clarksville in 1957. This 1963 picture shows the announcer's stand and spectators at the Occoneechee Marina with the twin smokestacks of Burlington in the background. (COE.)

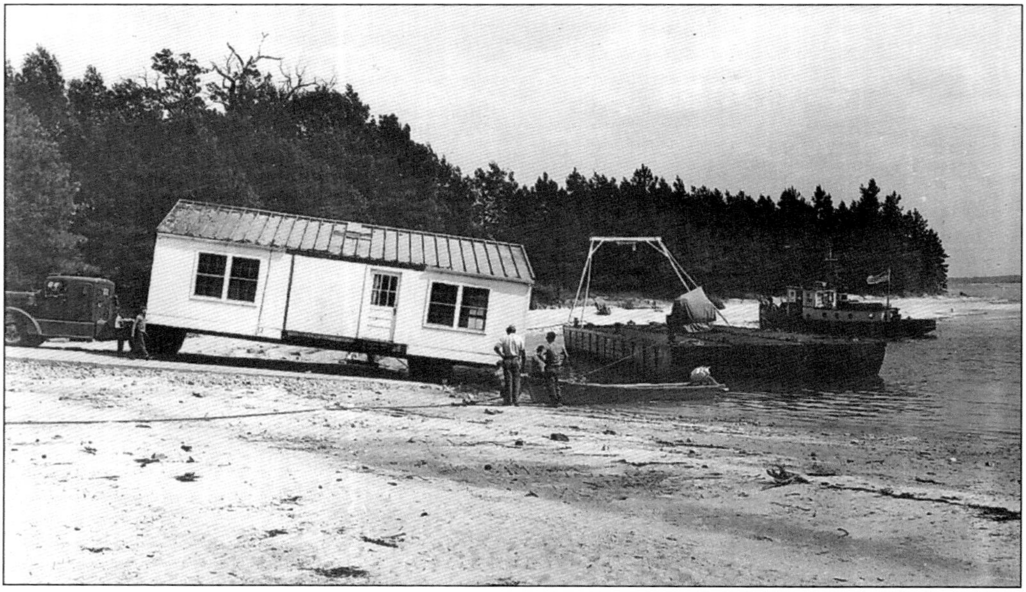

From 1956 through 1964, Castle Heights and Kerr Village were being sold and relocated. A number of homes in the county were originally there and moved for new residences in nearby communities. But many of the homes were hauled to the lake and placed on the barge; the three-man crew of the *Dan* would take them across to North Carolina or upstream to a new location. One of these houses was brought to North Clarksville and is the office of the Virginia Department of Fish and Wildlife. (COE.)

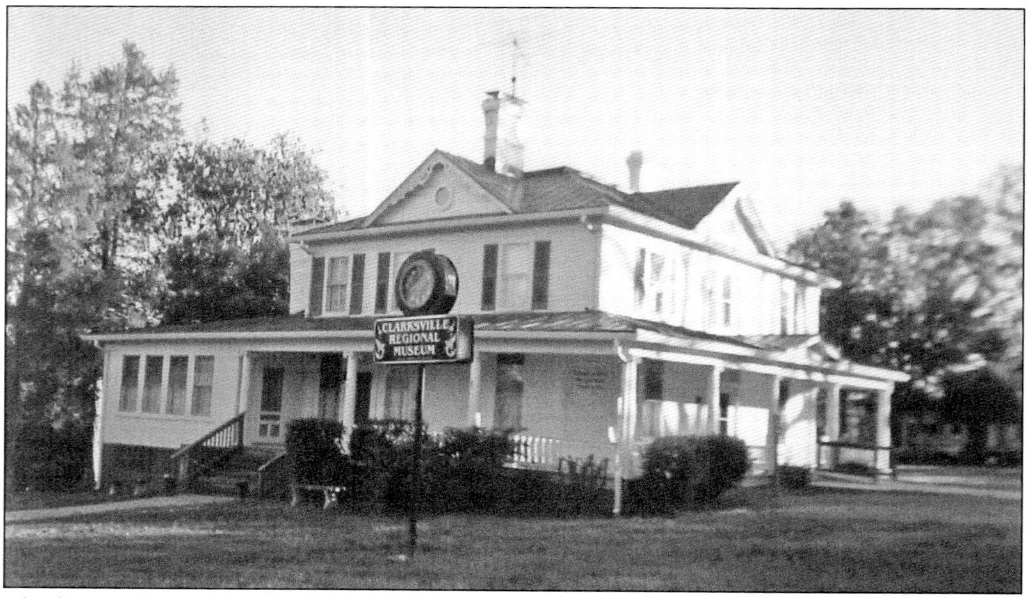

The former academy lot was purchased in 1903 by Sam Davis. By 1912, Davis had built his family a home. The Clarksville Regional Museum was organized in August 2005 and in 2008 moved into this home as their new location. It continues to add more to its collections weekly and is totally managed and operated by volunteers from the community. The museum is open afternoons Thursday through Sunday. (CRM.)

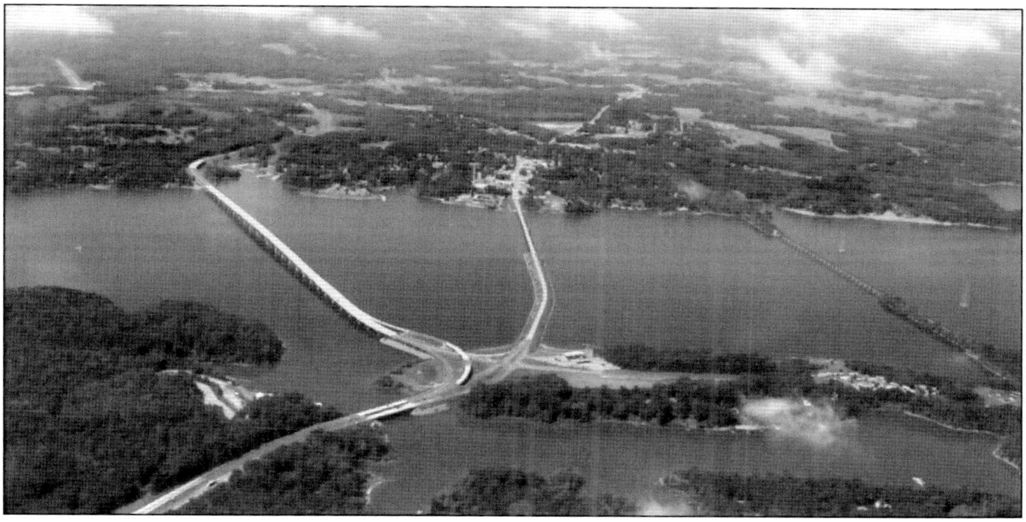

In 2006, a new Highway 58 bypass bridge was constructed, leading traffic around Clarksville. Note in this photograph how the new bridge lines up with the distant runway of Marks Municipal Airfield. North Clarksville is but a peninsula with one business at the intersection and Longs Mobile Home Park toward the new, relocated railroad bridge. Near the end of the bypass bridge on the left is the Clarksville Marina. The center bridge still serves Clarksville; at the end to the right is the Best Western Motel, and to the left is Lake Motel. Having lost its two major employers and the tobacco industry and with the bypass, Clarksville is rebounding again—the only town on the lake. (Joe Noah.)

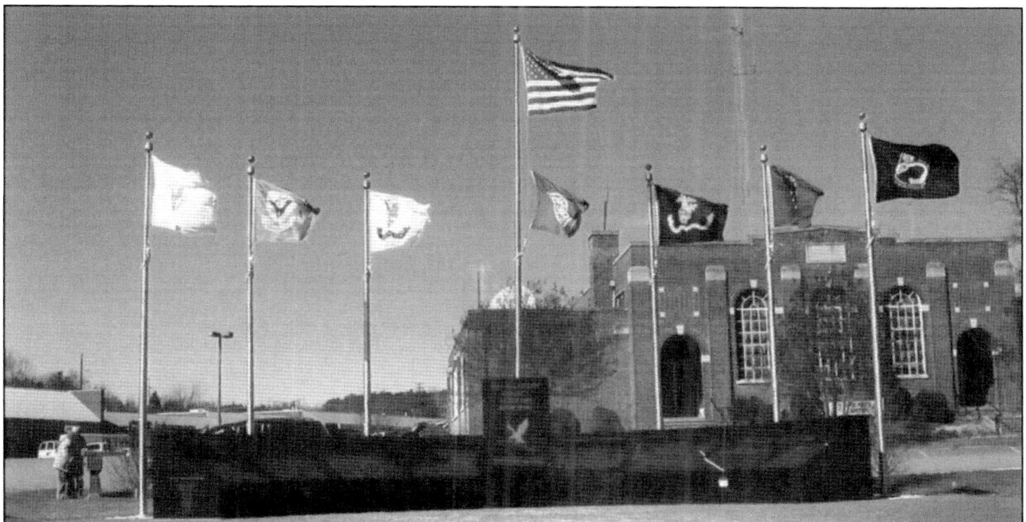

The County Veterans Memorial commemorates all the veterans in the county who died during service in every war from the Revolutionary War to the present. Commemorative bricks are available for those who wish to have a memorial for someone not on the walls. Books of the names on the wall have been compiled by war period and donated to all libraries in the county. The Memorial Committee consisted of Stuart and Marianne Buchanan, Mike and Iva Sizemore, Harrison and Winnie Blanks, Glen and Janice Edwards, J. T. and Grace Taylor, John Bowman, and Ronnie Bugg. (D. Stuart Buchanan.)